Environmental Impact Assessment Legislation:
Czech Republic, Estonia, Hungary, Latvia, Lithuania, Poland, Slovak Republic, Slovenia

Environmental Library 2

Environmental Impact Assessment Legislation:
Czech Republic, Estonia, Hungary, Latvia, Lithuania, Poland, Slovak Republic, Slovenia

published by

Graham & Trotman / Martinus Nijhoff
Members of the Kluwer Academic Publishers Group
LONDON/DORDRECHT/BOSTON

for the

European Bank
for Reconstruction and Development

Financed by the Government of Japan

Graham & Trotman Limited
Sterling House
66 Wilton Road
London SW1V 1DE
UK

Kluwer Academic Publishers Group
101 Philip Drive
Assinippi Park
Norwell, MA 02061
USA

ISBN 1-85966 036 3
Series ISSN 1351-8267

First Published 1994

British Library Cataloguing in Publication Data is available

Library of Congress Cataloging-in-Publication Data
Environmental impact assessment legislation: Czech Republic, Estonia, Hungary, Latvia, Lithuania, Poland, Slovak Republic, Slovenia.
p. cm. – (Environmental library)
Includes index.
ISBN 1–85966–036–3 : £55.00 ($95.00 U.S.)
1. Environmental impact analysis – Law and legislation – Europe, Eastern 2. Environmental impact analysis – Law and legislation – Baltic States. I. European Bank for Reconstruction and Development II. Series.
KJC6243.E58 1994
344.4'046–dc20
[344.0446] 94–36363
CIP

Typeset in Bodoni and Franklin Gothic by EXPO Holdings, Malaysia
Printed and bound in Great Britain by Hartnolls Ltd, Bodmin, Cornwall

Foreword

The countries of central and eastern Europe face considerable challenges in their quest to protect both the health and amenity of their populations and the natural resource base. They need to clean up the legacy of pollution which they have inherited from former regimes. They also need to ensure that the environmental consequences of present day decisions are well understood.

Environmental Impact Assessment (EIA) is perhaps the most important predictive tool which can prevent today's decisions resulting in unacceptable environmental impacts tomorrow. For over twenty years EIA has been used as an effective instrument for predicting the environmental impacts of projects and for mitigating any negative consequences that are identified. At the same time it has helped identify measures for enhancing the environmental benefits of projects. EIA is helpful to both investors and regulators. The European Bank, like other multilateral development institutions, has incorporated EIA within its environmental due diligence work.

Soon after the European Bank was established, we commissioned an initial study of EIA procedures in central and eastern Europe to assist investors to understand country-specific EIA legislation and regulations and to help the Bank's staff in setting EIA requirements on individual projects. The work has been updated for this volume.

I believe this publication will help those concerned with both development and environmental protection understand how EIA is evolving in the countries of central and eastern Europe. We look forward to working with these countries in the future in applying environmental assessment in their development and management programmes.

I would like to thank the Japanese Government for financing both the original study and this publication through the Japan–Europe Cooperation Fund. I would also like to thank Mr Duncan Fisher of East West Environment Ltd for his work in collecting and editing the material. Thanks are also due to Richard Macrory of the Imperial College Centre for Environmental Technology (London) and Mr Stanley Johnson of Environmental Resources Management (Oxford) for their review of the text. In conclusion, I would also like to thank my colleagues in the Bank's Environmental Appraisal Unit who initiated the idea for, and aided the development of, this book.

Jacques de Larosière
President
European Bank for Reconstruction and Development

Contents

Introduction*

The EIA process in central Europe and the Baltics: an overview

EIA is a process which provides decision-makers with an indication of the likely environmental consequences, both positive and negative, of their actions. When the EIA process includes the examination of alternatives (including the alternative of no action), as in the Czech Republic, Hungary and Slovenia, and when EIA is fully integrated from the earliest stages of the project design and planning process, as it is in all the countries covered in this review, it can play a more proactive role in encouraging the consideration of less environmentally damaging alternatives or modifications to the proposed project.

Legislation on environmental impact assessment (EIA) has recently been enacted or is planned in all the countries covered in this review:

- Latvia, Poland (1990)
- Lithuania (1991, 1993)
- Estonia, Czech Republic (1992)
- Hungary, Slovenia (1993)
- Slovakia (currently planned for 1994)

Prior to 1990, comprehensive socio-economic plans – economic plans for different sectors and spatial plans for regions and localities – provided the theoretical framework for development planning in these countries. Spatial planning provided the basis for integrating environmental considerations into development planning. The Slovak *Act on Land Use Planning and Construction Rules, No.50/1976* puts it thus:

> Land use planning is a prerequisite for ensuring the lasting harmony of all natural, human and cultural aspects in a territory, in particular with respect to the environment and the protection of its main components, soil, water and air. (Article 1.2)

Experience worldwide has shown, however, that the main determinant of the balance between conflicting economic, social and environmental considerations in development is the country's overall political and institutional framework. The socialist countries were no exception; both their politics and their administrative structures were heavily geared towards economic growth, with little consideration of social and environmental issues, both of which were weakly represented in politics. As a result, the centrally planned economic development tended to take place in designated localities, with few environmental and social constraints. This left a mixed legacy for the future. On the one hand, industrial pollution is severe in these industrial areas, but on the other hand, most industrial areas are fairly distinct, and environmental damage is less widespread than it has been in western Europe. There is, therefore, much that remains to be protected in central and eastern Europe. If environmental resources can be valued in an appropriate manner – again ultimately a function of politics – EIA may become a valuable tool for the integration of environmental protection into economic development.

* By Duncan Fisher, East West Environment Ltd (London)

Spatial planning regulations still exist in some of the countries covered in this review. In Poland, the Czech Republic and Slovakia, regional plans must still be referred to in the EIA process, even if they are outdated and subject to enforcement only at the discretion of the local authority.

There is an understandable resistance to the reintroduction of any form of social and economic planning in the transition economies. This is unfortunate. In developed countries there is a growing realisation of the value of conducting EIAs within the context of regional development plans. A development plan for an area, itself drawn up with a 'strategic environmental impact assessment', provides the baseline data needed for cost-effective EIAs, and facilitates due consideration of the impacts of projects both individually and collectively. In Slovenia, the new *Environmental Protection Act 1993* requires former regional plans to be replaced by 'environmental vulnerability studies' covering all ecological regions in the country. These will provide the basis for future development planning, including EIAs.

Structure of country reviews

Each chapter of this review describes the EIA process in one country, and includes translations of the relevant legislation. Although the process varies from country to country, the basic structure is the same, and follows that previously developed in western countries, particularly western Europe.

The vocabulary used in the review follows that of the EC Directive on Environmental Impact Assessment (1985).[1] A glossary of these terms is given on page 241.

Each chapter has the same structure:

1. Introduction: background information about the country and its environmental policy
2. The legislative and institutional framework for EIA
3. The EIA process, presented in sequential order
4. Monitoring of a project after implementation
5. EIA in practice
6. Possible changes in the near future
7. Contacts for further information
8. Copies of EIA legislation in translation.

The reference material on EIA laws and procedures was compiled by consultants in each country during 1992. On the basis of this, country reports were written by Duncan Fisher of East West Environment Ltd (London) and reviewed by Richard Macrory of the Imperial College Centre for Environmental Technology (London).

During 1993 the reports were updated and rewritten by Duncan Fisher for publication, and reviewed again by Stanley Johnson of Environmental Resources Management (Oxford), and Julie Scott of East West Environment Ltd (London).

Regulatory context for EIA

In all countries EIA is linked to applying for siting, building or operating permits. Only in Lithuania does the EIA result in an integrated 'Natural Resource Use Permit', incorporating

[1] Directive 85/337/EEC, 'On the assessment of the effects of certain public and private projects on the environment', *Official Journal of the European Communities* No. L175, 5.7.85, pages 40–48.

all individual environmental permits, such as air pollution, water use, waste-water discharge and production of solid wastes. In the other countries, these permits have to be obtained individually, in addition to the approval of the EIA. In Hungary, the EIA approval is given only when all environmental permitting requirements have been met. In Estonia, the EIA process is the basis for a number of individual environmental permits.

Responsibilities for preparation of EIA documentation

A form of quality control has been introduced in some countries by the requirement that the Environmental Impact Statement be produced by independent government approved experts. This is the situation in Estonia, Poland, the Czech Republic, Slovakia, and Slovenia.

Activities subject to EIA

In all the countries, EIA is required not just for construction projects, but also for the modification and liquidation of facilities. Specific lists of those projects requiring an EIA exist in the Czech Republic, Estonia, Hungary, Lithuania and Poland, sometimes divided into projects which must be assessed at the national level and those at the local level. The Slovenian *Environmental Protection Act 1993* requires such lists to be drawn up during 1994.

The lists are similar to those which have been adopted elsewhere in the world, and typically divide projects into different sectors such as agriculture, mining, energy, transport and waste treatment.

In the countries covered in this review except Estonia and Hungary, the national and local environmental authorities are given discretionary powers to require an EIA, even for projects not explicitly covered by legislation.

In the Czech Republic, Latvia and Slovenia, EIA can be required for changes in technologies and processes, and for the introduction of new technologies and products.

Scope of EIA and environmental impact statement

There is no scoping procedure at the beginning of the EIA process in any of the countries covered by this review. In Slovenia, the public may demand a wider scope for an EIA than that required in the law; in such cases, the Ministry of Environment adjudicates. The introduction of a scoping process is being considered in Poland and the Czech Republic. A formal scoping process is sometimes carried out in the context of multilaterally financed projects: the World Bank and the European Bank for Reconstruction and Development require this for certain categories of projects. The lack of a scoping procedure can cause problems at the public consultation stage of the EIA, if the interested parties find themselves in disagreement over the terms of reference of the discussion.

EIA is generally confined to an assessment of compliance with existing regulations and standards. In Estonia, Latvia and Lithuania, the old system of former USSR standards is still in operation. In Poland, emission standards are calculated on the basis of maximum permissible ambient pollutant concentrations in air and water. This means that permissible emissions will be lower in already polluted areas.

In Poland the impact on the 'natural beauty' of a site is specified in the legislation, and the Czech legislation considers the impact on cultural monuments. In Hungary, the social and economic consequences of changes in environmental conditions must also be considered. In Latvia, special cultural protection measures exist in one particular region,

Līvod rānda. In Lithuania, cultural and historic assets must be inventoried in the Environmental Impact Statement. The legislation in Latvia and Lithuania is vague and could be interpreted to include more than purely physical impacts.

Various elements of the EC Directive on EIA are incorporated into EIA legislation and regulations. The Czech, Hungarian and Slovenian EIA Environmental Impact Statement must contain a non-technical summary, to make it more accessible to the decision-makers and public who will read it. In Slovenia, the entire Environmental Impact Statement is required to be accessible to the public. The Polish, Czech and Slovenian legislation specifies direct and indirect, short and long-term environmental effects. The Czech, Hungarian and Slovenian legislation require a statement of data sources and limitations in the process of predicting environmental impacts.

Public participation

In all countries except Poland, there is a requirement for the EIA proceedings to be made public. In all the countries except Poland, there is a also a requirement for consultation with the affected public. The form of this public consultation is generally left vague; it is most explicit in the case of the Czech Republic. In Hungary, there is an exemption from public consultation where military secrecy is involved (in common with the EC Directive on EIA). In Poland, there is an independent national 'EIA Commission' of experts, and some equivalent regional bodies, which advise the environmental authority on EIAs. The Commission provides a mechanism for consultation with the public, although it does so at its own discretion.

Review and approval

An independent expert review of EIAs is required in Estonia and the Czech Republic, and is optional in Latvia and Slovakia. In Poland there is a permanent EIA Commission of 75 experts, set up by the Minister of Environment, which reviews all EIAs. Three district equivalents have been established, and there are plans to extend the practice throughout the country.

Implementation of EIA

There have been a number of problems with the implementation of EIA in EC countries. The EC Directive on EIA (1985) required a study of its implementation after five years. This study was undertaken by the EIA Centre of Manchester University.[2]

A number of key problems were identified.

- The Directive is designed to be an anticipatory instrument to prevent pollution at source by taking the environment into account from the earliest stage of planning. In EC countries, however, the EIA often begins late. Often it is not clear how the results of the EIA are integrated into the project plan.
- EIA is intended to be a technical instrument, requiring sound scientific and technical data and expert advice. Environmental statements, however, show inconsistent quality. The methodology is frequently unclear, project alternatives are often excluded, as are measures to mitigate environmental impacts. Consultants and municipalities who conduct and review EIAs often lack sufficient experience.

[2] Commission of the European Communities COM(93)28. 2.4.1993.

- EIA is also intended to be a participatory instrument, requiring consultation with the public. Few opportunities exist, however, for the public to analyse the EIA documentation effectively and comment on its content.

There is no indication that these problems will not recur in central and eastern Europe. Undertaking an EIA and evaluating the resulting information demands of local governments in the region an untested degree of flexibility and administrative capability. The test of this flexibility and capability will be the degree to which meaningful public participation is assured. The lack of experience on the part of both the public and the administration in mutual consultation, and the inherited perception of the planning process as a technical analysis rather than a process of negotiation, will make the task of ensuring effective public participation exceptionally difficult. In addition, the lack of a scoping process often results in argument about the scope of the EIA when it is too late to introduce new issues into the EIA process.

Czech Republic*

EIA regulation	Czech Act on Environmental Impact Assessment, No.244/1992 (Document A)
EIA authority	Ministry of Environment. District Environmental Offices (part of local government).
Responsibilities for EIA	The developer covers the cost of preparing the Environmental Impact Statement and the expert review. The Environmental Impact Statement must be prepared by registered experts.
Regulatory context for EIA	EIA is part of the process of applying for siting and building permits.
Activities subject to EIA	Two lists of mandatory projects. EIA is optional for projects not on these lists, at the discretion of the EIA authority.
Consultation	Discussions with the municipal construction office about whether an EIA is required and at what level it must be reviewed – Ministry of Environment or District Environmental Office ('competent environmental authority').
Scoping	None.
Environmental Impact Statement	The Environmental Impact Statement is drawn up by certified experts, and submitted to the competent environmental authority.
Public participation: comment	Consultation with public and concerned administrative departments.
Expert review	Submission of Environmental Impact Statement to the competent environmental authority, with the opinions of the public and other administrative bodies. Expert review of the Environmental Impact Statement.
Public participation: hearing	Public hearing: discussion of expert review. The views of the public are taken into account during the approval procedure.
Approval	Competent environmental authority issues its opinion on the EIA taking into account the expert review and the second public discussion.

* Reference material provided by Dr. Václav Mezřický, Institute for Environmental Policy (Prague)

Development consent	EIA result submitted with other documentation as an application to the municipal construction office for the building location and/or construction permits. A positive EIA is not compulsory, unless the EIA shows thatenvironmental regulations will be contravened. It is compulsory, however, that the EIA process is carried out.
Transboundary EIA	Interstate negotiations are required when transboundary impacts are likely (*Act on Environmental Impact Assessment, No.244/1992*, Article 13). The documentation is stipulated in Annex 3. The Czech Republic has signed the Espoo Convention on EIA in a Transboundary Context.

1. Introduction

Population: 10.4 million
Area: 78,900 sq km
Currency: Czech crown

Principal environmental problems
The main environmental problems in the Czech Republic are:

- air pollution and forest damage – 60% of forests affected;
- drinking water contamination – 50% of sources do not meet legal standards;
- waste management – 600 million tonnes of industrial waste are produced each year.

Environmental policy
The Ministry of Environment is currently preparing a new policy document, outlining its goals.

2. Legislative and institutional framework for EIA

2.1 Administrative structure and responsibilities for EIA

The Czech Republic is divided into 76 districts, of which the City of Prague is one. At the local level there are 6,000 self-governing municipalities.

Central government
The Ministry of Environment is responsible for drafting environmental legislation, formulating environmental policy and enforcing environmental laws, including EIA laws.

For EIA, the Ministry of Environment:

- reviews projects specified in annex 1 of the *Act on Environmental Impact Assessment, No.244/1992*;
- keeps a list of persons authorised to prepare Environmental Impact Statements and to carry out expert reviews;
- keeps a register of EIAs;

- expresses its position on drafts of programmes and policies which will be submitted to EIA;
- reviews Environmental Impact Statements for district-level projects which influence a territory larger than that of a district, or which are located in a territory with severely polluted environment or in protected areas.

The Ministry of Environment enforces environmental laws through the Czech Environmental Inspectorate. The Inspectorate has 42 branches, and has separate divisions for water, air, waste management, forestry and nature protection. It monitors compliance, issues administrative orders and imposes penalties in some sectors. Its powers are broadest in the air sector where it is authorised to issue permits.

The Ministry of Economy is responsible for land use planning, as of 31 October 1992. This task was formerly carried out by the Ministry of Environment.

The Ministry of Health is responsible for regulation of noise and toxic substances, as well as for general health and safety issues. It executes its responsibilities through Hygiene Offices at the District Level.

Local government

District Offices are part of the state administrative structure, answerable to the Ministry of Interior.

District Offices have environmental protection departments ('District Environmental Offices'), which are part of local government.

District Environmental Offices, and the Metropolitan Authority of the Capital City of Prague, have the following responsibilities for EIA:

- require an EIA for proposed projects specified in annex 2 of the *Act on Environmental Impact Assessment, No.244/1992*, and carry out review;
- send a copy of the EIAs to the Ministry of Environment's register.

District Environmental Offices can delegate to municipalities, where the latter have sufficient resources and expertise.

2.2 Sources of legislation relating to EIA

The Czech Republic has adopted all the laws of the former Federation, including its environmental laws.

2.2.1 Legislation on EIA

- Czech *Act on Environmental Impact Assessment, No.244/1992* (Document A)

The Act relates to the assessment of buildings and construction, technologies, development plans and new products. In general terms it identifies cases when EIA is mandatory (Annexes 1 and 2) and when it is optional. (These lists are based on the lists in the Federal *Act on the Environment, No.17/1992*, but are more specific.) The extent and contents of the EIA are defined in Annex 3.

- Czech *Decree on Professional Qualification in EIA and on the Means and Form of Public Discussion of Expert Reports, No.499/1992* (Document B)

The Decree specifies conditions for obtaining a licence to perform EIAs and expert reviews of EIAs. It also defines conditions for public hearings for EIAs.

- Federal *Act on the Environment, No.17/1992* (Document C)

The Act has an almost constitutional character, summarising the principles of environmental protection and natural resource use to be observed by the legislature of the Federation and the republics. One of these principles is pollution prevention (Article 17).

The Act states that all human activities must be evaluated in terms of their potential impact on the environment and natural resources. Such activities include investment activity and the introduction of new technologies, products and substances into production or into circulation.

The Act provides criteria binding upon bodies that will perform the EIA (Articles 20–23). It empowers Republic Parliaments to specify these bodies and the EIA procedure. In appendices it defines activities submitted to EIA in the ČSFR. The appendices also specify the content of the Environmental Impact Statement. The Act incorporates fundamental principles of the Espoo Convention on Transboundary Environmental Impact Assessment into Czechoslovak Law (Articles 24–26).

2.2.2 Legislation on planning

- Czechoslovak *Act on Land Use Planning and Construction Rules, No.50/1976* (Document D), amended by *Act No.262/1992*

The Act specifies basic rules for land use planning and construction. The amendment contains some details of land use planning in relation to the public interest, and in relation to expropriations and other particular circumstances.

The Act, as amended, defines the basic requirement that the developer must obtain a decision from the competent authority with any application for locating a building and for using land.

- Czechoslovak *Decree on General Technical Requirements of Construction, No.83/1976* (Document E), as amended by *Decree No.376/1992*

The Decree provides criteria for how buildings are located on various kinds of land. These criteria are binding for both state authorities and developers. The Decree defines general requirements for environmental protection.

- Czechoslovak *Decree on More Detailed Regulation of Land Use Planning and Construction Rules, No.85/1976* (Document F), as amended by *Decree No.378/1992*

The Decree specifies certain provisions of the *Act on Land Use Planning and Construction Rules, No.50/1976*. It sets requirements for location of buildings and for building permits.

The amendment states that if a facility is going to use unusual technology, or if it is not possible to reliably predict its negative environmental impacts, the developer must obtain the expert opinion of an appropriate specialised unit, university or judicial expert.

2.2.3 Legislation related to EIA

(For environmental permits, see box on page 8 below.)

- Czechoslovak *Act on Human Health Care, No.20/1966*

The Act provides basic principles for the preservation of sound living conditions, especially sound quality of water, soil, air. It empowers health service bodies to check on compliance with these principles from the point of view of citizens' interests.

- Czechoslovak *Regulation concerning the Safeguarding and Protection of Healthy Living Conditions, No.45/1966*, as amended by *Act No.548/1991*

The Decree defines conditions for establishing 'health zones' protected against pollution of air and drinking water.

- Federal *Clean Air Act, No.309/1991*, as amended by *Act No.318/1992*

The Act defines rights and obligations in relation to air pollution. The amendment specifies pollution sources and deadlines for complying with emission limits.

- Czech *Act on the Administration of Air Protection and Charges for the Pollution of Air, No.389/1991*

The Act specifies basic responsibilities of the state administration, including the Environmental Protection Inspectorate, in the field of air pollution control.

It specifies documents that must be presented with the application for a building permit.

- Czech Ministry of Environment *Decree Establishing Regions Requiring Special Air Protection, and Establishing Principles for the Creation and Operation of Smog Regulation Systems, and Other Measures for Protection of the Air, No.41/1992*

The Decree outlines more stringent protection measures to be followed for industrial construction in polluted regions. The Inspectorate defines these measures for large and medium size pollution sources.

- Czechoslovak *Water Act, No.138/1973*

The Act regulates the balance between the demand and supply of water resources. It protects the quality of water and its rational use, and assures protection from floods. At the same time, the Act respects the requirements of nature conservation.

- Czech *Act on the State Administration in Water Economy, No.130/1974*, as modified and amended by *Act No.23/1992* and restated as *Act No.458/1992*

The Act defines responsibilities of water management authorities to implement the Czechoslovak *Water Act, No.138/1973*.

- Federal *Waste Act, No.238/1991*

The Act defines rights and obligations of the state administration and of legal and physical persons in waste treatment.

- Czech *Act on the State Administration of Waste Treatment, No.311/1991*, as amended by *Act No.466/1992*

The Act defines responsibilities of the state administration in the field of waste treatment in the Czech Republic.

- Czech *Act on the Protection of the Agricultural Soil Fund, No.334/1992*

The Act protects agricultural soil as a fundamental part of the Republic's natural wealth, as the means of agricultural production, and as one of the main components of the environment. The Act establishes basic criteria for the protection of agricultural land during building, mining and industrial activities.

- Czech *Act on the Responsibility of the Agricultural Soil Fund Protection Authorities of the Czech Republic, No.77/1976*

The Act defines responsibilities of the Ministry of Environment as the agricultural soil protection authority.

- Czechoslovak *Decree Defining Some Details of Agricultural Soil Protection, No.36/1987*, as amended and modified by later regulations, in particular the *Decree of the Ministry of the Environment of the Czech Republic, No.528/1991*

The Decree specifies details of protection of agricultural land in land use planning and in building design.

- Czechoslovak *Act on Forests, No.61/1977*

The Act protects forests and timber species as a permanent source of wood and as a fundamental part of the natural environment.

- Czech *Act on Forest Management and on the State Administration of Forest Management, No.96/1977*

The Act defines forms of forest management and responsibilities of the state administration in forest management.

- Czech *Act on Nature Conservation and Landscape Protection, No.114/1992*

The purpose of the Act is to contribute to the maintenance and restoration of the balance of the landscape, to the protection of the diversity of life forms, to the protection of natural values and features, and to the rational use of natural resources.

3. Environmental impact assessment process

3.1 Activities subject to EIA

An EIA is mandatory for construction and modification projects listed in Annexes 1 and 2 of the *Act on Environmental Impact Assessment, No.244/1992* (Document A). Projects listed in Annex 1 are reviewed by the Ministry of Environment; those in Annex 2 are reviewed by the District Environmental Office. (The authority to review can be transferred between the Ministry of Environment and District Environmental Office.)

An EIA is optional for projects not in these lists, if required by any administrative body or local government. An EIA is necessary in regions governed by special regulations. In such cases the EIA is reviewed by the District Environmental Office.

(The Ministry of Environment or District Environmental Office are referred to below as the 'competent environmental authority'.)

The law states that the developer must supply an environmental impact statement when applying for any land use or building permit (*Act on Environmental Impact Assessment, No.244/1992; Act on Land Use Planning and Construction Rules, No.50/1976, amended by Act No.262/1992; Decree on More Detailed Regulation of Land Use Planning and Construction Rules, No.85/1976*, as amended by *Decree No.378/1992*).

An EIA is also required for new products and technologies. Details of EIA for new products are given in Articles 15–18 of the *Act on Environmental Impact Assessment, No.244/1992.*

3.2 Regulatory context for EIA

The EIA process is defined in detail in the *Act on Environmental Impact Assessment, No.244/1992* (Document A).

The EIA takes place as part of the process of applying to the municipal government for siting permission, and for a building permit. Siting permission is needed if the proposed project is on a greenfield site or involves expansion of an existing facility.

A building permit is also required for the modification, maintenance and removal of any building (*Act on Land Use Planning and Construction Rules, No.50/1976*, amended by *Act No.262/1992*).

The full requirements for these permits are outlined in the *Decree on More Detailed Regulation of Land Use Planning and Construction Rules, No.85/1976*, as amended by *Decree No.378/1992.*

The EIA process must be completed before siting and building permission can be given, but the review of the EIA need not be positive for these permissions to be given.

Land use planning requirements

Developers planning to build new facilities on greenfield sites or to expand or redevelop existing facilities must comply with the land use and building regulations of the Czech Republic. The principle law governing this area is the *Act on Land Use Planning and Construction Rules, No.50/1976*, as amended by *Act No.262/1992.*

The 1992 amendment provides for new public participation provisions. The public participants are defined as neighbours, private individuals or businesses which may be affected by the construction, and concerned administrative authorities. This public participation requirement is separate from the public participation requirement in the EIA process; it takes place even when an EIA is not required.

During project planning, land use planning regulations need to be carefully observed. The *Act on Environmental Impact Assessment, No.244/1992* states the necessity to consult the municipal construction office about how the project complies with the 'General Plan of the Area'. These plans, however, are for the most part outdated, incomplete or invalidated by economic and political reforms. Thus, the binding nature of the land use planning documents depends on the attitude of the municipality or higher authority.

Environmental permits

Closely related to the EIA process, but separate from it, are applications for various operational permits. (See section 2.2.3 for relevant legislation.)

Air

Certain air pollution sources require a permit from the Ministry of Environment or its Environmental Inspectorate.

The Ministry of Environment must approve projects which introduce new production and technologies at large and medium pollution sources (Article 2, *Act on the State Administration of Air Protection and Charges for the Pollution of Air, No.389/1991*; Article 11.1c, Federal *Clean Air Act, No.309/1991*).

The Environmental Inspectorate grants approval, which includes conditions for air pollution control, for the siting and construction or modification of large, medium, and small pollution sources involving new technologies (Article 3.2a, *Act on the State Administration of Air Protection and Charges for the Pollution of Air, No.389/1991*; Article 11.1a, f, Federal *Clean Air Act, No.309/1991*).

Special air protection zones are defined in the *Decree of the Ministry of Environment of the Czech Republic Establishing Regions Requiring Special Air Protection, and Establishing Principles for the Creation and Operation of Smog Regulation Systems and Other Measures for Protection of the Air, No.41/1992*.

Where permits are required, there is no formal application procedure. Details of air emission sources and other relevant information must be provided. The permit should be provided within 60 days, according to the *Act on Administrative Procedure, No.71/1967*.

Water

When proposing a new project, the developer must ask the water management authority for its opinion on the proposed use of water (Czechoslovak *Water Act, No.138/1973*).

Permits from the District Environmental Office are required for use of surface and groundwater, for discharge of waste water, and for discharge of pre-treated water into the public sewage system. If the project significantly alters the water resources of an area, the Ministry of Environment must approve the construction.

Where permits are required, there is no formal application procedure. The permit should be provided within 60 days, according to the *Act on Administrative Procedure, No.71/1967*.

The affected public has access to documentation on permits, including the opinions of the authorities. Information on compliance, however, is confidential.

Noise and health

The District Hygiene Office issues noise permits. Information on noise levels is given to the District Hygiene Office, which can obtain an expert opinion. New noise laws are in preparation.

In certain cases, a health review of the proposed project is necessary. These cases are specified in the *Act on Human Health Care, No.86/1992*. The District Hygiene Office must give an approval.

Waste
Documentation must be presented to the District Office with the application for the decision concerning building location or for a construction permit. Waste management plans must be prepared if annual output is more than 100 tons or 50 kg of hazardous waste (*Act on the State Administration of Waste Management, No.311/1991*). The contents of the waste management plan are outlined in the Public Notice on Waste Management Programmes, No.401/1991. The public has access to these plans.

The District Office gives its opinion on the installation of waste treatment equipment, and construction concerned with waste treatment. (Federal Waste Act, No.238/1991; Act on the State Administration of Waste Management, No.311/1991)

A permit is required from the Ministry of Environment for transport of waste, including import and export.

Chemical storage
An EIA is required in certain cases. The Act on Environmental Impact Assessment, No.244/1992 specifies the following:

- underground storage of natural gas and other gases with a capacity exceeding 1 million m^3; surface storage of natural gas and other gases with a capacity exceeding 100,000 m^3; storage of oil, oil products and chemicals with a capacity exceeding 1,000 m^3;
- storage of poisons and pesticides in amounts exceeding 1 tonne, and the storage of pharmaceutical products, paints and varnishes exceeding 100 tonnes/year.

Agricultural land
If a project takes land out of agricultural use, permission is required for temporary or permanent exemption from agricultural land classification. In practice this type of permission is very difficult to obtain. The District Office grants this permission (*Act on the Responsibility of the Agricultural Soil Fund Protection Authorities of the Czech Republic, No.77/1976*).

Forests
A project which anticipates permanently or temporarily taking forest land out of use, or limiting forest land use, requires the approval of the forestry authority (Czechoslovak *Act on Forests, No.61/1977*). The District Office must also grant approval (*Act on Forest Management and on the State Administration of Forest Management, No.96/1977*).

Nature conservation
If the nature conservation authorities request it, developers must, at their own expense, carry out an analysis of the project's impact on land, flora and fauna. The nature conservation authority then issues a permit. (*Act on Nature Conservation and Landscape Protection, No.114/1992*)

3.3 Responsibilities for EIA

The costs of producing the EIA documentation and the expert review are covered by the developer.

The Environmental Impact Statement must be prepared by qualified experts certified by the Ministry of Environment and the Ministry of Health (*Act on Environmental Impact Assessment, No.244/1992*). These qualifications are defined in the *Decree on Professional Qualification in EIA and on the Means and Form of Public Discussion of Expert Reports, No.499/1992*. The Ministry of Environment has a list of certified experts.

If a project has an unusual design or incorporates new technology, and if it is difficult to assess its environmental impact accurately, the developer must solicit the opinion of a specialised institute, university or judicial expert (*Decree on More Detailed Regulation of Land Use Planning and Construction Rules, No.85/1976*, as amended by *Decree No.378/1992*).

3.4 Scope of EIA and environmental impact statement

There is no scoping process, although the introduction of this step into the EIA process is being considered.

The EIA covers the following issues:

- direct and indirect, short-term and long-term impacts of the project on the environment, natural resources, cultural monuments and the town and community environment, including the aesthetic value of the area;
- comparison of impacts of alternatives if these are required by the competent environmental authority;
- proposal of measures to mitigate impacts;
- evaluation of consequences of not proceeding with the project.

The developer begins by announcing the project to the competent environmental authority. When an EIA is required, the developer must present an Environmental Impact Statement according to a carefully defined format given in Annex 3 of the *Act on Environmental Impact Assessment, No.244/1992* (Document A). The format includes a non-technical summary.

3.5 Public participation: comment

The competent environmental authority passes the Environmental Impact Statement to the concerned administrative bodies and the affected communities without undue delay. (The competent environmental authority decides which communities are affected.) Within five days, the community must announce when and where the Statement will be available for public inspection. Written comments may by submitted by the public within 30 days of publishing the Statement, and these must be passed on by the community within 14 days after this. Concerned administrative bodies have 50 days to make written comments on the Statement.

The *Act on Environmental Impact Assessment, No.244/1992* makes special provision for participation of 'civil initiatives' and 'civil associations'.

A civil initiative is a group of more than 500 people over the age of 18 who support an opinion on the project. Along with the affected public, the civil initiative can submit written comments within 30 days of the Environmental Impact Statement being published. (It can also take part in the second public hearing – see 3.7). A civil initiative can institutionalise itself into a 'civil association', such as a registered environmental organisation. An already existing association may also participate in the EIA process.

3.6 Expert review

The competent environmental authority contracts independent authorised experts (see 3.3), but different from those who produced the Environmental Impact Statement, to review the Statement, taking into account the opinions of the public and other administrative bodies. The developer is required to provide further information, if required by the experts. The review must take place within 60 days, which can be extended for another 150 where this is justified.

The review evaluates the following:

- completeness of the Environmental Impact Assessment;
- opinion of all concerned bodies;
- adequacy of evaluation of positive and negative impacts;
- methods and data used;
- proposed measures to eliminate or reduce pollution, with reference to state of the art technologies;
- alternative measures to eliminate or reduce pollution;
- proposals to mitigate the environmental impact.

3.7 Public participation: hearing

A public hearing is organised within one month after the expert review. The basis of discussion is the developer's Environmental Impact Statement, the comments of the community, administrative bodies and civil initiatives and associations, and the expert review.

The time and place of the meeting is made known by the competent environmental authority with a minimum of seven days notice. A report of the discussions at the hearing is distributed to the relevant parties.

3.8 Approval of EIA

On the basis of the expert review and the report of the public hearing, the competent environmental authority issues a statement of its opinion. The statement must include specific information outlined in Annex 4 of the *Act on Environmental Impact Assessment, No.244/1992*. The statement grants or withholds approval, recommends which variant if there is more than one, and specifies conditions.

According to the *Act on Administrative Procedure, No.71/1967*, the opinion should be issued 30 to 60 days after the public hearing.

The opinion of the competent environmental authority is not binding on the municipal building authority (unless an infringement of environmental regulations is involved), although no permits can be issued by this authority until the EIA process has been completed.

4. Monitoring

Plans for monitoring and analysing environmental impacts once the project has begun must be included in the Environmental Impact Statement (Annex 3 of *Act on Environmental Impact Assessment, No.244/1992*). The final approval of the EIA by the competent environmental authority may contain requirements to implement monitoring procedures. The Environmental Inspectorate is responsible for environmental monitoring.

5. EIA in practice

About 170 EIAs have taken place in the Czech Republic. (Since the EIA takes place at the beginning of the permitting procedure, some of these projects are still being reviewed for other permits.) No projects have been refused as a result of a negative EIA review, although environmental conditions have been included as a result of EIAs.

An EIA for a spent nuclear fuel dump has been particularly controversial, and has stimulated considerable public interest. For some other projects there has been public apathy, and no interest was shown in the public hearing, despite being announced in the required way.

Because of the lack of familiarity with public consultation, on the part of both administrative and public bodies, controversy often arises. This is exacerbated by the lack of a scoping procedure, which can lead to disagreement about the scope of the EIA at an advanced stage of the process. The developer must often take additional steps to reach a consensus with the public participants.

6. Possible changes in the near future

The introduction of a scoping procedure into the EIA process is being considered.

7. Sources of further information

Ing. Václav Obluk
Director
EIA Department
Ministry of Environment
Vršovická 65
100 10 Prague 10
Czech Republic
tel: (42-2) 6712 1111
fax: (42-2) 6731 0308

Dr. Eva Kružíková
Director
Institute for Environmental Policy
U dvou srpů 2
150 00 Prague 5

Czech Republic
tel: (42-2) 534 833
fax: (42-2) 527 808

Ing. Jiří Dusík
Public Environmental Assessment Centre
Soukenická 30
110 00 Prague 1
Czech Republic
tel: (42-2) 231 0894
tel/fax: (42-2) 231 3057

Ing. Vladimír Rimmel
Regional EIA Centre
Chelčického 4
701 00 Ostrava 1
Czech Republic
tel: (42-69) 610 4296/4297/4111
fax: (42-69) 611 3855

Dr. Jan Horák
North Czech EIA Centre
Nám. Míru 37
400 01 Ustí nad Labem
Czech Republic
tel/fax: (42-47) 22528

Dr. Jiřina Vargová
EIA Consultation
ul. J. Hory 13
466 04 Jablonec n.N.
Czech Republic
tel: (42-428) 28062

8. EIA legislation

Terms used in law	*Terms used in book*
Report/documentation	Environmental Impact Statement
Involved body	Competent authority
Statement	Decision by authority

CZECH REPUBLIC A

Czech National Council Act on Environmental Impact Assessment

Act No.244/1992 S.B., 15 April 1992

The Czech National Council has passed the following Act:

Part one. Introductory provisions

Article 1. Subject of regulation

The Act regulates the environmental impact assessment of planned constructions, their changes and changes in their use[1] (hereinafter referred to as 'constructions'), activities[2], technologies[3], development concepts and programmes[4] (hereinafter referred to as 'concepts') and products[3]. The Act determines the bodies of State Administration that are competent in environmental impact assessment[5].

Part two. Assessment of constructions, activities and technologies

Article 2. Subject of assessment

1. Subject of assessment are constructions, activities and technologies listed in Appendices Nos. 1 and 2 of this Act.

2. Subject of assessment are also constructions, activities and technologies listed in Appendices Nos. 1 and 2 of this Act which do not achieve the limit values mentioned in the Appendices in case they are to be carried out in areas that are protected under separate regulations[6], if so decided by the body that is competent in environmental impact assessment (hereinafter referred to as the 'competent authority'), on its own initiative or on the initiative of:

2.2.a. the Construction Office to which a proposal has been submitted to issue a territorial decision on the location of a construction, or on the use of an area, or to which an application has been submitted to issue a permit;

[1] Act No.50/1976 S.B. on Territorial Planning and Construction Regulations (The Construction Act), in the wording of subsequent regulations; Decree No.85/1976 S.B. on More Detailed Regulations of Territorial Procedures and Construction Rules, in the wording of subsequent regulations.

[2] Article 17.2 of Act No.17/1992 S.B. on the Environment.

[3] Article 17.3 of Act No.17/1992 S.B.

[4] Article 20.2 of Act No.17/1992 S.B.

[5] Articles 21.1 and 2 of Act No.17/1992 S.B.

[6] E.g. Act of the Czech National Council No.114/1992 S.B. on the Protection of Nature and the Landscape, Government Decree of the Czech Socialist Republic No.40/1978 S.B. on Protected Areas of Natural Water Reservoirs of Beskydy, Jeseníky, Jizerské hory, Krkonoíe, Orlické hory, Sumava and Žďárské vrchy; Government Decree of Czech Socialist Republic No.10/1979 S.B. on Protected Areas of Natural Water Reservoirs of Brdy, Jablùnkovsko, Kruíné hory, Novohradské hory, Vsetínské vrchy and Žamberk-Králíky.

2.2.b. another body of the State Administration or a community, within the area of which or in the vicinity of which the construction, activity or technology is to be carried out.

Extent of assessment
Article 3. The assessment shall include in particular:

3.a. an identification, a description and an evaluation of the assumed direct and indirect impact of the construction, activity or technology on:

3.a.1. climatic conditions, ambient air, surface and groundwater, soil, rock environment, manner of utilisation of the landscape, protected areas, flora, fauna, functions and stability of ecological systems, population;

3.a.2. the utilisation of natural resources;

3.a.3. cultural monuments;

3.a.4. the town and community environment;

3.b. a comparison of proposed alternative solutions in case they are required to be prepared (Article 6.2) and a selection of the best alternative;

3.c. a proposal of measures and conditions which shall exclude or reduce the assumed negative impact, or which shall increase the positive impact of the construction, activity or technology;

3.d. an evaluation of the consequences, should the construction, activity or technology not be carried out.

Article 4
4.1. The impact of a construction, activity or technology shall be assessed for the period of their development, implementation and use (operation), of their removal and if necessary for the period after their removal.

4.2. When assessing the impact of construction, activity or technology, the conditions of a given area are taken into account.

4.3. When assessing the use (operation) of a construction, activity or technology, the assumed environmental impact shall be evaluated both in case of normal operation and in case of possible accidents.

Article 5. Notification
5.1. Anybody who intends to carry out a construction, an activity or technology listed in Appendices Nos. 1 and 2 of this Act (hereinafter referred to as the 'notifier') is obligated to notify the competent authority of this (Article 19).

5.2. The notification shall include:

5.2.a. basic data on the construction, activity or technology, in particular name, location, purpose, characteristics, extent, starting and finishing date;

5.2.b. a brief description of the technical and technological designs;

5.2.c. basic data on the impact of the construction, activity or technology on the environment, in particular claims on land occupation, on energies, on raw materials, the rate of pollution or damage to the individual components of the environment;

5.2.d. the opinion of the competent Construction Office on the compliance of the proposed construction, activity or technology with the approved Territorial Planning Documentation.

5.3. Documentation on the evaluation of the impact of the construction, activity or technology (hereinafter referred to as 'documentation'; see Appendix No. 3) will be added to the notification in six copies. The competent authority may, in justified cases, request more copies to be submitted.

5.4. Within 30 days after delivery of an initiative following Article 2.2, the competent authority shall decide whether the impact assessment shall or shall not be carried out and it will inform the body which presented the initiative for an assessment as well as the respective proposer[7] or building contractor[8]. In case of an impact assessment, the proposer or building contractor shall submit notification and documentation following Articles 2 and 3 to the competent authority.

5.5. Authorities of those communities on the territory of which a construction shall be located, an activity carried out, or a technology implemented, or the territory of which, following the elaborated documentation, is affected by a construction, activity or technology (hereinafter referred to as the 'affected community') shall ensure, upon initiative of the competent authority, the publication of information, in the usual local manner, that the construction, activity or technology shall be assessed following this Act.

Article 6. Documentation

6.1. The content and extent of the documentation is determined in Appendix No. 3 of this Act.

6.2. The competent authority may require the documentation to be supplemented, in particular, with alternative solutions.

6.3. The documentation may only be elaborated by persons with a certificate of professional competence (hereinafter referred to as 'authorised persons'). The certificates are issued by the Ministry of the Environment of the Czech Republic (hereinafter referred to as 'the Ministry') with the consent of the Ministry of Health of the Czech Republic.

6.4. The basic requirements of professional competence are relevant university education, six years of practical experience and passing of a special examination. Exemptions from educational or practical requirements may be granted by the Ministry. The Ministry shall determine in a decree further conditions regarding the professional competence, the procedure of its verification and regarding the issuing of certificates.

6.5. The Ministry shall keep a list of authorised persons.

[7] Article 34.1 of Act No.50/1976 S.B.
[8] Article 59.1 of Act No.50/1976 S.B.

Article 7. Publication and discussion of the documentation

7.1. The competent authority shall, without delay, dispatch the documentation to the concerned bodies of State Administration and to the affected community. The community shall, within five days of receiving the documentation, announce in the usual local manner, when and where it will be possible to examine the documentation, to make excerpts, transcripts or copies. Public examination of the documentation must be made possible for a period of 30 calendar days; within this period a written opinion on the documentation may be submitted (hereinafter referred to as 'public opinion').

7.2. In case of doubt whether a community is affected or not pursuant to Article 1, the competent authority shall decide. The competent authority can also determine that, should there be a large number of communities affected following Article 1, the documentation can only be examined in communities selected by the competent authority; the remaining affected communities must announce when and where it will be possible to examine the documentation.

7.3. The affected community shall send the public opinion and its own opinion to the competent authority within 14 days after the period determined in Article 1 has expired.

7.4. The concerned bodies of the State Administration shall send their opinion to the competent authority within 50 days after having received the documentation.

7.5. In case the documentation contains facts which are protected following separate regulations[9], the provisions of Articles 1 through 4 shall not apply.

7.6. In case no opinions following Articles 1, 2 and 4 are delivered within the determined period, it shall be considered that there are no comments on the documentation.

Article 8. Participation of the civil initiative and civil associations

8.1. A civil initiative, which for the purposes of this Act is to be understood as a group of at least 500 natural persons older than 18 years who support in writing the public opinion pursuant to Article 7 is entitled, through representation of a mandatory following Article 3, to take part in the discussions on the documentation following Article 7 and in the public discussions pursuant to Article 10.

8.2. A civil initiative pursuant to Article 1 shall present a list of signatures, including name, surname, permanent address, birth certificate numbers and signature of the persons who support the respective public declaration. The list of signatures must be submitted together with the public opinion pursuant to Article 7.

8.3. The mandatory of the civil initiative who is authorised to act on its behalf and to receive written material, is the person who is appointed as a mandatory in the list of signatures. In case such designation is missing or incorrect, the person who is mentioned first on the list of

[9] E.g. Act No.12/1971 S.B. on the Protection of State Secrets, in the wording of Act No.383/1990 S.B.; Government Decree of the CSFR No.419/1990 S.B. on Basic Facts Constituting the Subject of State Secrets; Government Decree of the CSFR No.420/1990 S.B. which amends Government Decree of the CSSR No.148/1971 S.B. on Protection of Economic and Professional Secrets.

signatures shall be considered as the mandatory of a civil initiative. The mandatory can appoint in writing a deputy, who will act for him or her within the scope of the mandate.

8.4. The mandatory of a civil initiative may be replaced by another person on the basis of a written declaration to the competent authority. This declaration must be signed by a majority of the members of a civil initiative. The same procedure is also valid in case such a mandatory of a civil initiative withdraws.

8.5. If a majority of the persons mentioned in Article 2 establishes a civil association following separate regulations[10], for further support of the opinion of the civil initiative, such an association is participant in an administrative procedure, if in this procedure decisions are made on a permit for a construction, activity or technology that are assessed following this Act. A civil association which has been established previously and which has submitted an opinion pursuant to Article 7.1 is also participant in the same administrative procedure.

Article 9. Expert opinion

9.1. The competent authority shall without delay ensure the elaboration of an expert opinion based on the documentation, taking into account the public opinion, the opinion of the affected community and the opinion of the concerned bodies of the State Administration, within a period of 60 days after these materials have been submitted. This period can be extended in reasonable cases, however, for not longer than another 150 days.

9.2. An expert opinion can be elaborated by authorised persons only, pursuant to Articles 6.3 and 6.4.

9.3. Authorised persons who have taken part in the elaboration of documentation are excluded from elaboration of the expert opinion.

9.4. The notifier is obligated to provide the persons that are elaborating the expert opinion at their request, with additional information necessary for the elaboration of the expert opinion.

9.5. The expert opinion shall evaluate in particular:

9.5.a. completeness of the documentation;

9.5.b. public opinion, opinion of affected community and opinions of the concerned bodies of the State Administration;

9.5.c. completeness of identification of all positive and negative environmental impacts of the construction, activity or technology, including their mutual interactions;

9.5.d. applied evaluation methods and completeness of input information;

9.5.e. proposal of technical solutions concerning the elimination of limiting of pollution or damage to the environment with regard to the contemporary level of knowledge;

9.5.f. alternative solutions;

[10] Act No.83/1990 S.B. on Civil Associations.

9.5.g. proposal of measures and conditions for the exclusion or reduction of negative environmental impact of the construction, activity or technology, or for the implementation of the construction, activity or technology and for the use (operation) of the construction, activity or technology.

9.6. An expert opinion shall always contain a proposal for a statement of the competent authority.

Article 10. Public discussion

10.1. Within one month at the latest from the receipt of the expert opinion pursuant to Article 9, the competent authority shall ensure public discussion on the contents of the expert opinion, and on the public opinion, including civil initiatives, on the opinion of communities and concerned bodies of State Administration, which it receives pursuant to Article 7.

10.2. The competent authority shall at least one week in advance announce in writing the time and place of the public discussion to the notifier, the communities, the concerned bodies of the State Administration, the civil initiatives and to the persons who elaborated the expert opinion. If the proposed construction, activity or technology concerns more communities, concerned bodies of the State Administration or civil initiatives, the competent authority can ensure separate public discussions in territorial districts determined by the competent authority.

10.3. In particular experts and persons who can present important information on the discussed subject can be invited to participate in the public discussion.

10.4. The Ministry shall determine the manner and procedure of public discussions in a public notice.

10.5. The participants, mentioned in Article 1 shall receive the minutes of the results of the public discussion.

Article 11. The statement

11.1. Based on the expert opinion and on the minutes of the public discussion, the competent authority shall issue a statement, the contents of which are described in Appendix No. 4 of this Act. Without this statement, an administrative body cannot issue a permitting decision or measure following separate regulations[11].

11.2. In case a construction, activity or technology is for purposes of state defence, the competent authority shall issue a statement after discussions with the relevant body of the Czechoslovak army.

Article 12. Settlement of costs and records

12.1. The costs of the elaboration of an expert opinion shall be covered by the notifier.

12.2. The competent authority keeps records of issued statements.

[11] E.g. Act No.50/1976 S.B., Act No.138/1973 S.B. on Water (The Water Act), Act No.135/1961 S.B. on Ground Roads (The Road Act), in the wording of subsequent regulations, Act No.51/1965 S.B. on Railways, in the wording of subsequent regulations, Act No.47/1956 S.B., on Civil Aviation (The Aviation Act), in the wording of subsequent regulations.

Article 13. Transboundary environmental impact assessment

13.1. In case of assessment of the impact of constructions, activities or technologies and of their consequences for the environment exceeding state borders as determined in separate regulation[12], Part Two of this Act applies with the following restrictions:

13.1.a. the content and extent of the documentation on evaluation of impact and consequences on the environment are governed by a separate regulation[13] and by Appendix No. 3 of this Act;

13.1.b. the competent authority shall submit a proposal of a statement to the Federal Committee for the Environment;

13.1.c. the competent authority shall issue a final statement after it has been notified of the result of interstate negotiations[14].

Part three. Assessments of concepts

Article 14

14.1. Under this Act a 'concept' is a concept submitted and approved at the level of the central authorities of State Administration (hereinafter referred to as the 'approving authority') in the field of energy, transport, agriculture, waste treatment, mining and processing of minerals, recreation and tourism. Territorial planning documentation[15] and the General Water Management Plan[16] are also considered to be concepts.

14.2. The submitter of a concept (hereinafter referred to as the 'submitter') must ensure that environment impact assessment, elaborated to an adequate extent according to Appendix No. 3 part C, items 3 and 4 of this Act is a part of the concept.

14.3. The submitter must ensure in a suitable manner and in agreement with the Ministry publication of the concept proposal, or its principles, at least 60 days prior to its discussion.

14.4. The submitter shall send the concept proposal, prepared with respect to public comments if there are any, to the competent authority, which shall issue its statement within 30 days from the date of delivery, with the exception of the case that the competent authority is the submitter itself.

14.5. The approving authority shall not discuss the concept without a statement of the competent authority.

[12] Appendix No. 3 of Act No.17/1992 S.B.

[13] Appendix No. 4 of Act No.17/1992 S.B.

[14] Article 26.1 of Act No.17/1992 S.B.

[15] Article 13 of Act No.50/1976 S.B.

[16] Article 3 of Act No.138/1973 S.B.; Article 8 of Act No.130/1974 S.B. on the State Administration of Water Management, in the wording of subsequent regulations.

Part four. Assessment of products

Principles of assessment

Article 15

15.1. The assessment of products includes a comparison of the characteristics of the product from the point of view of their environmental impact and the requirements determined by legal regulations and technical standards.

15.2. Subjects of assessment are products which are determined by the competent authority on its initiative in co-operation with the Central Authority of the State Administration[17] for State Testing (hereinafter referred to as 'determined products'). Determined products are announced in the Ministry Bulletin.

15.3. The assessment is carried out for both domestic and imported products, except for foodstuffs.

15.4. The assessment is carried out in the form of certificates following separate regulations[18].

Article 16

16.1. The determined products cannot be distributed without a certificate pursuant to Article 15.4.

16.2. The certificate can be replaced by indicating an imported product with an appropriate foreign certification mark or by a foreign certificate recognised in the territory of the Czech Republic.

16.3. In case it is found out that imported products, despite designation by a foreign certification mark or a foreign certificate pursuant to Article 2 have negative impact on the environment, the competent authority shall propose to the Central Authority of State Administration for Foreign Trade[19] to take measures to prevent their import.

16.4. Determined products which are already distributed and for which the application for a certificate was made within a period of 30 days after their announcement pursuant to Article 15.2 can be distributed until the completion of their assessment by an authorised legal or natural person[20]. Determined products which have not been reported for certification within this period, may not be distributed after the period has expired.

Article 17. The costs related to the certification and control of distributed products or to their withdrawal from distribution pursuant to Article 20.1.j) are covered by their producer or importer.

[17] Article 117 of Act No.194/1988 S.B. on Jurisdiction of Federal Central State Administrative Authorities, in the wording of subsequent regulations.

[18] Act No.30/1968 S.B. on State Testing, in the wording of subsequent regulations.

[19] Article 61 of Act No.194/1988 S.B.

[20] Article 6 of Act No.30/1968 S.B.

Article 18. Penalties
18.1. The competent authority shall impose a penalty of up to three hundred times the minimum wage as determined in a separate regulation[21] upon a person who:

18.1.a. has distributed a determined product which was not granted a certificate or the certificate of which was withdrawn;

18.1.b. has not ceased to distribute determined products pursuant to Article 16.4.

18.2. When imposing a penalty pursuant to Article 1, the weight of the consequences to the environment which were or could have been caused is taken into account.

18.3. A penalty pursuant to Article 1 can be imposed within one year of the date the competent authority learned of the infringement of an obligation, at the latest, however, within three years from the date on which the infringement of an obligation occurred.

18.4. All revenues from the penalties shall be paid into the State Environment Fund of the Czech Republic[22].

Part five. The competent authorities

Article 19. The competent authorities are:

19.a. the Ministry;
19.b. the Czech Environment Inspection;
19.c. District Offices.

Article 20
20.1. The Ministry

20.1.a. assesses constructions, activities and technologies listed in Appendix No. 1 of this Act and issues a statement on them;

20.1.b. keeps a list of authorised persons;

20.1.c. keeps comprehensive records of issued statements;

20.1.d. issues statements on proposed concepts;

20.1.e. determines products subject to assessment pursuant to Article 15.2 and announces them in the Ministry Bulletin;

20.1.f. keeps a list of determined products which were not granted a certificate or from which a certificate was withdrawn and announces them in the Ministry Bulletin;

20.1.g. keeps a record of granted certificates;

20.1.h. determines regulations and technical standards for the assessment of products pursuant to Article 16.3;

[21] Government Decree of the Czech and Slovak Federative Republic No.53/1992 S.B. on Minimum Wages.
[22] Article 2.1.g of Act No.388/1991 S.B. of the Czech National Council on the State Environmental Fund of the Czech Republic.

20.1.i. proposes measures pursuant to Article 16.3;

20.1.j. based on a proposal from the Czech Environmental Inspection, decides on the withdrawal from distribution of a determined product which was not granted a certificate or from which a certificate was withdrawn pursuant to Article 15.

20.2. The Czech Environment Inspection

20.2.a. controls whether determined products which were not granted a certificate, or from which a certificate was withdrawn are not distributed;

20.2.b. imposes penalties pursuant to this Act;

20.2.c. proposes the withdrawal from distribution of a determined product which was not granted a certificate or from which a certificate was withdrawn.

20.3. District Offices

20.3.a. assess construction, activities and technologies listed in Appendix No. 2 of this Act and constructions, activities and technologies following Article 2.2 of this Act and issue statements on them;

20.3.b. send one copy of their statement to the Ministry for comprehensive records.

20.4. In the capital city of Prague, the municipal authorities of the capital city of Prague carry out the activities of the District Office pursuant to this Act.

20.5. The Ministry may reserve the right to issue a statement on a construction, activity or technology when a District Office is the competent authority, in case the construction, activity or technology is to be carried out in areas protected under separate regulations[6].

20.6. The Ministry can transfer its activity to assess a construction, activity or technology listed in Appendix No. 1 of this Act to a District Office when, in an individual case this would contribute to the speed and economisation of the assessment.

Part six. General, temporary and final provisions

Article 21. The Ministry shall, with the consent of the Ministry of Health of the Czech Republic, determine binding provisions through a decree for the use of products or substances which may significantly influence the environment in a negative way.

Article 22. Administrative procedures following separate regulations[11] initiated before this Act came into force are not affected by this Act.

Article 23. General regulations on administrative procedures[23] do not apply to Part Two and Part Three of this Act.

Article 24. This Act comes into legal force as of 1 July 1992.

Signed: V. Bureová, P. Pithart

[23] Act No.71/1976 S.B. on Administrative Procedures (The Administrative Act).

Appendix 1

Constructions, activities and technologies assessed within the competence of the Ministry of the Environment of the Czech Republic

1. Agriculture and forestry

1.1. Deforestation of an area exceeding 5 hectares;

1.2. Amelioration activities (drainage, protection of soil from erosion, land alternations, technical forest amelioration) on an area exceeding 500 hectares.

2. Mining industry

2.1. Extraction and processing in situ of ore, magnesite, coal exceeding 100,000 t/year, stone, gravel, bituminous shale and industrial minerals exceeding 200,000 t/year, natural gas exceeding 100 million m^3/year, and peat;

2.2. Extraction and processing of uranium ore, waste banks and sludge beds including recultivation;

2.3. Extraction and refining of crude oil, including plants for regeneration of used mineral oils, facilities for thermal and chemical processing of coal and shale.

3. Power industry

3.1. Electric power plants, other industrial facilities for production of electricity, steam, hot water, and other facilities with an installed output exceeding 100 MW;

3.2. Hydroelectric power plants with a peak output of 50 MW and more;

3.3. Nuclear power plants and other facilities with nuclear reactors.

3.4. Facilities for conversion, enrichment and production of nuclear fuel;

3.5. Interim spent nuclear fuel storage facilities;

3.6. Processing and final depositing of highly radioactive waste;

3.7. Processing and depositing of low and medium radioactive waste from operating and shut-down nuclear power plants and from facilities using radionuclides.

3.8. Long distance gas, oil, steam, hot water and other pipelines, including their facilities (pumping, exchange and compressor stations), long distance power transmission lines (110 kV and more);

3.9. Underground storage of natural gas and other gases with a capacity exceeding 1 million m^3, above ground storage of natural gas and other gases with a capacity exceeding 100,000 m^3, of oil, oil products and chemicals with a capacity exceeding 1,000 m^3.

4. Metallurgy

4.1. Production and processing of crude iron, cast iron and steel with a capacity exceeding 30,000 t/year, production and processing of non-ferrous metals (non-ferrous metallurgy) with a capacity exceeding 3,000 t/year;

4.2. Surface processing of metals with a capacity exceeding 10 million m^2/year of processed surface.

5. Water and paper industry

5.1. Production of cellulose and paper.

6. Other industries

6.1. Processing of asbestos and asbestos products;

6.2. Cement factories and lime factories with a capacity exceeding 100,000 t/year;

6.3. Chemical production with a capacity exceeding 200 t/year;

6.4. Production of toxic substances, pesticides and pharmaceutical products in an amount exceeding 1 t/year;

6.5. Facilities for processing, neutralising and incinerating hazardous waste in an amount of 1,000 t/year and more, and facilities for storing and disposing hazardous waste in an amount of 10 t or more.

7. Infrastructure

7.1. Construction of highways, first category roads, railways, airports, and permanent racing tracks for motor vehicles with hardened surface, water ways including ports;

7.2. Dams and water reservoirs, if the height of the dam exceeds a level of 10 m above the footing bottom, or if the total volume exceeds 10 million m^3;

7.3. Facilities for groundwater withdrawal if the annual volume of withdrawn water exceeds 10 million m^3;

7.4. Facilities for municipal waste treatment with a capacity exceeding 100,000 t/year[24].

Appendix 2

Constructions, activities and technologies assessed within the jurisdiction of the District Offices

1. Agriculture and forestry

1.1. Facilities for animal production, including waste deposits, for cattle breeding facilities with a capacity exceeding 100 animals, for pig breeding facilities with a capacity exceeding 200 pigs, for poultry farms with a capacity exceeding 25,000 broilers or 25,000 hens;

1.2. Storage facilities for agricultural products with a capacity exceeding 20,000 tonnes;

1.3. Amelioration activities (drainage, irrigation, protection of soil from erosion, land alternations and technical forest amelioration) on an area from 10 hectares to 500 hectares.

[24] Article 2.2 of Act No.238/1991 S.B. on Waste Management.

1.4. Landscape interventions which may cause fundamental changes in the biological diversity and in the structure and function of eco-systems.

2. Food industry

2.1. Breweries, malting houses and non-alcoholic drinks production with a capacity exceeding 10,000 hl/year;

2.2. Slaughter houses and meat processing plants with a production capacity exceeding 5,000 t/year;

2.3. Starch producing plants with a capacity exceeding 50,000 t/year of processed potatoes;

2.4. Sugar refineries with a capacity exceeding 15,000 t/year of processed raw materials

2.5. Frozen food factories with a capacity exceeding 100,000 t/year of frozen products;

2.6. Distilleries with a capacity exceeding 1,000 t/year;

2.7. Oil industry (production of vegetable oil and grease) and production of detergents with a production capacity exceeding 20,000 t/year;

2.8. Dairies and milk products facilities with a capacity exceeding 100,000 t/year of processed milk;

2.9. Canning factories with a production capacity exceeding 100,000 t/year.

3. Power industry

3.1. Electric power plants, other industrial facilities for production of electricity, steam, hot water and other facilities burning fossil fuel, with an installed output from 20 to 100 MW;

3.2. Hydroelectric power plants with a peak output from 10 to 50 MW.

4. Metallurgy

4.1. Surface processing of metals with a capacity from 5 to 10 million m^2/year of processed surface;

4.2. Machinery and electrotechnical production area exceeding 5,000 m^2;

4.3. Production and assembly of motor vehicles, railway carriages and tanks with a capacity exceeding 1,000 items/year;

4.4. Production of passenger and cargo ships for river transport;

4.5. Production and repair of airplanes with a capacity exceeding 100 items/year.

5. The wood and paper industry

5.1. Impregnation of wood with toxic chemicals in an amount exceeding 1,000 t/year;

5.2. Production of fibreboard and plywood with a production capacity exceeding 50,000 m^2/year;

5.3. Production of furniture, with a capacity exceeding 10,000 m^3 of processed raw material per year.

6. Other industries

6.1. Processing of textiles, dye works, with a capacity exceeding 10,000 t/year of used chemicals;

6.2. Tanneries with a capacity exceeding 50,000 m^2/year of processed raw material;

6.3. Production of glass or glass fibres with a capacity exceeding 50,000 t/year;

6.4. Use and recycling of contaminated chlorinated hydrocarbons in an amount exceeding 10 t/year;

6.5. Polygraphic facilities with a capacity exceeding 1 tonne/year of used chemicals;

6.6. Storage of toxins and pesticides in an amount exceeding 1 t/year, liquid fertilisers, pharmaceutical products, paints and lacquers in an amount exceeding 100,000 t/year;

6.7. Production of construction materials with a capacity exceeding 100,000 t/year;

6.8. Asphalt production exceeding 10,000t/year.

7. Infrastructure

7.1. Facilities for withdrawal water of an annual volume of withdrawn water exceeding 3 million m^3;

7.2. Waste-water treatment plants and sewerage with a capacity exceeding 100,000 inhabitant equivalents;

7.3. Sludge basins and sludge beds with a capacity exceeding 100,000 m^3, and others with an embarkment height over 10 m above the footing bottom;

7.4. Facilities for municipal waste treatment with a capacity from 10,000 to 100,000 t/year;

7.5. Rendering plants and veterinary decontamination plants;

7.6. Modifications of water courses that fundamentally change the character of the water course and the nature of the landscape;

7.7. Cableways, a part of which is the construction of ski pistes of a total area exceeding 5 hectares;

7.8. Trade and storage complexes of a total built-on area exceeding 3,000 m^2;

7.9. Camp sites, sports and military shooting ranges affecting interests protected by separate regulations;

7.10. Airports and permanent racing tracks for motor vehicles without hardened surface.

Appendix 3

Documentation on environmental impact evaluation

Part A. Basic data[25]

- name
- character (new construction, modernisation, reconstruction, repair)
- location (district, community, cadastral territory)
- reason for locating in the given location (continuation of an already started project, availability of raw materials, labour force, others)
- applicant
- project developer
- user
- starting and finishing date
- brief description of the technical and technical designs (main characteristics of the production process, capacity, number of shifts, number of employees)
- level of proposed technical designs
- total costs
- list of community territories which will be affected by the presumed impacts

Part B. Data on direct environmental impacts[25]

I. Input data

1. Land

- occupied land (hectares, soil quality); total area, of which temporarily occupied land and permanently occupied land, of which agricultural land use and forest land use
- protected areas
- protective zones

2. Water

- total amount of withdrawn water (m^3/hour, m^3/year)
- of which for operation use
- total water consumption (m^3/hour, m^3/year)
- water source (public water supply, surface source, others)

3. Other sources of raw material and energy

- type, annual consumption, manner of acquirement (own source, import)

4. Claims on transport and other infrastructures

[25] Basic data are given for each variant.

II. Output data

1. Air

a. main point sources of air pollution

- technological process of pollution production
- amount of emitted pollutants in t/year (in particular solid emissions, sulphur oxides, nitrogen oxides, CO, heavy metals, hydrocarbons, halogen derivatives of hydrocarbons and other characteristic pollutants)
- manner of emission separation (type of separator, planned capacity, effectiveness)

b. main areal air pollution sources (dust, raw material storage, construction works, etc.)

- type of source
- corresponding technological process
- extent of areal source (in m^2)
- source of activity (permanent, regular, incidental)
- amount of emitted pollutants (t/year)

c. main mobile pollution sources (transport, etc.)

- type of source
- amount of emitted pollutants (t/year)

2. Waste water

- total volume of discharged waste water in m^3/year (of which directly to recipient, to waste-water treatment plants)
- technological process which produces waste water
- type, planned capacity and effectiveness of waste-water treatment plants for the main indicators of pollution
- character of recipients (waterworks streams, level of pollution)
- amount of discharged pollutants in t/year; mg/l; average maximum values (in particular BOD_5, COD_{Cr}, phosphorus, nitrogen and other characteristic chemicals, biological and microbiological indicators of radioactivity, temperature of water).

3. Waste (not included in air or in waste water)

- type of waste (municipal waste, hazardous waste, radioactive waste)
- technological process which produces waste
- amount of waste in t/year
- manner of waste treatment

4. Noise, vibrations

5. Radioactive and electromagnetic radiation

Part C. Complex description and environmental impact evaluation

I. Description of proposed alternative solutions (e.g. of a geographical or technological character – localisation, type of technology), description of comparative alternatives (e.g. alternative without activity, active zero alternative, best environmental alternative) including their comparison.

II. Brief description of the probably significantly affected environment.

A. Basic characteristics

1. air (climatic factors, air quality)

2. water (groundwater, water courses, water spring areas, water yield, flow rate, withdrawal of water, water quality)

3. soil (type, soil quality, soil contamination)

4. environmental geo-factors (geological conditions, hydrogeology, relief of the terrain, seismic conditions, erosion)

5. fauna and flora (species and habitats, in particular endangered and protected species and habitats)

6. territorial system of ecological stability and the nature of the landscape

B. Other characteristics

1. landscape (manner of utilisation of the landscape, settlements, production and recreation)

2. character of town quarters, functional characteristics of suburban zones

3. protected areas, nature reserves, national parks

4. areas of raw material resources and other natural riches

5. protective zones

6. architectural and historical monuments, archaeological findings

7. other characteristics of the environment

8. location of constructions in relation to territorial planning documentation (basics)

III. A complex description of the presumed environmental impacts and an estimation of their significance (presumed direct, indirect, secondary, cumulative, synergic, short-term, temporary, long-term and permanent impacts).

A. Impacts on inhabitants

– health risks, social consequences, economic consequences
– number of inhabitants affected by the construction, activity or technology
– detrimental consequences of construction, activity or technology
– factors detrimental to comfort

B. Impacts on ecosystems, their components and functions

1. impacts on air and climate

- amount and concentration of emissions and their impact on the near and distant surroundings
- significant odour
- other impacts on air and climate

2. impacts on water

- impact on the character of drainage of the area
- changes in hydrological characteristics (groundwater levels, flowing rate, yield of water sources)
- impact on water quality

3. impacts on soil, land and geological conditions

- impact on the extent and manner of land use
- soil contamination
- changes in local topography, impact on the stability and erosion of the soil
- impact on rock environments and mineral resources
- changes of hydrogeological characteristics
- impact on the protected parts of nature
- impact in consequence of depositing waste

4. impacts on flora and fauna

- damage to and extinction of plant and animal species and their biotopes

5. impacts on ecosystems

C. Impacts on the anthropogenic systems, their components and functions

- impact on buildings, architectural and archaeological monuments and other human creations
- impact on cultural values of a non-material nature (local traditions, etc.)
- damage and loss of protected geological and paleontological objects and areas

D. Impacts on the structure and functional use of an area

- impact on transport (local transport, road, railway, air, and water transport)
- impact of connected construction and activities (construction of new roads, engineering works, housing construction)
- development of connected infrastructure
- impact on the aesthetic quality of the area
- impact on the recreational use of the landscape

E. Other impacts

- biological impacts
- impact of noise and radiation
- other ecological impacts

F. Large-area impacts in the landscape

- suitability of localisation of the individual alternatives with regard to the ecological capacity of the area
- the present and potentially resulting situation of the ecological burden of the area (comprehensive effect of all spatial phenomena and factors)

IV. A description of the proposed measures to prevent, eliminate, minimise or compensate environmental impacts

- territorial planning measures
- technical measures (elimination of pollution, recycling of waste, protective survey of archaeological findings, measures for the protection of cultural monuments)
- compensatory measures
- other measures

V. A description of the operational safety risks

- possible occurrence of accidents
- impacts on the surroundings
- preventive measures
- consequential measures

VI. Outline of monitoring and management programmes and post-project analysis plans.

VII. Presentation of the applied methods of prediction and the basic principles used in the impact evaluation, and the manner of acquiring data on the present and future conditions of the environment in the locality where a construction, activity or technology is to be realised.

VIII. Statement of insufficient knowledge and uncertainties which emerged in the course of elaborating the documentation.

IX. Summary of a non-technical character, if necessary, supplemented with diagrams, maps, etc.

X. Conclusion.

Appendix 4

Statement on impact evaluation

1. Identification data

- name
- brief purpose
- locality (district, community, cadastral territory)
- starting date
- finishing date
- applicant
- project developer
- total costs

2. Description of the course of the evaluation

- where and by whom was the documentation elaborated
- where and by whom was the expert opinion elaborated (conclusions)
- when and how was the public discussion held (conclusions)

3. Conclusions

- statement (approval, disapproval)
- recommended alternative
- recommended conditions for the stage of
  a. preparation
  b. implementation
  c. operation

Stamp of the competent authority

Signature of the responsible representative of the competent authority

CZECH REPUBLIC B

Decree of the Ministry of the Environment of the Czech Republic on Professional Qualification in Environmental Impact Assessment and on the Means and Form of Public Discussion of Expert Reports

Decree No.499/1992, 1 October 1992

On the basis of Articles 6.4 and 10.4 of Act of the Czech National Council No.244/1992 S.B., on environmental impact assessment, the Ministry of the Environment of the Czech Republic decrees:

Part one. General provisions

Article 1. The subject of the decree
The decree specifies

a. detailed conditions of professional qualification (competence) for assessment of the impact of constructions, activities and technologies on the environment, the procedure to be followed in determining such qualification and the issuing of certificates;
b. the means and form of public discussion of expert reports.

Part two. Conditions for professional qualifications, the procedure to be followed in determining professional qualification and the issuing of certificates

Article 2. Professional qualification
2.1 Professional qualification in environmental impact assessment (hereinafter 'professional qualification') is to be understood for the purposes of this decree as professional qualification (competence) to draw up documents on assessment of the impact of constructions, activities or technology on the environment[1] (hereinafter 'documents') and professional reports[2].

2.2 A legal individual or a natural individual who is a businessman and who does not hold a certificate of professional qualification (hereinafter 'certificate') may draw up documents and professional reports only through an individual who holds such a certificate.

Article 3. Conditions for professional qualification
3.1. The Ministry of the Environment of the Czech Republic (hereinafter 'The Ministry') in accordance with the Ministry of Health of the Czech Republic will issue a certificate[3] to an individual who:

a. is fully competent to carry out legal acts;
b. has a university education in the appropriate field;
c. has at least six years of practical experience connected with environmental protection;

[1] Article 5.3 of Art of the Czech National Council No.244/1992 S.B. on Environmental Impact Assessment.
[2] Article 9 of Art of the Czech National Council No.244/1992 S.B.
[3] Articles 6.3 and 9.2 of Art of the Czech National Council No.244/1992 S.B.

d. has a clean criminal record;
e. has successfully completed an examination of professional qualification (Article 5).

3.2. An individual with a clean criminal record is considered for the purposes of this decree to be an individual who has not been found guilty of a crime connected with endangering of the environment[4].

Article 4. Procedure to be followed in determining professional qualification
4.1. Professional qualification is to be determined on the basis of an application submitted to the Ministry.

4.2. The application is to include:

a. the name and forename(s), professional titles, address of permanent residence, date of birth and birth certificate number of the individual submitting the application;
b. the education completed by the individual including the field of study and any specialisation;
c. the length and nature of any professional experience and any relevant specialisation in the field of environmental protection;

4.3. The following are to be included with the application:

a. excerpts from the criminal records, which must not be more than three months old;
b. a notarised copy of documents on completed university education;
c. documents on the completion of at least six years of practical experience (Article 3.1.c);
d. a list of any work published by the individual, scientific or any other work and professional experience, especially in relation to the environment.

Article 5
5.1. Professional qualification is to be determined through an examination by an examining commission which is to be set up by the Ministry.

5.2. The examining commission is to consist of a chairman, secretary and other members to be named by the Minister of the Environment of the Czech Republic, to be selected from professionals in the field. The knowledge required for the examination is defined in Appendix No. 1 to this decree.

5.3. Every individual who submits an application for certification of professional qualification as Articles 4.1–4.3 and who fulfils the conditions as Article 3.1.a–d (hereinafter 'candidate') will be invited to undergo an examination.

5.4. The rights and obligations of the examining commission and also the means of carrying out the examination and the assessment of the results of the examination are defined in the examination rules given in Appendix No. 2 of this decree.

5.5. The examining commission is to orally inform the candidate(s) of the results of the examination on the same day as the examination was carried out (Appendix No. 2, Part III, item 2).

[4] Articles 181a and 181b of Penal Act No.140/1961 S.B., in the wording of later regulations (complete wording Act No.392/1992 S.B.).

Article 6. Issuing of certificates

6.1. The Ministry is to issue a certificate of professional qualification at the latest three weeks after successful completion of the examination.

6.2. The certificate is to contain:

a. The name and forename(s), titles, permanent residence address, date of birth and birth certificate number of the individual who has successfully undergone the examination;
b. the official number and date of the issuing of the certificate;
c. the stamp of The Ministry;
d. the signatures of the chairman and secretary of the examining commission.

6.3. An individual who has been issued with a certificate and is a holder of such a certificate (hereinafter 'qualified individual') is to see that the completed documents and expert report include not only his (her) name, forename(s), address and signature, but also the date and official number of the certificate issued to him (her).

Article 7. Changes in and withdrawal of certificates

7.1. A qualified individual is obliged to notify The Ministry of all important changes connected with the information and documents as given in Articles 7.3 and 7.4, within 30 days of the occurrence of any such changes.

7.2. The Ministry will withdraw the certificate from an individual who,

a. has been deprived of his (her) legal rights or whose legal rights have been in any way limited;
b. has been legally convicted for an international crime carried out in connection with carrying out his (her) professional activities;
c. was the recipient of a certificate based on information given in the application or appendices thereto that he (she) knew to be false.

7.3. The Ministry can withdraw a certificate if:

a. an individual does not adhere to the notification obligations as in Article 7.1;
b. it is demonstrated that documents or assessments (reports) are imperfect or distorted or there is some other major neglecting of obligations in carrying out professional work.

Article 8. Termination of validity of a certificate

A certificate becomes invalid if:

a. the qualified individual dies;
b. the qualified individual surrenders the certificate.

Article 9. Payment of costs

A candidate who has been invited to submit to an examination is to pay in advance an amount equal to 2000 CK to cover costs connected with the examination. This amount is also to be paid in case of repeated tests.

Article 10. The Ministry is to keep a complete list of qualified individuals and to publish this list twice annually in the Ministerial Bulletin.

Part three. Means and form of public discussion of expert reports

Article 11
11.1. The appropriate authority[5] is to request posting of the notification of the place and time of public discussion of expert reports (hereinafter 'public discussion') on the official notice board to the municipality or, in the Capital City of Prague, the City of Brno, the City of Ostrava or the City of Plzeň on the official notice board of the appropriate part of the city in which the given construction is to be carried out, activity carried out or technology introduced or which would be affected by such construction, activity or technology.

11.2. Notification of the site and time of the public discussion is considered to be published as Article 11.1 if such notification is posted on the official notice board for a period of at least seven days prior to the public discussion.

Article 12
12.1. The public discussion is to be chaired by an individual authorised to do so by appropriate authority[5], whose knowledge and experience are to provide a guarantee of professional leadership (hereinafter 'authorised person').

12.2. The authorised person is to manage the course of the public discussion so that the impact of the construction, activity or technology on the environment is considered in all its important aspects and so that it includes the viewpoints of the representatives of the municipality and the general public, that exercised their right to express a standpoint on the documents[6], and also those of the representatives of civic movements[7].

12.3. The authorised person can interrupt the public discussion for serious reasons, especially if important questions or objections cannot be discussed or if it is necessary to obtain additional information that is essential for the discussion. The public notification of the place and time of the continuation of the public discussion is to be carried out by the appropriate authorities as Article 11.

Article 13. The authorised person is to draw up a protocol on the results of the public discussion within a time period of ten days after the end of the public discussion.

Article 14. The organisation and technical details of the public discussion are the responsibility of the appropriate authority[5] in cooperation with the appropriate municipality as Article 11.

Part four. Final and temporary provisions

Article 15. The Ministry can authorise selected legal individuals to draw up documents and expert reports in the period up to 31 March 1993.

Article 16. This decree comes into legal force on the day of its promulgation.

Signed by The Minister: V. Benda M.Eng. Ph.D.

[5] Articles 20.1, 3 and 4 of Act of the Czech National Council No.244/1992 S.B.
[6] Article 7 of Act of the Czech National Council No.244/1992 S.B.
[7] Article 8.3 of Act of the Czech National Council No.244/1992 S.B.

Appendix No. 1 to Decree No.499/1992 S.B.

Knowledge required in examinations of professional qualification to draw up documents and expert reports

– on the protection of water, protection of the air, protection of nature, the landscape and soil, protection of mineral resources, waste handling;
– a survey of the main kinds of environmental impacts;
– a survey of the principal technical measures for the protection of the individual components of the environment;
– on the subject of basic legal regulations governing care for the health of the population and care for the creation and protection of healthy living conditions;
– the environmental laws;
– the Act of the Czech National Council on Environmental Impact Assessment;
– generally valid regulations issued for implementation of the Act on the Environment and the Act of the Czech National Council on Environmental Impact Assessment;
– basic legal regulations related to the individual components of the environment (water, soil, air, rocks, nature) and waste management;
– the importance, goals and methodology of environmental impact assessment.

Appendix No. 2 to Decree No.499/1992 S.B.

Examination rules for examinations of professional qualification in environmental impact assessment

I. The rights and obligations of the examining commission, its chairman and its secretary

1. The examining commission

a. is to make decisions on matters of contention connected with the examination;
b. can exclude a candidate from the examination for serious reasons;
c. makes decisions on evaluation of the results of the examination;
d. signs the minutes on the progress and evaluation of the examination.

2. The chairman of the examining commission

a. is to chair the meeting and work of the examining commission;
b. is to ensure the uniform and correct procedure of the examining commission;
c. is to sign the certificate of professional qualification.

3. The secretary of the examining commission

a. is to notify the candidates of the form, organisation and proceedings in the examination, of their rights and obligations and of the manner of evaluation of examinations;
b. is, prior to the beginning of the examination, to verify the identity of the candidate(s) on the basis of their personal documents and submitted application, as well as the fulfilling of obligations as Article 9 of this decree;

c. is to ensure that written minutes are drawn up on the proceedings and evaluation of the examination;
d. is to sign the certificate of professional qualification.

4. The examining commission is always to have an odd number of members, equal to at least five persons. Decisions are to be made on the basis of a majority vote.

II. Examinations to determine professional qualification

1. The candidate is to be invited to undergo the examination at least 30 days in advance of the date of the examination.

2. The examination is to consist of a written part (hereinafter 'written examination') and an oral part (hereinafter 'oral examination').

3. The writtten examination is to have the form of a written test.

4. The written examination is to be assessed and evaluated by the examining commission at the latest before commencement of the oral examination.

5. The examining commission is to notify the candidate of the results of evaluation of the written examination at the latest during the oral examination.

6. During the oral examination the candidate generally is to answer three examining questions. The members of the commission can ask complementary questions.

III. Evaluation of the results of the examination

1. The examination is to be evaluated on the basis of the criterion 'satisfactory' or 'unsatisfactory'.

2. Written minutes are to be drawn up on the examination and are to include the evaluation of the written and oral examinations and the overall results of the examination as 'satisfactory' or 'unsatisfactory'.

3. The certificate is to be sent to the candidate by registered mail to be delivered into the hand of the addressee at the latest 30 days after successful completion of the examination.

4. A candidate who was classified as 'unsatisfactory' is to be informed by the examining commission of the possibility and conditions for repetition of the examination and the commission is to decide whether the candidate is to repeat the whole examination or only part thereof.

IV. Re-examinations and setting of the date for re-examination

1. If a candidate fails to pass an examination, then (s)he may repeat the examination or part thereof. The date for the re-examination is to be set for the candidate by the examining commission so that the re-examination is to take place at the earliest three months after the date of the previous examination; the candidate is to be informed of the date of the re-examination at least one month prior to this set date.

2. A candidate who was unable to attend an examination for an important reason or who properly excused himself from the examination is to be excused from the examination and the examination commission is to set a new date for the examination.

3. If the candidate does not appear for the examination without properly excusing himself and without providing an important reason for so doing, then he can be accepted for examination only on the basis of a newly submitted request.

V. Documents on examination of professional qualification

Documents connected with examinations of professional qualification and records of the issuing of a certificate of professional qualification are to be kept by the Ministry.

CZECH REPUBLIC C

Federal Act on the Environment

Law No.17/1992; 5 December 1991

The Federal Assembly of the Czech and Slovak Federal Republic, recognising the fact that human beings, together with other organisms, are an intrinsic part of nature, considering the natural interdependence of human beings and other organisms, respecting humanity's right to transform nature in accordance with the principle of permanent and sustainable development, aware of its responsibility for securing a favourable environment for future generations, and emphasising the right to a favourable environment as one of humanity's principal rights, has approved this Act:

Article 1. The purpose of the Act
The Act defines basic terms and determines basic principles of environmental protection and obligations of legal and natural persons in the process of protecting and improving the environment and in the utilisation of natural resources; this Act follows the principle of permanently sustainable development.

Principal terms

Article 2. Environment
The environment is everything that provides natural conditions for the existence of organisms, including human beings, and is the precondition of their future development. Its major components are air, water, rocks, soil, organisms, ecosystems and energy.

Article 3. Ecosystem
The ecosystem is the functional set of living and inanimate components of the environment which are interlinked by metabolism, energy flow and the exchange of information and which influence one another and develop within a certain space and time.

Article 4. Ecological stability
Ecological stability is the ability of the ecosystem to balance changes caused by external factors and to maintain its natural properties and functions.

Article 5. Acceptable regional load
The acceptable regional load is such load exerted upon a region by human activity which does not damage the environment, particularly its components, the function of ecosystems or its ecological stability.

Article 6. Permanently sustainable development
Permanently sustainable development of the society is the development which preserves for present and future generations the possibility of meeting their basic needs, and at the same time, does not reduce the diversity of nature and preserves the natural functions of ecosystems.

Article 7. Natural resources
7.1. Natural resources are those parts of living and inanimate nature which are or can be used by humanity to satisfy its needs.

7.2. Renewable natural resources have the capability of partial or complete regeneration while being gradually consumed either with or without human assistance. Non-renewable natural resources become extinct by consumption.

Article 8. Pollution of and damage to the environment

8.1. Pollution of the environment means the introduction of physical, chemical or biological agents into the environment through human activity which by their nature or their quantity are foreign to the given environment.

8.2. Damage to the environment means aggravating the state of the environment by pollution or other types of human activity in excess of the limits determined by special regulations.

Article 9. Environmental protection

Environmental protection consists of activities that prevent pollution or damage to the environment, or that reduce or eliminate pollution and environmental damage. It includes the protection of individual components of the environment, organisms or specific ecosystems and their inter-relationships, as well as protection of the environment as a whole.

Article 10. Ecological damage

Ecological damage is the loss or impairment of the natural functions of ecosystems, caused by damaging their components or disturbing their internal relations and processes owing to human activity.

Principles of environmental protection

Article 11. The territory must not be burdened by human activity in excess of the level of acceptable load.

Article 12

12.1. The acceptable level of environmental pollution is determined by limit values stipulated by special regulations; these values are determined in accordance with the existing state of knowledge in such a way as to prevent damage to human health, other living organisms and other components of the environment.

12.2. Limit values must be determined with regard to the possible cumulative effects or synergistic effects of pollutants or polluting activities.

Article 13. If, considering all circumstances, it can be assumed that irreversible or serious damage could threaten the environment, any doubt concerning the realistic nature of such threat cannot be a reason for postponing measures intended to prevent such damage.

Article 14. Everyone has the right to true and accurate information about the state and development of the environment, the causes and consequences of that state, activities which are being prepared and which could change the environment, as well as to information about measures taken by the authorities responsible for environmental protection in order to prevent or remedy environmental damage. A special regulation may stipulate cases in which such information can be restricted or withheld.

Article 15. Everyone may approach the relevant authority and claim, in a prescribed manner, his or her legal rights stipulated by this Act and other laws and regulations concerning the environment.

Article 16. Education is implemented in such a way as to promote thinking and activity which comply with the principle of permanently sustainable development, and which encourage awareness of responsibility for maintaining the quality of the environment and its individual components and of respect for life in all its forms.

Obligation with regard to environmental protection

Article 17
17.1. Everyone is obliged, primarily through measures taken at the pollution source, to prevent environmental pollution or to minimise the unfavourable environmental impact of his or her activity.

17.2. Everyone who uses an area or natural resource, designs, builds or removes structures, is obliged to carry out such activities only after assessing their impact on the environment and the load exerted on the territory to the extent stipulated by this Act and by special regulations.

17.3. Everyone intending to launch the production, circulation or consumption of technologies, products and substances, and everyone intending to import them, is obliged to ensure that these technologies, products and substances comply with the conditions of environmental protection and, in cases stipulated by this Act and by special regulations, to provide for the assessment of their potential impact on the environment.

Article 18
18.1. Everyone who in the course of his or her activity pollutes or damages the environment or exploits natural resources is obliged at his or her own expense to provide for monitoring the activity involved and to know the potential environmental impact of the activity.

18.2. Legal and natural persons authorised to conduct business are obliged to provide information about the environmental impact thereof to the extent and under the conditions stipulated by special regulations.

Article 19. Everyone who learns about a threat to the environment or about environmental damage is obliged to take such measures as are within his or her powers to eliminate the threat or minimise its consequences, and to report the facts without delay to the state administrative authorities. This obligation does not apply where such measures would threaten the life or health of the person or persons closely related to him or her[1].

Environmental impact assessment of activities

Article 20
20.1. Plans to execute activities listed in Articles 17.2 and 17.3 (hereafter 'plans'), are subject to assessment of their potential impact on the environment (hereafter 'assessment of plans') prior to their approval under special regulations[2].

20.2. The principles of environmental protection and assessment of the environmental impact of activities shall also be adequately applied in the course of preparing development concepts and programmes and drafts of legal norms.

[1] Section 116 of the Civil Code.

[2] E.g., Act No.50/1976 on regional planning and construction regulations (The Construction Act).

Article 21
21.1. Assessment of plans mentioned in Appendix 1 of this Act is conducted by the appropriate state administrative authorities appointed by the Czech National Council and the Slovak National Council (hereafter 'assessing authorities'), following discussions with other concerned state administrative authorities, with communities whose territory is to be affected by the impact of the plans, and with the general public. The evaluation of the environmental impact of the plans is executed according to Appendix 2 to this Act.

21.2. Details shall be established by Acts of Law passed by the Czech National Council and the Slovak National Council, which may also extend and specify the activities listed in Appendix 1 of this Act (namely determining the extent of these activities) and define more stringent requirements for the documentation attached to the environmental impact assessments as listed in Appendix 2 to this Act.

Article 22. The assessing authorities shall scrutinise the plans according to the nature of the matter, particularly with regard to:

a. the environmental tolerance of the relevant territory;
b. the consequences of routine activity and possible accidents;
c. cumulative and synergistic phenomena in various time horizons and considering irreversible phenomena;
d. the prevention, minimisation and possible compensation of the environmental impact of the plans;
e. methods of handling the achieved result of the plans after the expiration of their lifetime or after their utilisation (possibilities of disposal, recycling, etc.);
f. applied methods of evaluating the completeness of information;
g. comparison with the best available technologies.

Article 23
23.1. Where a proposed plan, which is to be executed on the territory of one republic, could have a negative environmental impact on the territory of the other republic, the assessing authority shall ask for an opinion from the relevant central authority of the republic. Potential differences shall be resolved by agreement between the central authorities of both republics.

23.2. If an agreement cannot be reached, the difference shall be settled by an arbitration commission made up of representatives of the Czech and Slovak bodies responsible for environmental protection and the Federal Committee for the Environment. If the commission fails to reach an agreement, the plan cannot be executed.

Assessment of the environmental impact of activities and their consequences extending beyond national borders

Article 24
24.1. The proposers of the plans listed in Appendix 3 of this Act are obliged to submit the environmental impact assessment to the assessing authority (Article 21.1) prior to the issuance of a regional decision concerning the location of a construction site or the use of the territory.

24.2. The environmental impact assessment of plans extending beyond the national orders must contain the data listed in Appendix 4 to this Act.

Article 25. The extent of the environmental impact assessments shall be discussed by the assessing authorities with the relevant state administrative authorities, with the communities whose territory is to be affected by the impact of the plan and with the general public. The completed environmental assessment shall be subject to similar discussions.

Article 26

26.1. The assessing authorities authorised to issue the statement pursuant to Article 21.1 in cases stated in Appendix 3 of this Act, shall submit the draft statement to the Federal Committee for the Environment. Where the environmental impact of the proposed plan may extend beyond the national borders, the Federal Committee for the Environment shall arrange, in agreement with the bodies authorised to issue the statement, international negotiations in accordance with approved international commitments[3].

26.2. The relevant central authorities of state administration in both republics may determine, at the request of the Federal Committee for the Environment and based on international commitments (see footnote 3), that plans otherwise not subject to environmental impact assessment shall be assessed according to this Act.

26.3. The Federal Committee for the Environment, on the basis of information provided by authorities of other states concerning plans considered on the territory of other states, the consequences of which could damage the environment of the territory of the Czech and Slovak Federal Republic, shall organise, together with the responsible authorities of the republics, assessment of the plans in accordance with the adopted international commitments (see footnote 3).

Responsibility for the breach of obligations in environmental protection

Article 27

27.1. Everyone who by damaging the environment or by other criminal activity causes ecological damage, is obliged to restore the natural functions of the damaged ecosystem or of its parts. If this is not possible or if it is not for serious reasons desirable, he or she is obliged to compensate the ecological damage in a different manner (substitute compensation), if this is not possible, he or she is obliged to compensate the damage in money. The Act does not exclude simultaneous application of these types of compensation. The method of calculating ecological damage and other details shall be stipulated by a special regulation.

27.2. The imposition of the obligation according to Article 27.1 shall be decided by the relevant state administration authority.

27.3. The state is the authority in cases of the ecological damage; the details are determined by the laws of the Czech National Council and the Slovak National Council respectively.

[3] UN European Economic Commission Convention on the assessment of environmental impact reaching beyond national borders.

27.4. For the purposes of ecological damage, general provisions concerning the responsibility for damage and compensation for damage are to be applied unless Articles 27.1 and 27.3 state otherwise.

27.5. Provisions of Articles 27.1–3 do not affect general regulations stipulating responsibility for damage and compensation for damage.

Article 28. Sanctions imposed for environmental damage

28.1. Environmental authorities shall impose a fine of:

a. up to 1,000,000 Czechoslovak crowns upon a legal or natural person authorised to conduct business who in the course of his or her activity causes environmental damage by breaching legal obligations;
b. up to 500,000 Czechoslovak crowns upon a legal or natural person authorised to conduct business who does not take necessary corrective measures or does not notify the state administration authority (Section 19).

28.2. The fine may be imposed within one year from the day the environmental authority learns about the breach of the obligation, but at the latest within three years from the day on which the breach of the obligation was committed.

28.3. The imposition of the fine does not affect general regulations concerning the compensation of damage.

Article 29. The breach of obligations stipulated by special environmental protection regulations is subject to the imposition of a fine or to other penalties according to special regulations; this does not affect possible criminal liability or responsibility for damage incurred under general legal regulations.

Article 30. Where there is a threat of major environmental damage or where such damage has already been inflicted, the relevant state administrative authorities for the environment are authorised to temporarily close or restrict for up to 30 days the activity that may cause or has already caused the damage (preliminary measure), and at the same time may propose remedial measures to the relevant state administrative authorities. Details are stipulated by special regulations.

Economic tools

Article 31. Natural and legal persons pay taxes, fees, and other payments for polluting the environment or its components, and for economic exploitation of natural resources if required by special regulations.

Article 32. Special regulations stipulate the conditions under which legal and natural persons protecting the environment or utilising natural resources in accordance with the principle of permanently sustainable development can be granted tax relief, credits and subsidies.

Article 33. Environmental protection tools also include environmental funds; details are stipulated by special regulations.

Temporary and final provisions

Article 34
34.1. The use of territory, natural resources, buildings, technologies, products and substances which does not comply with the provisions of this Act and with the conditions ensuing from special regulations about the protection of individual components of the environment, shall be made to comply with these regulations within the standard period.

34.2. Unless the compliance stipulated by Article 34.1 is achieved within the stated period, the activity shall be restricted or terminated. This decision is issued by the relevant state administration authorities.

Article 35. This Act comes into legal force on the day of its publication.

Appendix 1

Activities subject to environmental assessment on the territory of the Czech and Slovak Federal Republic

1. Agriculture and forestry
1.1. Large-capacity facilities for animal husbandry, including waste disposal.

1.2. Large-capacity facilities for storing agricultural products.

1.3. Land improvement projects (drainage, irrigation, anti-erosion soil protection, re-allotment, technical improvements for forestry).

1.4. Interference in the landscape that may cause substantial changes in biological diversity and in the structure and functions of ecosystems.

2. Food industry
2.1. Breweries and malt plants

2.2. Slaughterhouses and meat-processing combines

2.3. Starch manufacture

2.4. Sugar factories

2.5. Refrigerating plants

2.6. Distilleries

2.7. Fat industry and the production of detergents

2.8. Manufacture of dairy products

2.9. Canning industry

3. Mining industry

3.1. Coal and lignite underground and open-cast mining

3.2. Crude oil and natural gas exploration

3.3. Peat mining

3.4. Uranium ore mining and processing, waste banks, sludge beds, including reclamation

3.5. Mining and enrichment of metallic ore

3.6. Bituminous shale mining

3.7. Mining of industrial minerals

3.8. Surface industrial facilities for the mining and processing of coal, natural gas, bituminous shale and industrial minerals

3.9. Crude oil refineries, including plants for the regeneration of spent mineral-oils and facilities for the thermal and chemical processing of coal

4. Energy industry

4.1. Power plants and other fossil-fuel burning facilities

4.2. Other industrial facilities for the generation of electricity, steam and hot water

4.3. Nuclear power stations and other facilities equipped with nuclear reactors

4.4. Nuclear fuel conversion, enrichment and production facilities

4.5. Burnt nuclear fuel intermediate storage facilities

4.6. Processing and final deposit of highly radioactive waste

4.7. Processing and deposit of low- and medium-level active waste from the operation and closure of nuclear power stations and utilisation of radionuclides

4.8. Gas, steam and hot water conduits and their facilities (including pumping and changer stations, electricity energy transmission by overhead circuits)

4.9. Oil, gas and other product pipelines, including operational facilities

4.10. Natural gas surface storage facilities

4.11. Underground storage facilities for inflammable gases, crude oil, petro-chemical and chemical products

4.12. Briquetting and coke plants

4.13. Hydro-electric power stations

5. Metallurgical industry

5.1. Ironworks and steelworks, including foundries, forges and rolling mills

5.2. Non-ferrous metallurgy works

5.3. Surface treatment of metals

5.4. Production and assembly of motor vehicles, train carriages and storage tanks

5.5. Shipyards

5.6. Facilities for construction and repair of aircraft

6. Wood and paper industry

6.1. Preservation of wood using toxic chemicals

6.2. Wood fibre board and plywood production

6.3. Cellulose and paper production

6.4. Furniture production

7. Other industries

7.1. Processing of asbestos and asbestos products

7.2. Textile preparation plants and dye houses

7.3. Tanneries

7.4. Glassworks

7.5. Chemical and pharmaceutical industry

7.6. Utilisation or regeneration of chlorinated hydrocarbons

7.7. Production and storage of poisons, pesticides, liquid fertilisers, pharmaceutical products, paints, varnishes and chemicals

7.8. Storage, processing, neutralisation and deposit of hazardous wastes

7.9. Long distance transport of radioactive and hazardous wastes

7.10. Crude oil and petrochemical products storage facilities

7.11. Cement works and lime works

7.12. Printing facilities

8. Infrastructure

8.1. Groundwater withdrawal

8.2. Waste-water treatment plants and sewage systems

8.3. Sludge beds and mud settling ponds

8.4. Facilities for communal waste treatment

8.5. Rendering plants, veterinary clearance facilities

8.6. Water reservoirs or dams rising to a height of over 3 metres measured from the foundation joint or with the total storage capacity over 0.5 million m^3

8.7. Waterways regulation

8.8. Construction and reconstruction of highways and roads

8.9. Railways

8.10. Cableways

8.11. Water routes and ports for inland shipping

8.12. Airfields

8.13. Shopping centres with a built-in area over 3,000 m^2

8.14. Camping sites with over 200 places

8.15. Structures and activities which could affect interests protected by special regulations.

Appendix 2

Contents of documentation and environmental impact assessment of plans on the territory of Czech and Slovak Federal Republic

1. Description of planning of the activity and its goals.

2. Description of suitable and substantiated alternatives of solution, including reference alternatives (alternative without the activity, zero alternative) and the optimum environmental alternative, and their mutual comparison.

3. Description of the environment likely to be significantly affected by the proposed plan (alternatives).

3.a. Basic characteristic features (air, water, soil, geological conditions, geomorphological characteristics, climatic factors, fauna, flora, ecosystems).

3.b. Other characteristics (utilisation of the landscape,, territory with exceptional civilisation impact, territory with a special protection regime, important landscape elements, environmental stability components, architectural and historical monuments, archaeological sites, material values, accord between the plan and valid territorial plans).

4. Description of the submitted environmental impact of the plan (alternatives) and estimation of their importance (not only assumed direct impact but also indirect, secondary, cumulative, synergic impacts, and not only short-term and temporary but also long-term and permanent impacts).

4.a. Impact on the population (health risks, social consequences, economic consequences).

4.b. Impact on ecosystems, their components and functions (geological, geomorphological and hydrological conditions, climatic conditions, hydrology, flora, fauna, processes, important landscape elements, ecological stability).

4.c. Impact on anthropogenic systems, their components and relationships (structures, monuments and other important human works, intangible cultural values – ethnic and local traditions, etc.).

4.d. Impact on the structure and function of the utilisation of the land (including the impact on the aesthetic quality of landscape).

4.e. Large-scale landscape impact of the plan – assessment of the environmental tolerance of the territory, suitability of the location of individual alternatives from the point of view of the environmental tolerance of the territory, existing and potential final environmental tolerance of the territory (overall effect of all territorial phenomena and factors).

5. Description of the measures suggested to prevent, eliminate, minimise and possibly compensate the environmental impact of proposed activity on the environment. Regional planning measure, technical measures (e.g. separation and deposit of pollutants, waste recycling, preservation research of archaeological sites, measures to protect cultural monuments, other measures).

Appendix 3

Plans subject to international discussion from the environmental impact point of view

1. Crude oil refineries (with the exception of plants producing only lubricants from crude oil) and facilities for gasifying and burning coal and bituminous shales with a daily capacity of 500 tonnes and more.

2. Thermal power stations and other combustion facilities, classified as large environmental pollution sources according to special regulations (Article 3.a) of the Act No.309/1991 on the protection of the air against pollutants (The Air Act).

3. Nuclear power stations and other facilities equipped with nuclear reactors (with the exception of research facilities for the production and conversion of nuclear fuel and nuclear fuel raw materials, the maximum capacity of which does not exceed 1 kWh of constant thermal load).

4. Facilities for the production or enrichment of nuclear fuel, other reprocessing of radioactive nuclear fuel, or the collection, storage and processing of nuclear waste.

5. Facilities for the primary production of cast iron and steel and production of non-ferrous metals with an annual capacity of over 30,000 tonnes.

6. Facilities for obtaining, processing and revising asbestos and asbestos products, for annual production of asbestos cement products exceeding 20,000 tonnes, for friction materials with an annual production exceeding 50 tonnes, and for other uses of asbestos exceeding 200 tonnes a year.

7. Complex chemical facilities where two or more combined chemical or physical processes are used for the production of olefins from crude oil products, sulphuric acid, nitric acid, hydrofluoric acid, chlorides or fluorides.

8. First-class roads, highways, national railways and airports with the main take-off and landing runways longer than 2,000 m.

9. Long-distance crude oil pipelines with pipes having an inner diameter of more than 500 millimetres and gas transmission lines with an inner diameter exceeding 300 millimetres.

10. Facilities for the neutralisation of toxic and hazardous waste, underground storage sites and surface storage sites for toxic and dangerous wastes.

11. Dams and reservoirs with dams rising to a height of more than 10 m above the foundation joint or with a total capacity of the reservoir exceeding 10 million m^3.

12. Facilities for the withdrawal of groundwater in case the annual volume of withdrawal equals or exceeds 10 million m^3.

13. Cellulose and paper production with a daily output of 200 tons or more, with air drying.

14. Inland water routes and ports for inland navigation, which enable the navigation of ships with a tonnage exceeding 1,350 tonnes.

15. In-situ mining, preparation and refinement of ores, magnesite and all types of coal, with an annual capacity exceeding 100,000 tonnes.

16. Large capacity storage facilities for storing crude oil (over 200,000 m^3), crude oil products (exceeding 50,000 m^3) and chemicals (over 2,000 m^3).

17. Changes in land utilisation relating to large-scale felling of forests exceeding and area of 5 hectares.

Appendix 4

Contents of documentation on environmental impact assessment of plans subject to international discussion

Information which should be included in documentation on environmental impact assessment must contain at least:

a. a description of the planned activity and its goals;
b. if necessary, a description of reasonable alternatives (e.g., of a geographical or technological nature) of the planned activities, including the alternative of withdrawing the activity;
c. a description of those elements of the environment which will probably be fundamentally affected by the planned activity or its alternative variants;
d. a description of all possible environmental impacts of the planned activity and its alternative variants and assessment of the magnitude of said impacts;
e. a description of the measures taken to minimise the extent of the harmful impact on the environment;
f. a statement of specific methods of forecasting and the initial postulates on which they are based, as well as the relevant environmental data used;
g. a listing of the shortcomings in knowledge and uncertainties which were revealed in the course of preparing the required information;
h. if necessary, a short summary of the monitoring and control programme, and of all post-project analysis plans;

i. a summary of a non-technical nature, if necessary, using visual methods of presentation (maps, diagrams, etc.).

Planned types of trans-boundary activity which may have a particularly damaging impact are assessed on the basis of one or several of the following criteria:

a. Volume: planned types of activity the volume of which is excessive for the given activity;
b. Area: planned types of activity executed in particularly sensitive or environmentally important areas or in their immediate proximity (e.g. heavily waterlogged soils as defined by the Ramsar Convention, national parks, protected nature areas, areas particularly interesting from the scientific or archaeological point of view, cultural or historical monuments); and further planned types of activity in areas where the features of the planned economic activity can have important impact on the population;
c. Consequences: planned types of activity which have an especially complicated and potentially harmful impact, including impacts resulting in serious consequences for the population and for important types of flora, fauna and organisms, jeopardising the existing or potential use of the relevant area and producing a burden exceeding the stability level of the environment with regard to the present impact.

The above is the objective of the assessment of the types of activities planned and executed in the immediate vicinity of national borders, as well as the types of activities planned and executed in more remote areas, which may have serious trans-boundary impact at great distance from the site of the economic activity.

CZECH REPUBLIC D

Act on Land Use Planning and Construction Rules
No.50/1976 S.B.

Excerpts

Unofficial translation by the Institute for Environmental Policy, Prague

Section 7. Territorial procedure

Article 32. Siting of buildings, utilisation of territory and protection of important interests on the territory

To site the buildings, to change the utilisation of a territory and to protect important interests on a territory can be realised only on a basis of territorial decision, which is:

a. the decision on siting of a building

Article 33. Jurisdiction

33.1. Only the appropriate surveyor's office is authorised to conduct the territorial procedure.

Article 34. Participants in territorial procedure

34.1. A participant in territorial procedure is the proposer, and organisations or citizens whose proprietary or other rights to the estates or buildings may be directly affected by the territorial decision. A participant in territorial procedure on nature reserve or protected zone or on building stoppage, is only the proposer.

34.2. The Local National Committee, unless it represents the surveyor's office, is also a participant in territorial procedure and in siting of a building; it defends important local interests in the territorial procedure.

Article 35. Opening of a territorial procedure

Territorial procedure is opened on written proposal of a participant, at the instance of the surveyor's office or other authority of the state administration. The proposal is proved by documentation provided by implementing regulations to this law, eventually by documents provided by special regulations. The proposal should list organisations and citizens coming into consideration as the participants in the procedure, and who are known by the proposers. The surveyor's office, in case of a territorial complexity, may request additional documents for the proposal, which are considered as necessary for reliable assessment of consequences of the proposed building or other provision on a territory, e.g. maps, layouts, studies, selected parts of preparatory documentation.

Article 36

36.1. The surveyor's office announces the opening of a building procedure to involved state administration authorities and to all known participants, and orders oral proceedings, usually connected with local investigation. At the same time, it advises the participants that they can apply their objections and comments not later than during the oral proceedings or else these will not be taken into account.

36.3. The involved state administration authorities will communicate their opinions in the same period in which the participants apply their objections and comments or else the surveyor's office may not take them into account. If any of the state administration authorities requires longer time for proper assessment, the surveyor's office, upon receiving an application, will adequately prolong the determined term before its elapsing.

Article 37. Documents for territorial decision
37.1. The documents for the issuing of a territorial decision are the territorial plans and territorial projects. In case the territorial plan has not been elaborated for a territory (or a territorial project), the surveyor's office secures other documents in the scope necessary for territorial decision, for example, territorial prognosis, territorial planning documents, and the facts determined by its own investigation and by local inquiries.

37.2. The surveyor's office will consider the proposal in territorial procedure, especially from the viewpoint of care for the environment, and the demands of the required measures on a territory, with possible consequences; it will review the proposal and its compliance with documents under Article 37.1 and with the preceding decisions on the territory, and consider whether it complies with the general technical requirements for construction, and finally with the regulations which provide the conditions for hygiene, fire safety, safety of work and technical facilities, transport, nature protection, care of historical monuments, protection of farm land fund, forest land fund, etc., unless such consideration is under the competency of other authorities.

Article 39. Territorial decision
In territorial decision the surveyor's office delimits the territory for the proposed purpose and determines the conditions which will safeguard the interests of society on the territory, especially harmony with the objectives and intentions of the territorial planning, material and temporal coordination of individual building constructions and other provisions on a territory, primarily the care for the environment, and decides on the objections of the procedure participants. In the decision on the building siting, the surveyor's office can, in justified cases, reserve the right to require more detailed project documentation or part thereof; according to these, the surveyor's office may additionally determine other conditions, which should be included in the building licence.

Section 3

Article 47. Products for building construction
For the building construction only such products may be used the properties of which secure economical construction, the requirements for health protection, fire safety, safety of work and technical facilities, and anticipated life service and utility of buildings.

Article 54. Buildings, their changes and adjustment work on them may be performed only in accordance with the construction permit or on the basis of an announcement to the construction office.

Article 55

55.1. The building licence is required, unless this law and regulations implementing it, or special regulations provide otherwise, in buildings of all types irrespective of their technical execution, purpose, and duration; the building licence is also required for building modifications, especially in building annexes, superstructures and readjustments.

Article 58. Application for building licence

58.1. The application for a building licence together with the prescribed documentation is submitted by the owner of the proposed building construction at the surveyor's office.

Article 59. The participants of building procedure

59.1. The participants of the building procedure are: the owner of the proposed building construction, and also the organisations and citizens with proprietary or other rights to the neighbouring estates or buildings and whose rights, rightly protected interests or obligations may be affected by the building licence.

59.2. The surveyor's office may invite to the building procedure also other organisations and citizens, especially the project designer and the organisation which will carry out the building construction or the works; these, however, are not the participants of the procedure.

Article 60. Construction procedure

60.1. If the presented application for a construction permit, especially building design documentation, does not provide sufficient basis for assessment of the proposed building or of adjustment works on it, or if the documentation does not meet conditions given by the territorial decision, the construction office asks the investor/financier to complete the application in a certain time, eventually to make it comply with territorial decision conditions, and lets him know that if he does not satisfy these requirements the office will stop the procedure.

Article 61

61.1. The surveyor's office announces the opening of a building procedure to the involved state administration authorities and to all known participants, and orders oral proceedings connected with local investigation. At the same time, it advises participants that they can apply their objections not later than during the oral proceedings or else these will not be taken into account. The comments and objections which were or could have been applied in the territorial procedure, or during discussions on a territorial zone plan or territorial zone project, are not taken into account.

61.5. The Local National Committee and other involved authorities of state administration always inform the surveyor's office individually. These authorities are obliged to inform about their standpoint during the same period in which the procedure participants can state their objections. The objections which are forwarded later need not be taken into account by the surveyor's office. If any of the state administration authorities requires more time for proper assessment, the surveyor's office, upon receiving an application, will adequately prolong the determined term.

Article 62
62.1. In the building procedure the surveyor's office will especially investigate whether

a. the documentation complies with the conditions of a territorial decision;
b. the documentation complies with the requirements relevant to the interests of society, primarily to the protection of the environment and corresponds to the general technical requirements for the building construction;
c. the complexity and continuity of the construction is secured and the technical and personal facilities necessary for proper utilisation are installed in due time;
d. the building construction will be implemented by authorised organisations, or whether in the case of buildings and works carried out by organisations for their own use or which will be realised by self-help cooperation (Article 44.2 and 44.3), a professional approach is secured or professional supervision safeguarded.

62.2. If the building is to be used for business purposes, the surveyor's office investigates the effects of future operation from viewpoints given under Article 62.1.b, and the technical and economic level of the technological equipment is not investigated.

62.3. The surveyor's office will secure the standpoints of the state administration authorities, their mutual harmony, and consider the attitudes of procedure participants and their objections.

62.4. If, by realisation or utilisation of the building, the interest of society could be endangered or the rights and justified interests of the participants infringed to a greater extent than had been considered in the territorial decision, then the surveyor's office will reject the application for a building licence.

Article 64
64.1. The construction office may reduce negotiation of the application with concerned authorities, and with participants whose opinions about the documentation presented in the construction procedure were given before the beginning of this procedure, to the extent to which their requirements were met.

Article 66. The building licence
66.1. In the building licence the surveyor's office will provide the binding conditions for the execution and utilisation of the building, and decides on the objections of the procedure participants. The surveyor's office secures by the determined conditions especially the protection of societal interests in construction and utilisation of the building, the complexity of the building, compliance with general technical requirements for the construction, eventually other regulations and technical standards and observance of the requirements provided by the involved authorities of the state administration, first of all the elimination or limitation of negative effects caused by the building construction and its utilisation with view to the environment.

Article 67
The building licence loses validity if the building is not started within two years of the day it was granted, unless the construction office, in reasonable cases, grants an extended deadline for beginning.

Article 68

68.1. The construction office can, at the request of the contractor in reasonable cases, license a change in the building if it is not yet completed.

68.2. If the change affects rights, legally protected interests or duties of participants in the construction procedure and interests protected by concerned state administrative authorities, the construction office considers the application and grants the decision approving the change of the building. At the same time, the construction office either decides also about potential objections of participants and specifies other mandatory conditions or refuses the application. Provisions on construction procedure apply equally to the procedure for changing a building.

CZECH REPUBLIC E

Czechoslovak Decree on General Technical Requirements of Construction No.83/1976 S.B.

Excerpts

Unofficial translation by the Institute for Environmental Policy, Prague

Article 4. Building plots
4.1. Plots determined for building should facilitate their properties, especially by position, shape, size and basic condition, the suitable and economical realisation as well as the safe utilisation of the buildings.

4.2. An estate will not be determined for building purposes, the building on which might cause unjustifiable harm to the interests of society, rightly protected interests of organisations or citizens, e.g. infringing or endangering of water economy, impairing of urban or architectonic character of landscape, of environment or endangering the defensive interest of the State.

4.3. The greenery of the estate unbuilt areas must be preserved to the greatest possible extent, and during building operations must be properly protected.

4.4. The unbuilt areas of building sites should be suitably arranged, especially by planting new greenery. This should be done before the building approbation, exceptionally before the next vegetation season after the building approbation.

4.5. Topsoil or deeper deposited arable soil should be removed from the building sites determined for construction, to be used in accordance with the requirements for protection of farmland fund.

Article 5. Building siting
5.1. If the building sites interfere with a protected zone or nature reserve or if there are other protected facilities on the estate, the construction must respect the conditions for the protected zone, nature reserve or protection for such facilities.

Article 8. Protection of the environment
8.1. The buildings according to their types should safeguard the required conditions for pleasant environment created especially by siting, space and functional solution, furnishings and facilities.

8.2. Negative effects and influences of the buildings and their furnishings – especially harmful exhalations, noise, heat, shocks, vibrations, dust, offensive odours, water pollution, dazzlement, overshadowing – should not damage the environment in buildings and in the vicinity of their reach above the admissible limit. The compliance with these requirements is verified by measurement results.

8.3. The buildings, the operation or utilisation of which results in production of wastes or trash, must be equipped with devices for their capture, neutralisation or disposal.

8.4. The equipment of buildings mentioned under Articles 8.1–3 should be reliable and safe, hygienically harmless and should be realised not later than simultaneously with the completion of the building.

CZECH REPUBLIC F

Decree of the Federal Ministry for Technical and Investment Development on More Detailed Regulation of Land Use Planning and Construction Rules

No.85/1976 S.B.

Excerpts

Unofficial translation by the Institute for Environmental Policy, Prague

Territorial procedure

Article 7. The proposal for obtaining a territorial decision
7.1. The proposal for obtaining a territorial decision is submitted by a proposer at the surveyor's office; the proposal includes:

7.1.a. proposer's name and address;

7.1.b. subject of territorial decision with brief characteristics of the territory and the way of its existing utilisation;

7.1.c. the list and addresses of all known participants in the territorial procedure;

7.1.d. types and building site numbers of the relevant building site according to real estate registration with stating of proprietary rights and users' rights.

7.2. In a proposal for obtaining a territorial decision in cases quoted under Article 36.4 of the law, the data according to Article 7.1.c and d, are not given in the proposal.

7.3. With the proposal for obtaining a territorial decision, the proposer encloses the following:

7.3.a. site layout of the existing territorial situation on the scale of estate map in estate registration, with the plotting of the subject of the territorial decision, its position indicating the relationships with the surroundings; if the territorial proposal involves especially large areas with large numbers of participants in the territorial procedure, or if it includes the siting of line building, then also a map documentation is required on scale 1:10,000 to 1:50,000, with indication of broader relationships with, and effects upon, its surroundings; site layout and maps are enclosed in duplicate;

7.3.b. with proposals for the siting of buildings of organisations, the documentation specified by special regulations is enclosed;

7.3.c. opinions, especially decisions of relevant authorities of state administration provided by special regulations, e.g. on protection of farmland.

7.4. If the proposal concerns a building in which nuclear facilities are to be installed, the proposer encloses with the proposal for obtaining a territorial decision, the approval of the Czechoslovak Commission for Atomic Energy, granted on the basis of assessment of the required safety report, which contains especially:

7.4.a. the assessment of the site from the nuclear safety aspect, preliminary evaluation of the nuclear facility's influence on the environment;

7.4.b. order for the project of the nuclear facility resulting from the requirements for nuclear safety in a specific locality.

7.5. If the submitted documents are insufficient for assessment of a proposal according to the territorial procedure, the surveyor's office determines the scope, method and terms of their completion. The surveyor's office may also determine the number of copies (and eventually the classification) of documents and opinions necessary for discussions with participants in territorial procedure and with the relevant authorities of state administration.

Article 8. Decision on construction siting
8.3. In the conditions for construction siting, the requirements are specially set out for the protection and creation of the environment, for securing the harmony of urban solution and architectural design of a building, to match the environment with relation to high-rise and position siting of the structure, including the setback from the estate border and neighbouring structures, the height of the building, requirements resulting from the viewpoints of concerned state administration authorities.

Article 20
20.2. The owner of the building under construction will enclose the following with the application:

20.2.a. documents with evidence of proprietary rights or other rights to the estate and buildings; if the construction modifications or maintenance work on it are carried out by a socialist organisation as the user, the written agreement with the owner of the building is to be enclosed;

20.2.b. prescribed documentation in duplicate; if the surveyor's office is not a municipal one or a Local National Committee, in triplicate;

20.2.c. documents on discussions with the state administration authorities and with the participants in the building procedure, if realised, and the opinions and eventually the decisions of relevant state administration authorities, if provided by special regulations;

20.2.d. the territorial decision, if issued by some other authority than the surveyor's office.

Article 21. The surveyor's office may determine that the owner of a building under construction will document the application for building licence by the opinion of a superior body or by the expertise of a scientific and research institute or a university, if it concerns:

21.a. a building with unusual technology in which a unique method of construction should be used, or a construction solution in which a unique technological facility should be installed, which facility is not comparable with other already tested (certified) facilities, and where it is not possible to determine in advance and reliably any negative effects of its operation on the environment, etc.;

21.b. experimental construction which should test the feasibility of a new method of design solution or building technique, new building technical lay-out solution, eventually new technical equipment or furnishing of a building.

Article 26

26.1. Under the conditions of the building licence, the surveyor's office determines:

26.1.a. protection of societal interests, primarily of the environment;

26.1.b. harmony of the project with general technical requirements for construction and other specifications and technical standards;

26.1.c. term of construction completion;

26.1.d. respecting the requirements of relevant state administration authorities applied in building procedure;

26.1.e. siting of the construction, if the territorial decision was consolidated with the building procedure.

26.2. The surveyor's office may, under the conditions of the building licence, the following requirements impose on the owner of a building under construction, or determine in the building licence:

26.2.a. the submission of more detailed documentation, before starting the construction, necessary to check on whether the conditions determined for the execution of the construction have been observed;

26.2.b. reporting at a certain stage of the construction in order to maintain expert supervision over the construction progress;

26.2.c. providing documents and professional expertise;

26.2.d. more detailed requirements for the execution of a construction, mainly from architectural and complexity aspects, especially to determine the type and colour of external parts of the building (roofing, plastering, coatings, etc.), connection into distribution network, roads, railways, surface draining and landscaping of the building environment, and conditions of protection and for planting out greenery belts;

26.2.e. necessary land area to form a part of a building site.

Estonia*

EIA regulation	Procedure for Carrying out Environmental Impact Assessment, No.314/1992 (Document A)
EIA authority	Ministry of Environment with 19 district Environmental Departments.
Responsibilities for EIA	Developer pays for Environmental Impact Statement and expert review. Registered experts are not required for the preparation of an Environmental Impact Statement.
Regulatory context for EIA	EIA required for approval of project design and siting, and for natural resource use and construction permits.
Activities subject to EIA	Two lists of mandatory EIAs.
Scoping	The district Environmental Department determines whether an EIA is necessary and on which level (national/district) it should be carried out, on the basis of the appendices of the Procedure for Carrying out Environmental Impact Assessment, 1992.
Environmental Impact Statement	If the project requires an EIA, an Environmental Impact Statement should be prepared, containing information on possible environmental impacts, and planned measures to mitigate pollution and reduce risks.
Review	Licensed experts contracted by the district Environmental Department or Ministry of Environment review the Environmental Impact Statement. The Environmental Impact Statement is then reviewed by the Ministry of Environment or district Environmental Department, as appropriate.
Public participation	EIA must be announced to 'relevant legal and natural persons'. Comments from the public have to be taken into account during the review, but no formal procedures exist.
Approval	A decision on whether or not the project may proceed is made on the basis of whether the predicted environmental impacts will remain within regulatory standards; background levels at the site are considered. Permits for air, water and waste are given on the basis of the EIA.

* Reference material provided by Pēteris Zilgalvis Esq, World Bank Office for the Baltic Countries (Rīga, Latvia), and Olavi Tammemäe, Head of EIA Department, Estonian Ministry of Environment (Tallinn)

Development consent	A construction permit can only be issued after the EIA is approved and all environmental permits issued.
Transboundary EIA	No legal provisions. Estonia has not signed the Espoo Convention on EIA in a Transboundary Context.

1. Introduction

Population: 1.5 million
Area: 45,215 sq km
Currency: Kroon

Principal environmental problems

The main environmental problems in Estonia are:

- environmental damage at former military sites;
- air pollution from two large power plants on the Russian border;
- water pollution because of lack of waste-water treatment facilities.

Environmental policy

The Ministry of Environment has the following priority projects:

- assessment and remediation of pollution at former military sites;
- reduction of water pollution through construction or completion of waste-water treatment facilities;
- reduction of air pollution at the two power plants on the Russian border, through the installation of filters and the improvement and replacement of the technology used at the plants.

The Ministry of Environment has the following policy goals:

- to maintain protection in protected areas currently being privatised;
- to enforce the use of EIA, and to carry out auditing as part of the privatisation process;
- to adjust the system of resource charges and pollution taxes in order to suit the new economic framework and to promote the efficient use of natural resources;
- to meet the requirements of international conventions and other policy documents, for example, the *Environmental Action Programme for Central and Eastern Europe* (approved at the conference of European Environment Ministers in Lucerne, April 1993), and the Baltic Sea Joint Comprehensive Environmental Action Programme (approved by members of HELCOM and multilateral banks in 1992).

2. Institutional and legislative framework for EIA

2.1 Administrative structure and responsibilities for EIA

Estonia is divided into 15 districts and over 200 municipalities. According to the reform of local government which is currently in progress, considerable changes are being made in the distribution of responsibilities between national and local authorities.

The Ministry of Environment in the capital city of Tallinn is the central environmental authority. There are 19 district Environmental Departments subordinate to the Ministry of Environment.

The competent bodies for organising EIA are the Ministry of Environment and its district Environmental Departments.

In relation to EIA, the Ministry of Environment:

- organises EIAs of nationally significant projects;
- organises EIAs at the district level if the district Environmental Department applies for this.

District Environmental Departments:

- organise EIAs for projects which have impacts only within their area of jurisdiction;
- present their opinion on national level EIAs in relation to impacts within their territory;
- issue permits for natural resource use and pollution discharge.

2.2 Sources of legislation relating to EIA

2.2.1 Legislation on EIA

- *Order on Environmental Impact Assessment, No.314/1992* (Document A)

The Procedure defines the process of and responsibilities for EIA in Estonia. Activities requiring an EIA, including national level EIA, are listed in Appendices.

In the preparation of this Procedure, the relevant environmental assessment laws of Great Britain, Denmark and Germany were considered, as well as materials from the European Commission and a draft of the Finnish EIA law.

2.2.2 Legislation on environmental permits

- *Temporary Distribution Order for Permission to Utilise the Environment and Natural Resources, No.13/1991* (Document B)
- *Temporary Order of Possession and Allotment of the Environment, Natural Resources and Objects submitted to the Competence of the Executive Body of the Primary Administrative Unit of Local Government, No.12/1991* (Document C)

The Orders determine the competence to grant permission for the use of the environment and natural resources. An EIA is the basis for applying for these permits. The following permits are defined.

- Use of surface, ground and sea water – permission from district Environmental Department and local government.
- Discharge of waste into water – permission from district Environmental Department.
- Research on or transport/export of flora and fauna – permission from district Environmental Department or Ministry of Environment.
- Extraction of mineral resources and geological research – permission from local government with agreement from district Environmental Department.
- Use of non-mineral resources in protected areas – permission from district Environmental Department or Ministry of Environment.

- Storage of wastes – permission from district Environmental Department and local government.
- Pollution of air – permission from district Environmental Department and local government (there is a list of air pollutants which must also be approved by the Ministry of Environment).

3. Environmental impact assessment process

3.1 Activities subject to EIA

The *Order on Environmental Impact Assessment, No.314/1992* (Document A) provides two lists of projects. The first list contains projects for which an EIA is mandatory, organised by the district Environmental Department, or the national Ministry of Environment if the expected impacts exceed the limits of a single district. The second list contains projects for which an EIA is mandatory, organised by the national Ministry of Environment.

No discretion is specified for the environmental authority to require EIAs for projects not on the two lists.

An EIA may be required for construction, extension and liquidation of industrial or business facilities.

3.2 Regulatory context for EIA

EIA is linked to the following:

- project siting;
- application for a permit to use natural resources;
- approval of project design;
- issuing a construction permit.

A favourable EIA review, and on the basis of this, environmental permits for air, water and waste, are all required before a construction permit can be given. (Plans for an integrated permitting system are being developed.) Details of environmental permits are given in section 2.2.2.

3.3 Responsibilities for EIA

The developer pays for the preparation of the Environmental Impact Statement and the expert review. The Ministry of Environment or the district Environmental Department organises the review.

3.4 Scope of EIA and environmental impact statement

There is no scoping process. The scope of the EIA is defined by the Ministry of Environment or district Environmental Department.

The Environmental Impact Statement consists of the following:

- a description of the project, containing information about its location, design and size;
- preliminary data on the tolerance of the surrounding environment;
- project alternatives under preparation;

- description of environmental protection measures;
- data to enable the estimation of possible damage through natural resource use and pollution of ground, air and water.

Environmental Impact Statements being reviewed at the national level must be presented with a written position of the district Environmental Department.

When an EIA is required, all other project documentation must also include relevant environmental information. The environmental information required for the Technical Economic Calculation (TEC), which constitutes the application for a construction permit, is as follows:

- emissions into air and water, water use, and waste discharges;
- environmental hazards and risk of accidents;
- measures planned for environmental protection, waste treatment and accident prevention or mitigation.

3.5 Public participation

According to the *Order on Environmental Impact Assessment, No.314/1992*, an EIA must be announced to 'relevant legal and natural persons'. The district Environmental Department or Ministry of Environment determines the manner of informing these persons, and announces the place and time of public consultations and discussions.

Comments from citizens have to be taken into account by the environmental authority, but no specific procedures have yet been drawn up.

3.6 Expert review

An independent review of the Environmental Impact Statement is carried out by experts licensed by the Ministry of Environment, at the expense of the developer. Sometimes a commission can be set up. (If there are no appropriately qualified Estonian experts, they have to be found abroad. Foreign experts and consultants have to present a letter of recommendation from their national ministry of environment.)

The review considers the following:

- project design – technology used, architectural form, use of materials and energy;
- measures to protect the environment and nature, and to treat wastes;
- use of natural resources;
- environmental risks and measures to deal with accidents and mitigate their impacts;
- measures to restore renewable natural resources.

The assessment period is one month, but can take longer if the expert considers that more information is required.

For EIAs carried out at the national level, the opinion of the district Environmental Department is included at this stage, before review takes place at the Ministry of Environment.

3.7 Review and approval

The EIA is then reviewed by the district Environmental Department, or by the Ministry of Environment for national level projects, as defined in the appendices of the *Order on*

Environmental Impact Assessment, No.314/1992. For national projects, the relevant district Environmental Department gives its opinion.

The review is carried out on the basis of the predicted pollution discharges. If the projected discharges exceed national standards then the project will not be allowed to proceed without modifications.

If the review is positive, an approval of the EIA is issued by the Ministry of Environment or the district Environmental Department, valid for two years. This can contain restrictions on and conditions for the proposed project.

Approval of the EIA provides the basis for permits for emissions into air and water, water use and waste discharges. These permits are a prerequisite for receiving a construction permit.

4. Monitoring

The Ministry of Environment and the district Environmental Department have the right to check on the implementation of conditions set in the EIA. The developer must guarantee environmental monitoring if it is required in the EIA.

The *Order on Environmental Impact Assessment, No.314/1992* makes it an offence to provide false information in relation to an EIA. An investor providing false information may be subject to administrative sanctions.

Local government has the right to halt any activity that violates the law or harms the environment beyond permissible limits, even if the approval has been given at the national level.

5. EIA in practice

About 60 EIAs have been carried out at the national level. There are no central records of EIA implementation at the district level.

No project has yet been forbidden as a result of an EIA. Rather, the environmental authority recommends modifications of the project. A process of negotiation takes place, until agreement is reached between the authority and the developer.

There has been little public participation in EIAs. In some cases, local scientists and local inhabitants have voiced opinions, but no formal process has yet been developed.

6. Sources of further information

Mr Olavi Tammemäe
Head
EIA and Standards Department
Ministry of Environment of the Republic of Estonia
Harju 11, B429
EE 0001 Tallinn

Estonia
tel: (372-2) 44 32 10
fax: (372-2) 45 33 10
telex: 17 32 38 METS SU

Licensed EIA review experts
Mr Väino Puura
Institute of Geology
Academy of Sciences
Estonia pst. 7
EE 0105 Tallinn
Estonia
tel: (372-2) 42 34 26 / 44 41 89

Mr Mart Külvik
Estonian Institute of Forestry and Nature Conservation
Rôômu tee 2
EE 2400 Tartu
Estonia
tel: (372-34) 36 375

Mr Edgar Karofeld
Institute of Ecology
Kevade 2
EE 0001 Tallinn
Estonia
tel: (372-2) 45 16 34

Mr Edgar Madis Metsur
MAVES (company specialising in geology, hydro-chemistry, waste water treatment)
Marja 4D
EE 0006 Tallinn
Estonia
tel: (372-1) 44 14 01

Mr Lembit Linnupôld
E-KONSULT (EIA management, water management, hazardous/solid waste, construction)
Harju 11
EE 0100 Tallinn
Estonia
tel: (372-2) 44 03 27

Mr Tônis Pôder
Estonian Sea Research Institute
Lai 32
EE 0001 Tallinn
Estonia
tel: (372-2) 45 35 74

Mr Ülo Heinsalu, licensed EIA expert specialising in geological aspects
Estonia pst. 7
EE 0001 Tallinn
Estonia
tel: (372-2) 45 47 60

Mr Timofejev Sidorkin, licensed EIA expert specialising in energy aspects
Elektriku 3
EE 2020 Kohta-Järve
Estonia

Mr Tõnu Oja, specialist in air pollution impact, landscape planning
Institute of Geography
Vanemuise 46
EE 2400 Tartu
Estonia
tel: (372-34) 30 605

Mr Aare Sirendi, air pollution, chemical analysis of environment
Marja 4D
EE 0006 Tallinn
Estonia
tel: (372-2) 53 83 01

Mr Kaarel Orviku, coastal environment
Estonia pst. 7
EE 0001 Tallinn
Estonia

7. EIA legislation

Terms used in law	*Terms used in book*
EIA	Review
Object of EIA	Project
Subject of EIA	Development
Materials for EIA	Environmental Impact Statement

ESTONIA A

The procedure for carrying out environmental impact assessment Sanctioned with Government Regulation No.314 of 13 November 1992

I. General provisions

Article 1. Definitions of the terms used:

'object of environmental impact assessment' means the sphere of activity or object requiring environmental impact assessment;

'subject of environmental impact assessment' means the legal or natural person whose sphere of activity or whose object requires environmental impact assessment;

'competent authorities' means the Ministry of the Environment and regional environmental protection departments within their scope of authority;

'expert' means a specialist carrying out assessment who has obtained a licence issued by the Ministry of the Environment;

'expert opinion' means assessment in the field of environmental protection given by an expert on the object of environmental impact assessment.

Article 2. The procedure for carrying out environmental impact assessment shall be binding on all subjects of environmental impact assessment and the competent authorities.

Article 3. The aim of environmental impact assessment is to assess the efficiency of the planned environmental protection measures, taking into account possible environmental impact related to the object of environmental impact assessment and to sustainability of the environment in the area under discussion, and to make proposals for organising monitoring, in case it is necessary.

Article 4. Environmental impact assessment is organised by competent authorities.

Article 5. Environmental impact assessment precedes the issuing of nature management and production permits, thus belonging to the system of endorsement and coordination of projects.

II. Rights and responsibilities of competent authorities

Article 6. The Ministry of the Environment organises environmental impact assessment at the national level concerning objects listed in Appendix 1 of this Procedure, the supposed impact of which exceeds the scope of authority of local authorities, as well as of all the objects listed in Appendix 2 of the current Procedure. Materials presented at environmental impact assessment shall on the national level include a written statement of a regional environmental protection department.

Article 7. Regional environmental protection departments organise environmental impact assessment of all the objects listed in Appendix 1 of the current Procedure, the impact of which does not exceed the scope of authority of local authorities.

Article 8. On the basis of results of environmental impact assessment, the competent authorities shall have the right to:

8.1. interrupt, set restrictions to, or terminate any activities harmful or dangerous to the environment as well as non-rational nature management, or to make this proposal to local authorities;

8.2. check the compliance with restrictions set on the basis of environmental impact assessment.

Article 9. Competent authorities shall have the right to obtain from the subject of environmental impact assessment environmental information concerning nature management, monitoring, waste treatment, and other relevant issues, as well as explanations from relevant officials, free and without reservation.

Article 10. Competent authorities and experts are obliged to comply with the rules and restrictions established by legislation and maintain the national, production, business and private secrets which have come to their knowledge during their assignment.

Article 11. Legal or natural persons connected with environmental impact assessment and storing information about materials to be presented at environmental impact assessment are obliged to forward it upon request of competent offices, free of charge.

Article 12. Environmental impact assessment shall be carried out within one month after the receipt of a request and of all necessary materials. This fixed term may be prolonged by competent authorities on the basis of reasonable application of the expert.

Article 13. Environmental impact assessment is financed at the expense of the subject of environmental impact assessment via a competent office. The competent office has also the right to organise environmental impact assessment at the expense of other sources of funding.

III. Materials to be presented for carrying out environmental impact assessment

Article 14. Materials presented by the subject of environmental impact assessment shall include:

14.1. a description of the object of environmental impact assessment containing information about its location, construction, dimensions and production technology;

14.2. initial data for assessment of the tolerance of the environment;

14.3. other (alternative) possible solutions being developed;

14.4. description of measures providing for environmental safety;

14.5. data necessary for assessment of the causes and consequences of possible environmental damage, including use of natural resources, waste products and hazardous compounds released into soil, atmosphere, and water.

IV. Proceedings of environmental impact assessment

Article 15. Environmental impact assessment shall be carried out:

15.1. concerning choice of a location (site) of an object;

15.2. concerning application for a permit on the use of natural resources and the environment;

15.3. concerning the approval of initial task and technical requirements, and concerning technical-economic reasoning of a project;

15.4. prior to approval of project documentation or prior to starting of construction activities.

Article 16. The requirements of this Procedure are also valid concerning reconstruction, expansion and liquidation (decommissioning) projects.

Article 17. Proceedings of environmental impact assessment include the following main phases:

17.1. competent office controls the completeness of materials delivered by the subject of environmental impact assessment for carrying out environmental assessment, determines the objectives of assessment, and enters into contracts with experts;

17.2. experts review and analyse documentation concerning the object of environmental impact assessment and assess the object from the point of view of environmental safety:

- reasons for the activity, or ways of implementation of the project (solutions of technical engineering and technological as well as architectural design, efficiency and complexity of the use of materials and power resources);
- environmental and nature protection measures and efficiency of utilisation of natural resources;
- consideration of possible consequences dangerous for the environment; suitability of solutions for mitigation of risks, accidents, and for remediation of their expected results;
- efficiency of the measures planned for environmental protection and waste treatment;
- guarantees for reproduction of renewable natural resources;

17.3. on the basis of expert opinion, the competent office makes proposals for decision-making concerning the object of environmental impact assessment.

Article 18. Proceedings of environmental impact assessment are made public by the competent office, who:

18.1. determines the ways of informing the relevant legal and natural persons;

18.2. announces the places and times of consultations (hearings) and discussions;

18.3. determines the procedure for collecting information and forwarding to the competent office;

18.4. stores materials concerning environmental impact assessment in its files.

In case essential additional information concerning the object of environmental impact assessment is submitted, the competent office may organise additional assessment.

Article 19. For carrying out environmental assessment, a commission of experts may be formed. A summarised assessment is compiled by the chairman of the commission on the basis of expert opinions of the members of the commission.

Article 20. Conclusions of environmental impact assessment shall be valid within two years.

Article 21. The competent office informs the relevant legal and natural persons and, in case of necessity, supervisory bodies of environmental protection, of the results of impact assessment. Materials which have been presented for carrying out impact assessment shall be returned to the subject of impact assessment.

V. Obligations and liability of the subject of environmental impact assessment

Article 22. The subject of environmental impact assessment shall be responsible for the completeness and correctness of the materials presented for carrying out environmental impact assessment.

Article 23. Upon request of an expert, the subject of environmental impact assessment is obliged to submit additional data concerning the materials being reviewed.

Article 24. The subject of environmental impact assessment is obliged to:

24.1. implement decisions made on the basis of environmental impact assessment;

24.2. guarantee consistent implementation of the environmental protection requirements, including the ones concerning liquidation (decommissioning) of the object;

24.3. guarantee environmental monitoring at its expense, according to the procedure determined by the competent office.

Article 25. Legal and natural persons violating with their activities or inactivity the requirements of this Procedure shall be held liable according to laws and other legislative acts.

Article 26. Appeals concerning decisions of environmental impact assessment on the national level shall be dealt with by the court.

Appendix 1 to the 'Procedure for carrying out environmental impact assessment'

List of the objects of environmental impact assessment

1. Nuclear industry.

2. Industry using radioactive materials and related fields of activities.

3. Biochemistry, biotechnology and pharmaceutics.

4. Chemical industry.

5. Production and use of mutagenic substances, including carcinogenic substances.

6. Power production and technological (engineering) networks.

7. Research activities where pathogenic microbes, electromagnetic radiation of high capacity, radioactive and other environmentally hazardous substances are used.

8. Production, storage, and use of mineral and organic fertilisers, pesticides and poisonous chemicals within areas with environmental protection restrictions.

9. Production using natural resources, including production of cement, glass and cellulose.

10. Mining and processing of mineral resources.

11. Processing of agricultural products.

12. Animal husbandry facilities for more than 10 cows or 30 pigs, and other cattle-sheds and poultry-farms with pollution loads equal to the former.

13. Waste treatment.

14. Storage, transportation and treatment of hazardous waste.

15. Storage sites of oil products (volume over 5 m^3), workshops providing technical services.

16. Activities causing noise, vibration and electromagnetic fields, including high capacity transmission lines.

17. Microelectronics industry.

18. Activities causing soil erosion and deflation or changes in coastline of water-bodies.

19. Regulation of flow on natural water-bodies, and amelioration.

20. Fish-rearing at natural water-bodies.

21. Utilisation of forests and other renewable natural resources.

22. Activities changing landscape, and recultivation activities.

23. Activities changing the purpose of land management (land use).

24. Planning concerning resorts and recreational areas.

25. Changing of sanitary conditions within recreation areas, and of natural conditions within nature conservation areas.

Appendix 2 to the 'Procedure for carrying out environmental impact assessment'

List of objects of national environmental impact assessment

1. National and departmental concepts, programmes, and master plans as well as planning, including management of the land fund, economic plans of water management, and management of forests and other renewable natural resources, waste management of districts or municipal towns related to nature management within the territory of Estonia.

2. Master plans and regional development plans, and reallocation of productive forces on the national level.

3. Master plans of regions and administrative units.

4. Plans of industrial regions and traffic schemes of municipal towns.

5. Establishment and zoning of nature conservation areas.

6. Establishment of communication lines and production facilities, planning of their settlements, changing the purpose (type) of land use, extraction of mineral resources.

7. Selection of location and route of, as well as design projects of national level communication networks (gas, communication, power transmission lines of 110 kW and more), railways, roads, airports and ports.

8. Dredging and dumping at sea, the Peipsi and Pihkva lakes, as well as at other water-bodies within national jurisdiction.

9. Terminals of oil products with the capacity of 5,000 m^3 and more.

10. Projects concerning regulation of waterways and water-bodies of national and regional importance.

11. Projects concerning treatment and storage sites of hazardous waste, including radioactive waste.

12. International and inter-regional schemes of nature management and conservation.

13. Electric power stations with the capacity exceeding 50 MW, and nuclear power plants.

14. Projects concerning establishment, reconstruction and liquidation of, as well as new technological schemes of enterprises using natural resources at a large scale, or producing environmentally hazardous waste.

15. Projects concerning the use and extraction of mineral resources of national importance.

16. Groundwater intake structures in groundwater layers of national importance.
17. Projects of waste treatment and experimental waste-water treatment facilities.
18. Plans for remediation of the consequences of large-scale accidents.
19. Projects connected with changing the gene-fund of livestock.

ESTONIA B

The Temporary Distribution Order for Permission to Utilise the Environment and Natural Resources

Government Decree No.13/1991 issued on 17 January 1991, Tallinn, Toompea

Unofficial translation

In accordance with part I article 7 of the Estonian Law covering 'The order of environment and natural resources utilisation', the Government of Estonia resolves:

The utilisation of water, water flora and fauna

Article 1. To establish that:

1.1. the right to use inland water-bodies and parts thereof (except those used for taking drinking water, everyday necessities, medical purposes or those being under State protection or having internal fish-farming or/and recreation status) situated on the territory of a settlement, a town or a region (volost) is carried out in accordance with the decision of the settlement, town or regional executive committee, it being in accordance with the opinion of the secondary local government institution for nature protection (district (yezd) or town) – in the text below: secondary nature conservancy institution;

1.2. the right to use inland water-bodies or parts thereof situated on the territory of several regions (volost) and one district (yezd) or town is carried out in accordance with the decision of the corresponding secondary local executive body, it being in accordance with the agreement between the primary local governments;

1.3. the right to use inland water-bodies or parts thereof situated on the territory of several regions and several districts or towns, is carried out in accordance with the decision of the Estonian Republic Department of Water, it being in accordance with the opinion of local executive body;

1.4. the right to use water-bodies or parts thereof used for taking drinking water, everyday necessities, medical purposes, and those taken under State protection or having internal fish-farming or recreation status, is carried out in accordance with the order established by the Ministry of Environment of the Republic of Estonia;

1.5. permission to use mineral water resources is given by the Department of Water of the Republic of Estonia in accordance with the decision of the Ministry of Public Health, Estonia Geology Centre and the secondary nature conservancy institution;

1.6. permission to use the surface, underground and sea-waters is given by the secondary nature conservation institution in the order established by the Ministry of Environment of the Republic of Estonia;

1.7. mooring permission for the owners of small-scale water transport is given by the primary executive body of the administrative unit which has self-governing status in accordance with the secondary nature conservancy institution;

1.8. permission to dump sewage into inland water-bodies, sea or soil is given by the secondary nature conservancy institution;

1.9. permission to fish or catch lamprey, crayfish and other water invertebrates is given by the organisation which has the right to use the above-mentioned resources; in case of its absence, permission is given by the Central State Institution in charge of fish resources if the fishing sites are Lake Chudskoye and Lake Pskovskoye, the Narva river, the Narva reservoir, the Estonian economic region in the Baltic Sea and the sea itself (at a distance of more than 2 sea-miles from the shore-line and at a depth of more than 20 metres), or by the corresponding secondary nature conservancy institution if the fishing site is the water-body situated on the territory of a district or town or the sea (at a distance of less than 2 sea-miles from the shore-line and at a depth of less than 20 metres).

Article 2. The use of water resources, being in the common use of several USSR republics and other states, and the sewage release into these resources, are regulated by international agreements.

The utilisation of land and animate nature

Article 3. To establish that:

3.1. the right to use land is carried out in accordance with the order established by the Department of Land of the Estonian Republic;

3.2. the right to the possession of forests is given on the basis of the order in force, until the implementation of the Estonian Republic Law relating to forests;

3.3. permission to conduct research into, to transport, etc., all flora and fauna species under State protection is given by the Ministry of Environment of the Republic of Estonia in accordance with the decision of the corresponding scientific institution and the secondary nature protection institution;

3.4. permission to import into Estonia new flora and fauna species, and also for the transportation within or outside the borders of Estonia of animal species inhabiting Estonia, is given by the Ministry of Environment of the Republic of Estonia in conformity with the decision of the Frontier Plant Quarantine Inspectorate of Estonia, the Veterinary Department of the Agriculture Ministry of the Republic of Estonia, and the secondary nature conservancy institution;

3.5. permission to export from Estonia plant and animal collections is given by the Ministry of Environment of the Republic of Estonia in accordance with the secondary nature conservancy institution;

3.6. permission for game shooting is given by the organisation possessing the hunting area for the sum demanded.

The utilisation of natural resources on the territories under protection

Article 4. To establish that permission to use the natural resources (with the exception of the earth's resources):

4.1. in State Reserves, in Lahemaa National Park and within other protected territories in the Republic of Estonia, is given in cases and on terms set out by legislation regulating the utilisation and protection of the above-mentioned territories, by the governing body (Heads, Directors) subject to the protected territories' dimensions and aims; and, on protected territories with no governing body, by the institution in charge of allotted natural resources in accordance with the secondary nature conservancy institution and the Ministry of Environment of the Republic of Estonia;

4.2. on the territories protected by the local self-governing body, is given by the corresponding secondary nature conservancy institution.

Waste products

Article 5. To establish that:

5.1. permission to store waste products in the provided places is given to those juridical bodies and their structural departments, in the activity of which waste products are generated, by the local secondary nature conservancy institution in conformity with the primary executive body of local government;

permission to store waste products is not given if the waste products are utilised, rendered harmless or handed over to specialised industrial works;

5.2. permission to release pollutants into the atmosphere is given by the secondary nature conservancy institution in conformity with the primary executive body of local government; besides that, such permission for juridical bodies possessing the sources of air pollution set out by the Ministry of Environment of the Republic of Estonia on a special list of air pollution sources having internal or international influence, must be coordinated with the Ministry of Environment of the Republic of Estonia;

5.3. the revised order for permission to release pollutants, providing the fulfilment of international agreements, is established by the Ministry of Environment of the Republic of Estonia.

Chairman of the Government of the Republic of Estonia, E. Savisaar

Minister of State of the Republic of Estonia, R. Vare

ESTONIA C

Temporary Order of Possession and Allotment of the Environment, Natural Resources and Objects submitted to the Competence of the Executive Body of the Primary Administrative Unit of Local Government

Government Decree No.12/1991 issued on 17 January 1991, Tallinn, Toompea

Unofficial translation

The present temporary order determines, in accordance with the 15 December 1989 Law of the Republic of Estonia 'About the order of utilisation of the environment and natural resources', the competence of the executive bodies of primary administrative units (region (volost), settlement, town) having self-governing status to possess the environment and natural resources, and also to set terms and to establish regulations for the right to use these.

Article 1. Within the competence of the executive body of the primary administrative unit concerning the possession of the environment, natural resources and objects and their distribution for utilisation are:

1.1. the granting of permission to extract rock and soil, not set out in a list of minerals of Estonia, subject to the agreement of the nature conservancy institution of the secondary administrative unit of local government (district (yezd) or town) – in the text below: secondary nature conservancy institution;

1.2. the granting of permission for peat extraction from peat-bogs with an area not exceeding 100 hectares, subject to the agreement of the secondary nature conservancy institution;

1.3. preliminary agreement concerning permission to utilise minerals that is given by the secondary nature conservancy institution and the right to stipulate special terms for this;

1.4. agreement to utilise land for carrying out geological research (time and place of the research), subject to the agreement of the secondary nature conservancy institution;

1.5. the granting of permission to transport soil outside the borders of land allotment;

1.6. the granting of the right to use inland water-bodies and parts thereof, with the exception of those used for taking drinking water, everyday necessities and medical purposes, and those being under State protection or having internal fish-farming and recreation status, subject to the agreement of the secondary nature conservancy institution;

1.7. preliminary agreement concerning permission, given by the secondary nature conservancy institution, to utilise water, and the right to stipulate special terms for this;

1.8. preliminary agreement on terms of contracts for hunting and fishing concluded by the secondary nature conservancy institution, and the right to stipulate special terms for these;

1.9. the granting of mooring permission for the owners of small-scale water transport, subject to the agreement of the secondary nature conservancy institution;

1.10. solving problems connected with the planting, guarding and maintenance of groups of trees, alleys, separate trees, and other elements of greenery, not being under State protection, not guarded by special regime, and not included in the forest fund, and also, the granting of permission for their liquidation;

1.11. the granting of permission to fertilise and protect plants from the air, and also to kill weeds along railway lines, gas pipelines, and electricity cables by means of chemicals;

1.12. the granting of permission to use territories for the organisation of different events, etc.

Article 2. The right to use land is carried out in accordance with the order established by the Department of Land of the Republic of Estonia.

Article 3. The self-governing bodies of primary administrative units exercise control over the observance of rights to utilise the environment, natural resources and objects, and to collect, transport, store and utilise household sewage and industrial waste, including dangerous waste products, by juridical bodies and citizens.

The self-governing bodies of the primary administrative units have the right to stop any activity that is against the law or causes harm to the environment; moreover, their directions are compulsory for juridical bodies and persons.

Article 4. Juridical bodies and persons are accountable to the self-governing organs of the primary administrative unit for the utilisation of the environment, natural resources and objects, and also for their condition.

Article 5. Permission to utilise the environment, natural resources and objects is given on the basis of written application, that must be presented to the regional, settlement or town executive committee in those cases mentioned in Article 1 of the present Temporary order.

Permission is signed, as a rule, by the Elder or Mayor of the region (volost) or settlement. In those cases when the utilisation of natural resources is connected with any activity requiring a licence, the applicant is supposed to produce the licence to the self-governing executive committee of the primary administrative unit.

Article 6. On the basis of the decision made by the self-governing executive committee of the primary administrative unit, the right to use the environment, natural resources and objects may require both a contract for utilisation, and permission to utilise.

Article 7. Disputes, connected with the signing, changing and repealing of contracts for utilisation of the environment, natural resources and objects and also with permission to utilise, are to be arbitrated according to the order established by the legislation of the Republic of Estonia.

Hungary*

EIA regulation	Government Decree No.86/1993 (VI.4.) on the Provisional Regulation of the Environmental Impact Assessment of Certain Activities (Document A)
EIA authority	Ministry of Environment and Regional Policy (MERP) and 12 regional Environmental Inspectorates.
Responsibilities for EIA	The developer pays for the preparation of the Environmental Impact Statement. There is no requirement to use registered experts.
Regulatory context for EIA	EIA is part of the process of obtaining siting, building, environmental and operating permits.
Activities subject to EIA	Two lists of mandatory EIAs.
Activities subject to EIA	Two lists of mandatory projects. EIA is optional for projects not on these lists, at the discretion of the EIA authority.
Scoping	The Regional Environmental Inspectorate defines the scope of the EIA.
Preliminary Environmental Impact Statement	The developer prepares a preliminary Environmental Impact Statement.
Review	The Regional Environmental Inspectorate reviews the preliminary Environmental Impact Statement.
Detailed Environmental Impact Statement	If required by law, or by the Regional Environmental Inspectorate, the developer prepares a detailed Environmental Impact Statement.
Public participation	The local government organises a public hearing involving the concerned authorities and affected public. The views of the public are taken into account during review and approval.
Review and approval	The Regional Environmental Inspectorate reviews the detailed Environmental Impact Statement, taking into account the views of the public. In certain cases the MERP is involved.

* Reference material provided by Dr. Judit Péter, Environmental Management and Law Association (Budapest)

Development consent	The Regional Environmental Inspectorate grants an environmental permit as a prerequisite for the siting and building permits granted by the municipality.
Transboundary EIA	No legal provisions. Hungary has signed the Espoo Convention on EIA in a Transboundary Context.

1. Introduction

Population: 10 million
Area: 93,033 sq km
Currency: Forint

Principal environmental problems
Environmental problems include:

- large increase in deforestation since the beginning of the process of land privatisation
- traffic pollution in cities
- groundwater pollution due to inadequate sewage systems, particularly in rural areas
- lack of law enforcement infrastructure

Environmental policy
The Ministry of Environment is focusing its activity in two areas:

- drafting a new environmental law
- introduction of environmental taxes (e.g. petrol, car tyres)

The Ministry is engaging in active consultation with NGOs, and has set up a unit responsible for this.

2. Legislative and institutional framework for EIA

2.1 Administrative structure and responsibilities for EIA

Hungary is divided into 19 counties and about 3,200 municipalities. The capital city of Budapest has the same status as a county.

Central government
The central environmental authority is the Ministry of Environment and Regional Policy (MERP). The MERP is responsible for the National Environmental Inspectorate, which has 12 regional offices.

The Regional Inspectorates have the following functions in relation to the EIA process:

- defining the exact scope of each EIA;
- organising public hearings for EIA;
- reviewing EIAs;
- enforcing conditions outlined in the EIA.

The *Ministry of Public Welfare* and its regional public health and epidemiological authorities are responsible for reviewing the human health aspects of the EIA.

The *Ministry of Transport, Telecommunications and Water Management* incorporates the National Water Management Authority and its 12 regional directorates. These are responsible for licensing projects for water supply, waste-water treatment and purification, and water management.

Other ministries grant various environmental approvals for projects in particular sectors.

Local government

Counties have a limited number of administrative powers, most of which do not concern environmental matters.

Municipalities are self-governing and are responsible for land use planning and projects involving construction. Municipalities draft regulations on environmental matters falling within their jurisdiction.

2.2 Sources of legislation relating to EIA

2.2.1 Legislation on EIA

- *Government Decree No.86/1993 (VI.4.) for Provisional Regulation of the Assessment of the Environmental Impact of Certain Activities* (Document A)

(Referred to below as '*Decree on Provisional EIA Regulation, 1993*')

The Decree lists the projects involving construction or modification for which an EIA is mandatory. There is a second list of projects for which an EIA is mandatory if the project is sited in a protected area.

The Decree is provisional until the new environmental law is passed (see section 6).

- *Act No.II/1976 on the Protection of the Human Environment*

The Act defines the principles of environmental protection in Hungary. It defines protected elements of the environment (ground, water, air, wildlife, landscape, urban environment) and rules for their protection. It outlines jurisdictions for environmental protection.

The Act defines the principle of EIA:

> The requirements of environmental protection shall be considered in determining the objectives of national economic plans. They shall be realised in regional planning and development, and in the siting, and economic and technical planning of facilities. (Article 5.11)

The Act emphasises the importance of considering environmental aspects in the process of economic planning and decision making (Article 5.2).

Other EIA related rules are included in the provisions relating to specific environmental components.

A revision of this Act has been in discussion since 1990. Several drafts have been drawn up. The process is stimulating intense professional and political debate.

- *Decree No.146/1992 (XI.4.) on the Provisional Regulation of Some of the Issues concerning the Investment of Facilities, and Equipment Used for Electric and Thermal Energy having Significant Impact on the Environment*

The Decree defines the requirements for building or modifying electric and thermal power stations greater than 50 MW. The Decree is the first piece of legislation in Hungary to require an EIA for specific projects.

The Decree is provisional until a new environmental law is passed. It is not affected by the later *Decree on Provisional EIA Regulation, 1993* (Document A).

According to the Decree, it is obligatory to make a feasibility study and undertake an EIA for a project to build or modify a power station which produces more than 50 MW of energy. The EIA has to be made in accordance with requirements of the MERP. (These requirements are listed in a document entitled *Technical Guidance* (1991).) A public hearing is required, but it has no legal force. The project, together with the EIA, is judged by a committee nominated by the Minister of Industry and Commerce.

2.2.2 Legislation on planning

- *Decree No.1/1968 (I.11.) of the Minister of Construction and Urban Development on the Procedure to Issue a Land Use Permit*

A developer must apply for a land use permit for any new building projects, not already included in a local plan. The permit is issued by the construction office of the municipality.

A survey of possible environmental impacts must be included in the application for a building permit (Article 5).

The Environmental Inspectorate reviews the permit application if the project involves hazardous waste, noise, vibration, air emissions or water emissions, or manufacturing (Article 7, and Appendix). The municipal construction office must refuse a permit if the project exceeds legal limits for water pollution, steam, gas, dust, heat, smell, smoke, noise, vibration, and radiation (Article 9.3.d).

- *Decree No.12/1986 (XII.30.) of the Minister of Construction and Regional Planning on the Permission Procedure for Construction and Starting Operations*

This Directive outlines the procedure for obtaining building permits and making projects operational. An assessment of the possible environmental consequences is required in this process.

If the project involves hazardous waste, noise, vibration, air pollution, or water pollution, the Environmental Inspectorate will participate in the decision making process.

- *Act III/1964 on Housing and Construction*, as amended in 1991, 1992, 1993

The Act and its executive orders cover all aspects of construction, including regional planning and land use. It describes different kinds of plan. It specifies that central government prepares regional plans and municipalities prepare local plans.

In making plans, the municipality must cooperate with local citizens and citizens' groups. If the municipality rejects the opinion of citizens, it must give a detailed explanation of why (Article 6.6).

The municipality must obtain an expert opinion from the MERP, although the details of this consultation are not defined.

- *Government Decree No.30/1964 (XII.2.); Executive Order of Act III/1964*

The Decree specifies that local plans contain provisions for protecting the environment, historical monuments and the landscape.

Executive orders for the amendments of *Act III./1964 on Construction* have not yet been passed.

- *Decree No.2/1986 (II.27.) of the Ministry of Housing and Construction on the National Regulations for Constructions*, as amended

The Decree contains specifications for construction, such as siting, structure, and safety. It describes various kinds of land use (habitation, recreation, industrial, traffic, green areas, forest, agriculture).

The Decree states that when a municipality issues a building permit, the environment should be taken into account through all the stages of a project, from construction to operation.

2.2.3 Legislation on environmental permits

(See box on page 92 below.)

- *Decree No.2/1980 (I.16.) on Preliminary Water Permit*, amended in 1982, 1984

A permit is required for building water treatment facilities and for consumption of water. A preliminary water permit is issued during project preparation, and a final permit just before the project becomes operational.

- *Decree No.4/1982.évi.4.tvr. of the Presidium with Statutory Force on Nature Protection*

The Decree establishes the process of creating local and national nature reserves and parks, protecting areas of special importance, regulating activities, and managing areas with protected species. The Decree describes the structure and administration of nature protection.

Projects in protected areas requiring an EIA are listed in the *Decree on Provisional EIA Regulation, 1993* (Document A).

- *Decree No.26/1985 (V.11.) on Procedures related to Toxic Substances, and its Executive Order No.16/1988 (XII.22.) of the Minister of Public Welfare and Health*

The Decree requires the classification of toxic substances according to the danger they represent to human life. The Decree also specifies that a permit is necessary to handle toxic waste. The Executive Order requires experts from the environmental and water management authorities to be involved in issuing the permit.

- *Act VII/1961 on Timber and Game Industry*, and its executive order, *Government Decree No.73/1981 (XII.29.)*

The Act sets basic principles for and regulations on afforestation, reforestation, the timber industry, and the game industry. One of the objectives of the Act is to protect forests which play a role in protecting soil, water, climate and human health.

The Decree requires a permit for any activity which may alter these protection functions of a forest. The Forest Inspectorate will only issue such a permit if the protection functions can be ensured by some other means.

- *Act XLVIII/1993 on Mining*

The Act regulates the construction, operation and termination of mining activity. It states that mining activity can only be pursued if it ensures protection of human life and health, the environment and property, and considers the economy of mineral and geothermal energy resources.

The Mining Inspectorate grants a mining permit, based on the operational plan for the mine. This plan includes landscape planning and measures to prevent and mitigate environmental damage.

This is the first Hungarian law which incorporated environmental aspects into permitting procedures.

A further permit from the nature protection authority is required if the mining activity affects protected areas.

- *Government Decree No.9/1961 (III.30.)*, and executive order of *Act III/1961 on Mining*

(*Act III/1961 on Mining 1961* was not repealed when *Act XLVIII/1993 on Mining* was passed.)

The Act specifies that the Mining Inspectorate designates the mining site for certain mineral resources. Before selecting a site, the Inspectorate is obliged to hold a public hearing at the site. The following have to be invited: the developer; the superior mining authority; the parish or town clerk; the water management authority; the owners of the mining equipment, facilities and real estate; Ministry of Environment and Regional Planning; the central authority for geology; the Registration Office of Real Estate; and other interested authorities. At the hearing, discussion will include the project's impact on the environment. The Mining Inspectorate makes its decision on the basis of the public hearing, and will set conditions in the mining permit in order to prevent or mitigate environmental impacts.

- *Government Decree No.12/1983 (V.12.) on Protection from Noise and Vibration*, as amended by *Decree No.88/1990 (IV.30.)*

The Decree regulates noise and vibration in order to protect the environment and human health. The developer of an industrial project must apply for a noise and vibration limit value. The application must include:

- sources of noise/vibration;
- local conditions;
- measures to reduce noise/vibration.

The permit is given after considering other noise emissions in the area. In certain areas (e.g. near schools) noise will be limited further. In case of very noisy activities, such as airports, a protective zone must be established.

- *Government Decree No.21/1986 (VI.2.) on the Protection of Clean Air*

The Decree sets rules and regulations for preventing, mitigating and eliminating air pollution, in order to protect human health and the environment.

The developer must ask the Environmental Inspectorate for a limit value on air pollution.

- *Government Decree No.27/1992 (I.30.) on Amending Government Decree No.56/1981 (XI.18.) on Controlling the Occurrence of Hazardous Waste and the Activities related to their Neutralisation*

The amendment decree requires the separation and collection of hazardous waste and sets a time limit for the amount that can be stored within a plant. The Environmental Inspectorate, however, can change the time limit if other authorities approve.

- *Government Decree No.104/1990 (XII.15.) on the Tasks and Authority of the National Atomic Energy Committee and the National Atomic Energy Office*

The National Atomic Energy Committee controls the production of nuclear energy and the enforcement of related laws. The National Atomic Energy Office has the right to issue permits related to building, operating, modifying and terminating facilities using nuclear energy.

3. Environmental impact assessment process

3.1 Activities subject to EIA

The *Decree on Provisional EIA Regulation, 1993* (Document A) lists 110 industrial and agricultural construction and modification activities for which an EIA is mandatory. Additionally there are 21 types of projects in national and local nature reserves and parks for which an EIA is mandatory. Both lists have to be reviewed by the Government at least every two years (Article 1.3).

The *Decree on Provisional EIA Regulation, 1993* describes a preliminary EIA and a detailed EIA. Some of the projects on the mandatory lists are marked as requiring a detailed EIA in all cases. Those not marked as requiring a detailed EIA, require it only if the Regional Environmental Inspectorate requests it, having reviewed the preliminary EIA (Article 4.2).

An EIA may be required for siting, construction, completion, and liquidation (Article 1.2).

3.2 Regulatory context for EIA

The EIA procedure fits into the overall planning procedure for building, modification and liquidation projects. Permits and approvals required to operate an industrial facility are as follows:

- permit from Land Registry if the project involves changes in land use;
- siting permit from municipality (after consulting with the Regional Environmental Inspectorate);
- favourable EIA review and environmental permits (see box);
- building permit from municipality, after all other necessary permits have been granted;
- permit from municipality to make the facility operational.

The *Decree on Provisional EIA Regulation, 1993* (Document A) defines an environmental protection permit. When the Regional Environmental Inspectorate grants the permit, in the form of a positive decision on the EIA, it must consider *all* other environmental requirements (Article 8.1.c). This is a step towards integrating the various permits required elsewhere in the legislation (see box).

Legislation predating the *Decree on Provisional EIA Regulations, 1993* has been incorporated into the formal EIA procedure:

The Regional Environmental Inspectorate participates in the process of granting siting and building permits if the project involves hazardous waste, noise, vibration, air pollution or water pollution. The

Regional Environmental Inspectorate can stop the permit from being issued if the project does not meet legal environmental requirements. (*Decree No.1/1968 (I.11.) of the Minister of Construction and Urban Development on the Procedure to Issue a Land Use Permit; Decree No.12/1986 (XII.30.) of the Minister of Construction and Regional Planning on the Permission Procedure for Construction and Starting Operations*)

Environmental permits

A positive EIA result can only be given when the requirements for all relevant environmental permits have been satisfied. (See section 2.2.3 for legislation on permits.)

New stationary air emission sources
Requirement: limit value on air pollution to be entered in building permit
Authority: Regional Environmental Inspectorate
Law: *Government Decree No.21/1986 (VI.2.) on the Protection of Clean Air*

Air pollution
Requirement: permit
Authority: National Public Health Service
Law: *Decree No.1/1968 (I.11.) of the Minister of Construction and Urban Development on the Procedure to Issue a Land Use Permit*

Water use and discharge
Requirement: permit
Authority: Water Directorate
Law: *Decree No.2/1980 (I.16.) on Preliminary Water Permit*, as amended in 1982, 1984

Water use and discharge
Requirement: approval
Authority: Ministry of Transport, Communications and Water Management
Law: *Decree No.1/1968 (I.11.) of the Minister of Construction and Urban Development on the Procedure to Issue a Land Use Permit*

Energy use
Requirement: approval
Authority: Ministry of Industry and Trade
Law: *Decree No.146/1992 (XI.4.) on the Provisional Regulation of Some of the Issues concerning the Investment of Facilities, and Equipment Used for Electric and Thermal Energy having Significant Impact on the Environment*

Waste storage, treatment, disposal
Requirement: permit
Authority: Regional Environmental Inspectorate
Law: *Government Decree No.27/1992 (I.30.) on Amending Government Decree No.56/1981 (XI.18.) on Controlling the Occurrence of Hazardous Waste and the Activities related to their Neutralisation*

Handling of toxic substances
Requirement: permit
Authority: National Public Health Service
Law: *Decree No.26/1985 (V.11.) on Procedures related to Toxic Substances*, and its *Executive Order No.16/1988 (XII.22.) of the Minister of Public Welfare and Health*

Noise
Requirement: limit value to be entered into construction permit
Authority: municipal government
Law: *Government Decree No.12/1983 (V.12.) on Protection from Noise and Vibration*

Impacts on soil
Requirement: approval
Authority: Ministry of Agriculture
Law: *Decree No.1/1968 (I.11.) of the Minister of Construction and Urban Development on the Procedure to Issue a Land Use Permit*

Changes to functions of forests
Requirement: permit
Authority: Forest Inspectorate
Law: *Act VII/1961 on Timber and Game Industry*, and its executive order, *Government Decree No.73/1981 (XII.29.)*

Mining activity: construction, operation, termination
Requirement: permit
Authority: Mining Inspectorate and nature protection authority if protected areas involved
Law: *Act XLVIII/1993 on Mining; Government Decree No.9/1961 (III.30.)*, and executive order of *Act III/1961 on Mining*
Application: must include landscape planning and measures to prevent or mitigate environmental damage

Use of nuclear energy
Requirement: permit
Authority: National Atomic Energy Office
Law: *Government Decree No.104/1990 (XII.15.) on the Tasks and Authority of the National Atomic Energy Committee and the National Atomic Energy Office*

3.3 Responsibilities for EIA

There is no requirement for the developer to use an independent expert to undertake the EIA. There is no list of accredited consulting firms. The EIA is arranged and paid for by the developer (Article 2).

3.4 Scope of EIA and environmental impact statement

The Regional Environmental Inspectorate defines the precise scope of the required Environmental Impact Statement (Article 4.1–2). There is no public consultation at this stage.

The preliminary Environmental Impact Statement should contain the following information (Article 5):

(a) purpose of the project, its location and alternative technologies that could be used;
(b) discharges into the environment for each alternative, and the use of natural resources, in particular water and land;
(c) preliminary estimation of the probable environmental effects and, in cases of a new project, the possible changes in landscape and ecology at the project site;
(d) list of questions that can only be answered on the basis of a further, detailed Environmental Impact Statement.

The contents of the detailed Environmental Impact Statement are (Article 6):

(a) parts (a) and (b) of the preliminary Environmental Impact Statement, as above;
(b) delimitation of the impact areas, and an indication of the environmental conditions in these areas if the activity were not carried out;
(c) forecast and evaluation of the expected changes to the environment;
(d) assessment of the probable health, social and economic consequences of changes in environmental conditions;
(e) description of measures taken to prevent, mitigate or avert possible pollution and damage;
(f) description of methods for monitoring pollution during the activity and monitoring of the impacts after the activity ceases;
(g) the source of data, methods of calculation and their limitations, probabilities of the predictions, shortcomings and uncertainties in scientific knowledge during the assessment;
(h) map of the affected area;
(i) list of studies made in the process and where they are available;
(j) an easily intelligible summary.

The Environmental Impact Statement can be extended to consider secondary operations such as transport, waste, and water treatment (Article 1.2).

3.5 Public participation

For the detailed Environmental Impact Statement, a public hearing is required, except when activity is subject to military secrecy (Article 7.1).

The local government invites the concerned authorities and the affected parties (the developer, and the population and municipality of the affected areas) to a public hearing. The time and place of the hearing, and the place where the detailed impact study may be seen, must be announced at least 15 days before the date of the hearing (Article 7.2–4).

Public opinion is taken into account during the review of the Environmental Impact Statement.

3.6 Review and approval

The Environmental Impact Statement is submitted to the Regional Environmental Inspectorate and reviewed within 30 days (Article 4.1–2). There is no requirement for an outside or independent expert review. The opinion of the public is taken into account. For projects with impacts in more than one region, or beyond the borders of Hungary, the review must be referred by the Regional Environmental Inspectorate to the MERP (Articles 4.3 and 9.2).

The purpose of the review is:

- to judge whether the Environmental Impact Statement meets the general EIA requirements and those specified during the preparatory phase by the Regional Environmental Inspectorate;
- to evaluate the project on the basis of environmental impacts forecast in the Environmental Impact Statements.

During the review, other statutory agencies (such as local and regional nature conservation and health services) are consulted (Article 4.2).

If the EIA results in a positive decision, the developer will receive an environmental permit, according to a specified format (Article 8.1). This permit is a prerequisite for receiving the siting and building permits from the municipality (Articles 8,9).

4. Monitoring

The establishment of a monitoring system may be entered as a condition in the environmental permits, or in the siting and building permits.

The Regional Environmental Inspectorate is allowed to repeat the EIA procedure if the developer supplies false information which affects substantially the EIA review.

If the developer breaks the conditions of the environmental permit, the Regional Environmental Inspectorate can suspend the project and require the restoration of original environmental conditions.

5. EIA in practice

No experience of the new EIA regulations has yet been recorded, given the short period that they have been in force. There is currently no system to determine whether the siting, building and the various environmental permits are being issued on the basis of an EIA as defined in the new regulations.

There is still a lack of knowledge of the new procedures at the regional level. The MERP is taking steps to enforce uniform interpretation of the Decree among the Regional Environmental Inspectorate

6. Possible changes in near future

A new environmental law has long been under discussion with an estimated 13–20 drafts during 1993. The process has stimulated vigorous professional and political debate. Whether the new law will be a comprehensive environmental law, or a short framework law has not yet been decided, although the latter appears the more likely. The *Decree on Provisional EIA Regulation, 1993* is provisional until the new law. Drafts of the environmental law contain few changes to the EIA process, but non-governmental organisations are pushing for strengthening of the EIA process in the new law.

7. Sources of further information

Ministry of Environment and Regional Policy
1394 Budapest
P.O. Box 351
1011 Fő utca 44-50
Hungary
tel: (36-1) 135 5921
fax: (36-1) 201 2846

Dr. Sándor Fülöp / Dr. Judit Péter
The Environmental Management and Law Association (EMLA)
1137 Budapest
Szt. István krt. 20.I/1
Hungary
tel: (36-1) 111 6830
fax: (36-1) 269 2466

8. EIA legislation

Terms used in law	*Terms used in book*
Activity	Project
Person initiating activity/applicant	Developer
Environmental impact study	Environmental Impact Statement

HUNGARY A

Government Decree No.86/1993 (VI.4.) for Provisional Regulation of the Assessment of the Environmental Impact of Certain Activities

By virtue of the powers given in Article 53.1 of Act No.II of 1976, the Government decrees as follows:

Article 1

1.1. Environmental impact assessment (hereinafter referred to as 'impact assessment') shall be carried out for the activities listed in the Appendix to this Decree, or the modification thereof, that have a significant impact on the environment.

1.2. The impact assessment shall comprise the investigation of the environmental impacts that may be expected because of:

- the siting and construction of the installation necessary for the activity;
- the completion of the activity;
- other operations directly connected to the activity, especially transport (in and out), and treatment of waste and effluent;

– the cessation of the activity; and
– possible failures or accidents occurring in any of the previous cases.

1.3. The list of activities requiring impact assessment shall be revised by the Government whenever necessary, but at least biennially.

Article 2. It shall be the duty of the person initiating the activity or the modification of the activity (hereinafter referred to as 'applicant') to complete the impact assessment (or arrange for its completion).

Article 3
3.1. The impact assessment shall consist of:

a) preliminary and, at all times in the cases listed in the Appendix, but otherwise depending on the decision of the environmental protection inspectorate (hereinafter referred to as 'inspectorate');
b) detailed assessment phases.

3.2. The results of the assessment phases shall be presented by the applicant:

a) in the preliminary environmental impact study (Article 5);
b) in the detailed environmental impact study (Article 6).

Article 4
4.1. The applicant must submit the preliminary environmental impact study to the inspectorate competent for the location of the activity.

4.2. On the basis of the preliminary environmental impact study, the inspectorate shall make a decision within 30 days with the cooperation of the competent nature conservation authority, the County (Budapest) Institute of the State Public Health and Sanitary Service and other specialised authorities having an interest in the matter, and shall:

a) order that a detailed environmental impact study be submitted, and determine the questions and requirements to be examined during the preparation of the impact study; or
b) issue the environmental protection licence necessary for the activity (or modification); or
c) refuse the application.

4.3. In the case of a project affecting the territories of more than one inspectorate, the competent authority shall be appointed by the second-tier authority.

Article 5
5.1. The preliminary environmental impact study shall contain:

a) a description of the purpose and the siting and technological possibilities of the planned activity;
b) a description of the emission into the environment of materials and energy originating from the realisation of the possibilities in point (a), and of the direct utilisation of environmental components, especially land use and water use;

c) a preliminary estimate of the probable environmental impacts and, in the case of a new project, a detailed description of the changes in the landscape and ecological conditions at the site of the project;
d) the questions that can only be answered on the basis of a further, detailed impact study.

Article 6. The detailed environmental impact study shall contain:

a) a detailed description (documentation) of the factors listed in points (a)–(b) of Article 5;
b) a delimitation of the impact areas, and an indication of the environmental conditions in these areas if the activity were not carried out;
c) a forecast and evaluation of the changes in the environmental conditions as a result of the activity;
d) an estimate of the probable environmental-health, economic and social consequences of the changes in the environmental conditions;
e) a definition of measures to prevent, reduce or avert possible pollution and damage;
f) the method of measuring and analysing environmental impacts in the course of the activity and the method for subsequent monitoring of these impacts after the activity ceases;
g) the source of the data used for carrying out the study, the methods used in the impact assessment, their limits and conditions of use, the limits of validity (probability) of the forecasts, and the gaps and uncertainties in scientific knowledge that have become apparent in the evaluation of the impacts and test results;
h) a map of the impact areas;
i) a list of the studies made during and used for the impact assessment, and the method of access to the studies;
j) an easily intelligible summary.

Article 7

7.1. If a detailed environmental impact study is submitted, the inspectorate – in order to involve the public – must hold a hearing, unless the activity is subject to military secrecy. Even in this case, the inspectorate shall inform the relevant local authority about environmental impacts affecting civilian areas as a result of military activity.

7.2. The location(s) of the hearing shall be the official premises of the local authority notary(ies) competent for the location of the activity or for the place(s) most affected. The inspectorate shall invite the specialised authorities having an interest in the matter (Article 4.2) and the affected parties to these premises. The affected parties in these proceedings are:

- the applicant;
- the population and local authority in the places that according to the detailed environmental impact study bear the impact (hereinafter referred to as 'affected place(s)').

7.3. The population of the affected place(s) shall be informed about the date and location of the hearing, and about the place where the detailed environmental impact study can be seen, in the manner customary for the place, by means of an announcement by the notary(ies) of the affected local authority(ies).

7.4. The announcement must be made at least 15 days before the date of the hearing.

7.5. Before reaching a decision, the inspectorate must examine, on their merits, the comments that are significant from the point of view of judging the environmental impact.

7.6. The inspectorate shall make its decision on the basis of the available data and the views of the specialised authorities, and shall:
a) issue the environmental protection licence needed for the activity or the modification thereof; or
b) refuse the application.

Article 8
8.1. The decision concerning the issue of the environmental protection licence shall contain:

a) the name of the licensee and the licensed activity;
b) the data characterising the activity that were used as a basis for the impact assessment, in detail, as required by Article 1.2;
c) the environmental protection requirements to be satisfied with regard to the siting, execution, completion or cessation of the licensed activity; and also the views of the specialised authorities with regard to environmental protection;
d) the fact that the licence is valid for an unlimited period; or the period of validity of the licence if this is necessary because of uncertainty concerning the likely environmental impacts, and the requirements under point (c) therefore include a requirement for the establishment of an observation/monitoring network.

8.2. The explanation of the reasons for the decision shall give details of the circumstances which were taken into account by the inspectorate in issuing or refusing the licence, and which were the basis of the decision.

Article 9
9.1. In cases where the activity requiring impact assessment also requires a licence from another authority, even if this licence is held, the activity (siting, execution, completion, cessation) or the modification thereof cannot be started without holding the environmental protection licence.

9.2. The authorities dealing with the matter must immediately inform the Ministry of the Environment and Regional Policy (hereinafter referred to as 'Ministry') if an impact going beyond the national frontier is to be expected. In this case the Ministry or the authorised agency, in tasks arising out of an international treaty or agreement, shall deal with the matter.

Article 10
10.1. This Decree shall enter into force 30 days after publication, and its provisions shall be applicable to proceedings starting after that date.

10.2. This Decree has no effect on Government Decree No.146/1992 (XI.4) for the provisional regulation of some aspects of the construction of installations that are used for the generation of electrical and thermal energy and have a significant impact on the environment.

Dr Antall József
with my own hand
Prime Minister

Appendix to Government Decree 86/1993 (VI.4)

A. List of activities requiring environmental impact assessment

Activities or facilities necessary for them

Agriculture, game-keeping, and forestry
Complete improvement of flat or hilly land, from 500 hectares
Partial improvement of hilly land, from 500 hectares
Local drainage, from 1,000 hectares

Mining
Surface mines
Deep mines
Mineral processing
Slag heaps, from 100,000 m^3 planned volume
Ore dressing, ore enrichment
Coal separation, preparation, briquette manufacturing works
Mineral oil and natural gas processing works
Self-supporting underground gas storage

Processing industry
Abattoirs
Fat processing, from 2 t/yr
Meat processing, from 500 t/yr
Processing of animal protein for feed purposes
Sugar manufacture
Vegetable oil manufacture
Distilleries
Starch and yeast production
Cellulose and paper manufacture
Manufacture of products containing asbestos (1)
Hide processing, tanning and currying factory, from 1,000 t hide/yr
Mineral oil refining (2)
Production of lubricants based on mineral oil, from 15,000 t/yr
Coking
Coal processing and coal distillation
CO_2 natural gas processing and technological utilisation
Nitric acid and sulphuric acid production (3)
Chlorine alkali electrolysis works (3)
Ammonia production (3)
Phosgene production (3)
Artificial fertiliser production (3)
Production of primary materials for plastics (3)
Synthetic cellulose fibre production (3)
Production of intermediate and active ingredients for pesticides (3)

Varnish and paint production, from 5,000 t/yr (3)
Pharmaceuticals manufacture (3)
Detergents manufacture, from 5,000 t/yr (3)
Cordite, explosives and ammunition manufacture (3)
Manufacture of chemicals used in the building trade from 100 t/yr (3)
Graphite and synthetic coal production (3)
Plastics processing
Rubber manufacture
Nuclear fuel processing and enrichment
Manufacture of nuclear heating elements, reprocessing of spent heating elements
Glassmaking
Manufacture of refractory bricks and concrete, from 20,000 t/yr*
Manufacture of fine pottery, from 5,000 t/yr
Cement manufacture
Asbestos cement manufacture (4)
Foundries (iron, steel, aluminium, other non-ferrous metals) (2)
Smelting works (iron, steel, aluminium, other non-ferrous metals)
Alumina production, corundum production
Red mud storage tanks
Surface treatment (galvanisation, degreasing), from 20,000 m^2 treated surface/yr
Workshops for repair and maintenance of motor vehicles, engines, railway vehicles and machines, from 50 vehicles, engines or machines repairable at a time
Battery manufacture
Production of printed circuits on an automated production line
Manufacture of road vehicles
Manufacture of railway vehicles

Electrical energy, gas, heat and water supply
Atomic power stations (2)
Atomic heating stations (2)
Thermal power stations, from 50 MW (2)
Hydroelectric power stations
Electrical transmission lines, from 120 kV
Fly ash heaps
Slurry tips
District heating stations, from 50 MW
Water reservoirs, from 1 million m^3 capacity or 2 m dam height
Barrages, from 2 m barrage height
Standing water and backwater regulation, from 5 hectares water area
River regulation, over a length of 3 km
Drainage of hilly land, from 5 km head-water flow length
Installing a piped water supply, if it exceeds 5% of the recipient surface water mass
Drainage of flat land, from 5 km main channel length
Water extraction below the surface, if the ground, stratum and karst water base is used, from 20,000 m^3/day capacity

Transport, warehousing, post and telecommunications
Passenger railway lines
Railway stations (passengers, goods, marshalling, transhipment)
Motorways etc (2)
Class I main roads
Class II main roads through woodland (from 50 hectares woodland)
Bus stations
Metro
Pipelines for mineral oil, natural gas and mineral oil products
Harbours and wharves (5)
Passenger airfields (6)
Airfields or landing places for helicopters or light planes

Real estate, letting and services supporting economic activity
Atomic reactors for research or teaching, from 1 kW continuous heat output (2)
Photographic unit, from 15,000 m^2 film development/yr or 50,000 m^2 paper copy production/yr
Type A isotope laboratories

Civil service, obligatory social insurance
Establishment of permanent barracks, in the case of an independent military battalion or a military detachment bigger than this, or from 20 hectares area
Shooting and practice grounds, in the case of an independent military battalion or a military detachment bigger than this, or from 100 hectares area
Military airfields

Other public social and personal services
Sewage works, from 20,000 m^3 capacity
Works using sewage for irrigation, from 100 hectares
Works discharging and discharging/treating sewage, from 250 m^3/day capacity
Filtration-field drying system, from 5 hectares
Sewage sludge dump, from 100 t/yr dry matter

Treatment of domestic and safe industrial solid waste
Landfill sites
Animal burial grounds
Incinerators

Treatment of dangerous industrial waste
Temporary storage sites for dangerous waste (2)
Establishments for preliminary treatment of dangerous waste (2)
Dumps for dangerous waste (2)
Incinerators for dangerous waste (2)
Installations which are not specialised for incinerating dangerous waste, but which do incinerate waste, from 1 t/day incineration (2)
Establishments that dispose of dangerous waste in some other way (2)

Treatment of radioactive waste
Final disposal of radioactive waste (2)
Independently established spent heating element stores (2)

Notes:
* Amount of final product released
(1) Always requires detailed environmental impact assessment from 200 t/yr asbestos utilisation upwards.
(2) Always requires detailed environmental impact assessment.
(3) Always requires detailed environmental impact assessment when a complete production line is set up.
(4) Always requires detailed environmental impact assessment when 20,000 t or more of final product/yr is released.
(5) Always requires detailed environmental impact assessment in the case of ships having a capacity of 1,350 t or more.
(6) Always requires detailed environmental impact assessment in the case of runways 2,100 m or more in length.

B. List of activities requiring environmental impact assessment in a nature reserve, of only national or local significance

Activities or facilities necessary for them
Every activity in the preceding list without stipulation of a limit value
Keeping game in enclosures
Establishments keeping animals
Places where game is released (in the case of aquatic game, moufflon and deer)
Roads built for permanent use
Agricultural and forestry railway lines
Radio and television transmitters
Aquatic and angling centres
Alpine skiing pistes, sled runs and associated facilities
Geothermal power stations
Fish breeding
Reed-growing ponds, fish ponds
Flood prevention
Main open-surface irrigation channels
Long-distance pipelines for water transport
Long-distance pipelines for sewage transport
Overhead cables
Facilities used for tourism or sport, with a capacity of 100 or more people/day
Mineral oil and natural gas production

Any modification to the activities listed in this Appendix requires environmental impact assessment if any of the following changes may result from the modification:

– a new release of material or energy subject to a limit value occurs;
– new dangerous or radioactive waste is produced;
– the previous (licensed) level of release of material or energy subject to a limit value increases;
– the previous (licensed) level of dangerous or radioactive waste increases;
– the previous (licensed) demand on the water supply increases;
– the previous (licensed) method of using the water changes;
– the volume of the activity exceeds the previous (licensed) capacity.

Latvia*

EIA regulation	Law on State Environmental Impact Assessments, 1990 (Document A)
EIA authority	Ministry of the Environment and Regional Development (MERD) and nine regional Environmental Protection Committees (EPCs).
Responsibilities for EIA	Developer pays for Environmental Impact Assessment and expert review. Registered experts are not required for the preparation of an Environmental Impact Statement.
Regulatory context for EIA	EIA is part of the process of obtaining building and environmental permits.
Activities subject to EIA	No lists. EIAs are carried out at the discretion of the EIA authority.
Scoping	The developer consults with the regional EPC to determine if an EIA is necessary and what environmental permits are required. The regional EPC specifies the scope and format of the Environmental Impact Statement and provides the relevant environmental permit application forms.
Environmental Impact Statement	The developer completes an Environmental Impact Statement, a Technical/Economic Calculation (as part of the application for a building permit), and applications for environmental permits.
Public participation	The developer must discuss the project with the local public. Public opinion is taken into account during review and approval.
Review and approval	The Environmental Impact Statement is reviewed by the regional EPC (or is referred to the MERD). For more complicated projects, a commission of independent experts may be set up. Within three months a 'State EIA Report' is produced, approving the EIA or requiring modifications to the project.
Development consent	The municipality issues a building permit. The regional EPC issues environmental permits. Without these permits, a project cannot be approved.
Transboundary EIA	No provisions in law. Latvia has not signed the Espoo Convention on EIA in a Transboundary Context.

* Reference material provided by Pēteris Zilgalvis Esq, Regional Environmental Specialist, World Bank Office for the Baltic Countries (Rīga)

1. Introduction

Population: 2.6 million
Area: 64,600 sq km
Currency: Lat

Principal environmental problems

The key environmental problems in Latvia are:

- industrial and vehicular pollution in urban and industrial centres, primarily Rīga;
- pollution of the Baltic Sea from point and non-point sources;
- localised groundwater pollution and contaminated drinking water.

Environmental policy

The National Report of Latvia to UNCED 1992 states that Latvia aims to achieve sustainable development. To this end, the Government has specified a number of tasks, which include:

- replacing environmentally damaging technologies in the region's main industries, for example, wood processing, building materials, light industry, food processing, technical appliances;
- implementing economic incentives for reducing pollution while developing a market economy;
- introducing certain command and control policy instruments to regulate the environment;
- developing strict environmental enforcement at the local level.

The Ministry of the Environment and Regional Development is aiming to create the preconditions for introducing European Community standards.

2. Legislative and institutional framework for EIA

2.1 Administrative structure and responsibilities for EIA

Latvia is divided into 26 districts and 593 municipalities.

The central environmental agency is the Ministry of the Environment and Regional Development (MERD). This was created in 1993 from the former national Environmental Protection Committee of the Supreme Council. (The Supreme Council has also now been replaced, by the Parliament.)

The legislation defining the role of the former national Environmental Protection Committee has not yet been updated. The roles have *de facto* been transferred to the MERD.

The MERD has nine regional Environmental Protection Committees (EPCs): Daugavpils, Jelgava, Liepaja, Madona, Ogre, Rezekne, Rīga, Valmiera, Ventspils. Each is responsible for three to four districts, with the exception of the Ogre regional EPC, which is responsible only for the Ogre district. The regional EPCs are directly subordinate to the MERD.

The MERD is responsible for performing 'State Environmental Impact Assessments' – the review of the developer's Environmental Impact Statement. Each regional EPC has an EIA department. The mandate of the MERD is defined in the *Law on State Environmental Impact Assessments, 1990* (Articles 12, 13).

State Environmental Protection Inspectorate

The State Environmental Protection Inspectorate was a division of the national EPC, with units in the regional EPCs. It has not yet been decided whether it will become part of the new MERD or become an independent body. The Inspectorate enforces environmental legislation in Latvia. It can halt activities which violate the law and can sanction those responsible. It can revoke environmental permits.

It is the duty of the Inspectorate to ensure environmental laws are followed when developers plan projects involving construction, expansion, new technology or production methods at new or existing facilities.

2.2 Sources of legislation relating to EIA

2.2.1 Legislation on EIA

- *Law on State Environmental Impact Assessments, October 1990* (Document A)

The Law establishes and regulates the EIA process in the Republic of Latvia.

The Law is soon to be revised following the replacement of the national EPC by the MERD, but this is unlikely to change significantly the substance of the EIA process.

- *Law on Environmental Protection, August 1991* (Document B)

The Law provides a framework for environmental protection in the Republic of Latvia. It delegates competence for environmental protection and natural resource use, and defines goals for protecting the environment and making rational use of natural resources.

Article 32 states that the aim of EIA is 'to evaluate economic or other types of activity as to the level of hazard that they present, to define the ecological situation of specific places and objects, and also to work out proposals for the improvement of environmental quality'.

The Law is due for revision following the replacement of the national EPC by the MERD.

- *Law on the Environmental Protection Committee of the Republic of Latvia, June 1990* (Document C)

The Law states that the national EPC is responsible for monitoring all environmental protection and natural resource use matters.

The Law defines the competencies of the national EPC in the field of EIA.

All the responsibilities of the national EPC have *de facto* been transferred to the new MERD. The law is due for revision to take into account the replacement of the national EPC.

- *Regulation on the Environmental Protection Committee Inspectorate, October 1990*

The Regulation will have to be changed in response to the replacement of the new administrative arrangement. The relationship between the Inspectorate and the MERD has not yet been decided.

It is the duty of the Inspectorate to ensure environmental laws are followed when developers plan projects involving construction, expansion, new technology or production methods at new or existing facilities.

2.2.2 Legislation on land use planning

- Council of Ministers' *Resolution on the State Specially Protected Cultural/Historical Territory Līwod rānda, October 1991*

The Resolution creates a special environmental and cultural protection zone on the northern coast of the Courland region of Latvia, in order to guarantee the preservation, existence and development of the Liv people in Latvia.

For projects planned in the Līvod rānda territory, the preservation of the cultural/historical landscape is an additional assessment criterion in the EIA.

- Council of Ministers' *Resolution on the Baltic Sea and Gulf of Rīga Coastal Protection Regime, June 1990*

The Resolution establishes a coastal protection belt along the coast of the Baltic Sea and the Gulf of Rīga. The protection belt stretches 300 metres and its goal is to 'guarantee the protection of the most significant part of the coast, including the beach and coastal formations (dunes, coastal sand shores, and sand hills) directly above the slope'. Activities are regulated and restricted in this zone. There is also a 300 metre offshore belt which is meant to 'conserve the underwater slope of the shore and the dynamic processes occurring there'.

The Resolution specifies how to plan and execute projects in this zone. All projects in the coastal region, including general planning and construction, have to be coordinated with the MERD. Certain activities listed in the Resolution, are allowed only after the developer prepares an EIA and consults with the MERD and the relevant municipal government.

2.2.3 Legislation on environmental permits

- *Law on Natural Resource Taxes, December 1990*

The Law establishes charges for the use of natural resources. If the emissions into the environment exceed stated limits, a schedule of fines is imposed.

Application for the air emissions permit requires information on point source emissions, from which an 'emission volume inventory' is calculated. Air quality standards apply for the surrounding atmosphere ('maximum permissible concentrations'). The impact of the proposed project's emissions on the surrounding atmosphere is calculated using simplified dispersion algorithms. Emissions are limited to levels which maintain specific ambient concentrations. This means that emission limits will vary according to the existing level of industrial development in the area.

- Environmental Protection Committee *Resolution on Water Use Permits, November 1991*

The Resolution regulates the utilisation of inland and sea water in Latvia, and defines the procedure for obtaining water use permits.

The application for a water use and discharge permit must include the source and volume of water to be consumed, and water discharge, including drainage system, volume, concentration of pollutants. For some pollutants, 'maximum permissible concentrations' apply, and the process for setting limits for emissions to water is similar to that for emissions to air.

- *Law on Hazardous Wastes, March 1993*

The Law authorises the national EPC (now replaced by the MERD) to serve as the chief authority in the field of hazardous waste regulation in Latvia. The Law will be amended to take account of the replacement of the national EPC.

Hazardous wastes are defined as wastes which are explosive, flammable, toxic, corrosive, chemically reactive or mutagenic. In order to produce, transport or dispose of hazardous waste, a declaration must be submitted to the municipality and to the regional EPC.

3. Environmental impact assessment process

3.1 Activities subject to EIA

The MERD and its regional Environmental Protection Committees (EPCs) have the right to demand an EIA for any industrial construction, or for modification or liquidation of an existing facility. EIAs may also be required for new technologies and materials. EIA and related legislation set no criteria for judging whether an EIA is necessary; there are no projects for which an EIA is mandatory.

Municipalities might also request the MERD or regional EPC to initiate an EIA, although the latter are not legally obliged to respond.

3.2 Regulatory context for EIA

EIA is incorporated into the process of applying for a building permit from the municipality or the Ministry of Construction and Architecture. The EIA procedure is used to apply for environmental permits from the regional EPC or the MERD. Permits[1] are required for air emissions, water use and discharge and hazardous waste (see section 2.2.3).

The sum of all these requirements is called the ‘Environmental Planning Requirement’.

3.3 Responsibilities for EIA

The developer organises and pays for the preparation of the Environmental Impact Statement, and also for experts contracted in by the environmental authority to review the Statement.

Preparation of the documentation for EIA does not have to be carried out by independent or government approved consultants, although professional state affiliated institutions can assist with drawing up Technical/Economic Calculations and making the calculations required for the environmental permits.

3.4 Scope of EIA and environmental impact statement

There is no scoping process. The MERD or regional EPC decides on the scope of the EIA.

According to the *Law on State Environmental Impact Assessments, 1990*, the goal of EIA is to evaluate the level of environmental hazard posed by economic activity, to assess the environmental conditions at particular sites, and to develop proposals for improving environmental quality.

[1] No permit is required for noise. Proof of remaining within permitted noise levels must be provided as part of the EIA.

The EIA focuses on compliance with existing legislative requirements, both national and those particular to a locality (e.g. the Baltic Sea coast). There is room for wider interpretation, however. The *Law on State Environmental Impact Assessments, 1990* allows more discretion on the part of the environmental authority. It states that the environmental authority must 'evaluate the effects of the impact of economic facilities on the surrounding environment'. Cultural impacts are not included in EIA, with the exception of projects in the Lĭvod rānda territory, where protection of the local culture is written into law.

The following information must be presented to the regional EPC in the Environmental Impact Statement:

- an evaluation of the planned activity's impact on the surrounding environment, on public health, and on public living conditions;
- a Declaration of Environmental Effects, which describes the measures that the developer will take to guarantee environmental quality during operation of the facility.

The developer must also submit a Technical/Economic Calculation (TEC) form for the project to the municipality. The TEC focuses on construction specifications, and includes a section on the planned environmental protection measures.

Applications for environmental permits (emissions to air, water use and discharge) are submitted to the regional EPC simultaneously with the Environmental Impact Statement. The application for hazardous waste production, transport and disposal must be submitted both to the regional EPC and to the municipality.

3.5 Public participation

During the three month review period (see section 3.6), the developer must discuss the project with representatives of local interest groups and residents. The regional EPC has the right to publish information about the Environmental Impact Statement and the outcome of the review in the media. Specific mechanisms for public consultation have not yet been prescribed.

The *Law on State Environmental Impact Assessments, 1990* states that one of the basic principles of EIA is openness and that the national EPC (now the MERD) is responsible for ensuring this.

Under the *Law on Environmental Protection, 1991* citizens and public organisations may demand that state institutions provide information on the environmental effects of any projects being proposed or under construction.

Public opinion is taken into account during the review and approval of the project.

3.6 Review and approval

The Environmental Impact Statement is reviewed by the regional EPC. The regional EPC can decide to refer the process to the MERD. For more complicated projects, a commission of independent experts may be set up. Members of the commission may include Latvian and foreign scientists, specialists, and representatives of government agencies, municipalities, public organisations and the public. The MERD/regional EPC is responsible for forming an expert commission.

The review determines whether the project will comply with environmental standards and legislation, and takes into account the opinion of the local public.

The review should take place within three months, unless the developer is required to provide further information.

After the review, the MERD or regional EPC produces a decision on the EIA called a 'State EIA Report'. The decision considers:

- experts' evaluations of specific questions;
- the regional EPC's report on the experts' conclusions;
- recommendations to the developer and to interested organisations regarding the requirement for the proposed economic activity.

A positive decision on the EIA enables the developer to obtain a building permit. If, however, the decision is negative because the project will exceed environmental standards, the project may still proceed, on condition that standards are met within a specified time period. In the case of a negative decision, the MERD and the regional EPC are able to prevent the issue of the building permit, on the grounds that such a permit would result in infringement of environmental regulations.

Permits

Applications for air and water permits are considered by the regional EPC during the same three month period as the developer's EIA is being reviewed. The hazardous waste permit is considered by the regional EPC and the municipality within a 15 day period from the date of application. Permits can last between one and five years, and may contain conditions, such as measures to reduce pollution. One-year temporary permits may be issued, for example in areas where the maximum permissible concentrations of pollutants are already exceeded (for air, this is the case in Rīga and Ventspils).

4. Monitoring

When a positive EIA contains conditions, there will be monitoring to verify that the conditions are met. The Inspectorate is responsible for monitoring compliance with the conditions and schedule outlined in the EIA; there are no formal procedures for how this is done.

The enforcement of environmental laws, standards, and EIA is carried out by the Environmental Protection State Inspectorate. Inspectors are responsible for monitoring compliance with environmental law when planning and siting projects, and when constructing, modifying, expanding or retooling facilities.

Submitting false information or concealing data results in administrative or criminal liability according to the Criminal Code and Administrative Violation Code of the Latvian Soviet Socialist Republic, which both remain in force until superseded by new legislation.

5. EIA in practice

Twenty full EIAs have been carried out since the EIA law was passed in 1990, and some have required modifications to the project. The Government has not hosted any public hearings, and there is little public interest in participating in EIAs. The World Bank has initiated an EIA for an energy sector project (converting a heavy fuel oil burner to wood and peat chips) and held a public hearing which was attended by non-governmental organisations. Public awareness of the importance of their participation in development planning is generally low.

6. Sources of further information

Board of EIA
Ministry of the Environment and Regional Development
25 Peldu Street
Rīga 226282
Republic of Latvia
tel/fax: (371-2) 228 159
telex: 11680 bitec su

Pēteris Zilgalvis
Gaujas ielā 5
Sigulda
Republic of Latvia
tel: (371-2) 36 49 12
fax: (371) 88 28 058

Zenico Ltd. (engineering consultancy)
Brīvības ielā 80
Rīga LV 1001
Republic of Latvia
tel: (371-2) 27 36 27 / 27 45 27
fax: (371) 88 28 072

Juris Circulis (EIA consultant)
E.S.Vide
Avotu ielā 29
Rīga LV 1009
Republic of Latvia

7. EIA legislation

Terms used in law	*Terms used in book*
State EIA	Review
Economic facility/industrial project/planned activity/ objects of State EIA/project	Project
Indicators of planned activity/documentation	Environmental Impact Statement
Developer/planner	Developer

LATVIA A

Republic of Latvia Law on State Environmental Impact Assessments

October 1990

Unofficial translation

Article 1. The goal of state environmental impact assessments

The goal of state environmental impact assessments is to evaluate the level of environmental hazard posed by economic activity and the environmental conditions at particular sites, and to develop proposals for the improvement of environmental quality.

Article 2. Basic operational principles of state environmental impact assessments

The carrying out of state environmental impact assessment is based on:

2.1. the principles of legality, comprehensiveness, scientific validity and openness;

2.2. integrated evaluation of social, engineering, nature protection, environmental planning, economic and other aspects;

2.3. generalised evaluation of the aggregate effect on the surrounding environment;

2.4. international obligations of the Republic of Latvia.

Article 3. Chief requirements of state environmental impact assessments

The chief requirements of state environmental impact assessments are:

3.1. to determine whether the level of potential environmental hazard has been correctly evaluated for a particular economic or other activity which directly or indirectly impacts, or in the future will or may impact, on the surrounding environment or public health and living conditions;

3.2. to provide or evaluate analysis of the environmental impact of the planned human-generated activity;

3.3. to evaluate the permissibility of economic activity, taking into account all environmental restrictions;

3.4. to establish, prognosticate and evaluate the effects of economic facilities' impact on the surrounding environment.

Article 4. The obligatory nature of state environmental impact assessments

The positive state environmental impact assessment report is an obligatory prerequisite for the realisation (financing) of any industrial project. If the state environmental impact assessment of a facility results in a negative report, state institutions of authority and administration will consider the question of whether to continue or halt the activity of this facility.

Article 5. The carrying out of state environmental impact assessments

Republic of Latvia state environmental impact assessments are carried out by the Environmental Protection Committee of the Republic of Latvia, which forms expert commissions independently or in conjunction with state institutions of authority and administration.

Article 6. The environmental planning requirement

The environmental planning requirement is the aggregate of all environmental protection demands and regulations which must be complied with by project developers and planners when preparing the project documentation.

Before planning is initiated, the developer submits to the Republic of Latvia Environmental Protection Committee the indicators of the planned activity in the required format. If necessary, the Republic of Latvia Environmental Protection Committee issues the environmental planning requirement within one month.

In the event of a negative report, planning may not be initiated.

Article 7. The objects of state environmental impact assessments

The objects of state environmental impact assessments are as follows:

7.1. pre-planning documentation (including state programmes) for all types of state and private economic development and territorial development;

7.2. planning and research materials which are related to environmental evaluation;

7.3. new technological developments, materials, occupational regulations, technological equipment;

7.4. draft regulations and methodical instructions for economic activity and natural resource use;

7.5. the environmental status of facilities, places and regions;

7.6. projects' economic substantiation (calculations); plans for the site selection; construction (reconstruction, expansion etc.) and liquidation of economic facilities;

Article 8. Operational guarantee of state environmental impact assessments

The developer submits to the Republic of Latvia Environmental Protection Committee documentation characterising the level of potential environmental hazard. The documentation must include an evaluation of the planned activity's impact on the surrounding environment and public health and living conditions, as well as a 'Declaration of Environmental Effects'. This is a document prepared by the developer describing the measures to guarantee environmental quality which the developer agrees to carry out throughout the duration of the planned activity.

Article 9. Responsibilities of the project developer and planner

The project developer and project planner are responsible for:

9.1. the completeness, scientific validity and accuracy of the information used;

9.2. the environmental effects of implementation of the project;

9.3. the organisation, financing and conducting of scientific research and planning efforts needed for evaluation of the planned activity's environmental impact;

9.4. full completion of all documentation required for the assessment;

9.5. discussion of the project concept and potential environmental effects with representatives of social organisations and local residents;

9.6. fulfilment of the recommendations included in the state environmental impact assessment report.

Article 10. Duration of state environmental impact assessments

State environmental impact assessments must be completed within three months.

Depending on the complexity of the submitted materials and the problem, the Chairman (in his absence the First Vice-Chairman) of the Republic of Latvia Environmental Protection Committee can extend the deadline.

Article 11. Responsibilities of the experts

The experts are responsible for:

11.1. the objectivity of the evaluation of submitted documentation;

11.2. the quality and completion on deadline of their report;

11.3. compliance with environmental protection laws.

Article 12. Rights of state environmental impact assessments

The Republic of Latvia Environmental Protection Committee, in conducting environmental impact assessments, has the right:

12.1. to identify those objects which must undergo environmental impact assessment;

12.2. to develop instructional/methodological documentation for conducting environmental impact assessment;

12.3. to prepare proposals for the improvement of regulatory and instructional/ methodological documentation;

12.4. to select the members of expert commissions (groups);

12.5. to involve in the conducting of assessments as non-staff experts, highly qualified Republic of Latvia and foreign scientists, specialists, and representatives of government agencies, local governments, social organisations and societies;

12.6. to use the submitted data and reports in its further work;

12.7. to monitor compliance with state environmental impact assessment reports;

12.8. to request and receive at no cost from all persons and legal entities within the nation's territory properly prepared information necessary for conducting environmental impact assessment;

12.9. to submit for publication in the mass media materials regarding the conducting and results of state environmental impact assessments;

12.10. to conduct other activities necessary for the exercise of its authority, in so far as these do not violate the law.

Article 13. Responsibilities of the Republic of Latvia Environmental Protection Committee

The Republic of Latvia Environmental Protection Committee, in conducting environmental impact assessments, is responsible for:

13.1. the validity of its conclusions;

13.2. the expert commission's make-up and qualifications, which must be appropriate to the level of complexity of the problem at hand;

13.3. the completeness of the information submitted to the experts;

13.4. the openness of the assessment;

13.5. the creation of working conditions which ensure an objective and integrated evaluation of the project under scrutiny;

13.6. compensation of non-staff experts;

13.7. losses to the property of persons or legal entities resulting from errors made in environmental impact assessments.

Article 14. Compensation of state environmental impact assessment commission non-staff experts

State environmental impact assessment commission (group) non-staff experts are compensated by the developer, with funds allocated for the planning and realisation of the project, according to the terms established by the Republic of Latvia's Environmental Protection Committee and the Finance Ministry.

Article 15. State environmental impact assessment reports

After receiving the materials, the Republic of Latvia Environmental Protection Committee prepares a state environmental impact assessment report, which is approved by the Chairman (in his absence, the First Vice-Chairman) of the Republic of Latvia Environmental Protection Committee, and which includes:

15.1. individual experts' evaluations of specific questions;

15.2. the Republic of Latvia Environmental Protection Committee's report on the conclusions submitted by the experts;

15.3. recommendations to the developers and to interested organisations regarding requirements for economic activity.

Article 16. Legal status of state environmental impact assessment reports

Republic of Latvia Environmental Protection Committee state environmental impact assessment reports are final; the Republic of Latvia Supreme Council can demand a second assessment.

Anatolijs Gurbunovs, Chairman of the Supreme Council of the Republic of Latvia

Imants Daudišs, Secretary of the Supreme Council of the Republic of Latvia

Rīga, 9 October 1990

LATVIA B

Republic of Latvia Law on Environmental Protection

August 1991

Excerpts

Article 8. Competence of the Republic of Latvia Environmental Protection Committee in environmental protection and natural resource use

In the fields of environmental protection and natural resource use, the Republic of Latvia Environmental Protection Committee:

- works out and, together with other State institutions, carries out a unified environmental development, protection, and natural resource use policy;
- performs State Environmental Impact Statements and determines requirements which guarantee environmental protection;
- on State territory, continental shelf, and the Republic of Latvia Baltic Sea economic zone, carries out State control of environmental protection and natural resource use;
- fulfils the functions of the Republic environmental protection fund manager and holder;
- works out and submits to the Republic of Latvia Supreme Council proposals for nationally significant nature reserves, national parks, a regional nature protection complex (system), cultural – historical and development of other specially protected natural objects;
- carries out other functions foreseen by the Republic of Latvia normative acts in the fields of environmental protection and natural resource use.

Article 9. Competence of the Republic of Latvia Council of Ministers in environmental protection and natural resource use

The Republic of Latvia Council of Ministers in the fields of environmental protection and natural resource use:

9.1. participates in the realisation of Republic of Latvia environmental protection and natural resource use policy;

9.2. in coordination with the Republic of Latvia Environmental Protection Committee:

- forms the ecological education system and provides for its implementation in all educational institutions;
- issues mineral deposit output and exploitation permits (licences);
- affirms the register of raw materials, material, technical processes, and finished products subject to ecological certification;
- defines and establishes ecological certification orders;
- determines the placement of the production process, and communal waste collection, storage, utilisation, and disposal sites of national significance;
- determines the placement of toxic and radioactive material disposal sites, and also this material's production, use, transport, storage, and disposal routine;

9.3. makes provision for State natural resource cadastre procedure;

9.4. coordinates and manages the permanent Republic of Latvia emergency commission for controlling the consequences of accidents, catastrophes, and sudden disaster;

9.5. affirms special natural resource economic activity district borders, environmental protection, and economic activity regimes;

9.6. realises the functions of the compensation fund's manager and holder in environmental protection, defines the fund's development and the order of the use of its finances;

9.7. solves disputes on questions of environmental protection and natural resource use, within their legal competence;

9.8. carries out other environmental protection and natural resource use functions foreseen in other Republic of Latvia normative acts.

Article 10. The competence of municipal governments in environmental protection and natural resource use

Municipal government institutions are responsible for environmental protection and natural resource use within their administrative territory. They:

- exercise control of environmental protection and the rational use of natural resources;
- propose that authorised State institutions limit, stop, or cease economic activity of object construction, reconstruction, and expansion, if necessary, when violations of the law have been allowed to occur, and also introduce corresponding proposals on how to remedy the violation;
- organise protection of district, city, city district, and civil parish environmental protection programmes preparation, construction of environmental protection objects, reconstruction, and expansion; if necessary, form a centralised, extra-budgetary fund for environmental protection and natural resource use;
- prepare proposals on how to differentiate natural resource use charges for those physical and juridical persons who pollute the air, soil, or water basin, or who do not provide for the rational utilisation or disposal of communal waste and of waste from general mineral mining process, and from production;
- allot or take away, within the legally defined competencies, land and other natural resource use rights, and decide disputes regarding land and natural resource use;
- carry out other environmental protection and natural resource use functions foreseen in the Republic of Latvia normative acts.

Article 13. Rights of inhabitants and public organisations of the Republic of Latvia to the implementation of environmental protection measures

Republic of Latvia inhabitants and public organisations on the territory of the Republic have the right to:

- demand from competent State institutions and officials information about the influence on the environment of proposed constructions and construction-in-progress on the environment, and state their objections and proposals;
- demand that competent State institutions publish and announce the results of Environmental Impact Statements and results of inquiries about environmental problems.

Article 32. State environmental impact statements

The aim of State Environmental Impact Statements is to evaluate economic or other types of activity as to the level of hazard that they present, to define the ecological situation of concrete places and objects, and also to work out proposals for the improvement of environmental quality.

The Law 'On State Environmental Impact Statements' regulates the Republic of Latvia Environmental Protection Committee's Environmental Impact Statement procedure.

A. Gorbunovs, Chairman of the Supreme Council of the Republic of Latvia

I. Daudišs, Secretary of the Supreme Council of the Republic of Latvia

6 August 1991, Rīga

LATVIA C

Republic of Latvia Law on the Environmental Protection Committee of the Republic of Latvia

June 1990

Unofficial translation

Article 1. The Environmental Protection Committee of the Republic of Latvia

The Environmental Protection Committee of the Republic of Latvia (RL EPC) is the central RL state executive and oversight organ for all questions of environmental protection and natural resource use which, according to RL laws, are within its competence.

Article 2. Basic activities of the RL EPC

Within its competence, the RL EPC

2.1. formulates and implements, together with other government agencies, a unified policy for environmental protection and natural resource use;

2.2. performs state environmental impact assessments and establishes environmental protection requirements;

2.3. oversees environmental protection and natural resource use throughout the nation's territory, the continental shelf, and that area of the Baltic Sea comprising the RL economic zone.

Article 3. Formation and membership of the RL EPC

The RL Supreme Council appoints the Chairman and elects the members of the RL EPC. The RL EPC membership comprises the Chairman, First Vice-Chairman, Vice-Chairmen, and members, whose number is determined by the RL Supreme Council and who operate collegially (by consensus).

Article 4. Accountability of the RL EPC

The RL EPC is accountable and subordinate to the RL Supreme Council. The RL EPC submits an account of its work to the RL Supreme Council not less than once annually.

Article 5. General questions of the competence of the RL EPC

The RL EPC, within its competence:

5.1. drafts and submits to the RL Supreme Council legislative proposals regarding environmental protection and natural resource use;

5.2. prepares and submits to the RL government and local government organs evaluations and proposals on questions of environmental protection;

5.3. approves environmental quality standards, reviews and evaluates national and local government projects relating to environmental protection and natural resource use;

5.4. performs environmental impact assessments for all proposed economic development projects;

5.5. organises the drafting of the Republic's environmental protection and natural resource profiles and long-term goals, approves the profiles and goals drafted by local government organs;

5.6. together with the RL Council of Ministers, establishes economic mechanisms for environmental protection, approves and supplements fees for natural resource use and pollutant emissions, establishes pollutant emissions standards, approves essential regulations and standards;

5.7. coordinates limits and standards for the obtaining and use of natural resources (including forests, fish populations and game animals), oversees compliance with these limits and standards;

5.8. oversees natural resource use and protection within the nation's territory, the continental shelf, and that part of the Baltic Sea comprising the RL economic zone; provides methodological leadership for environmental pollution control;

5.9. oversees compliance with ecological standards during the introduction of new techniques, technologies and materials, as well as the design of construction and renovation projects, which may affect the state of the environment and of natural resources;

5.10. coordinates the functioning of natural areas requiring special protection;

5.11. conducts ecological research upon the request of the government;

5.12. compiles data on the state of the environment;

5.13. participates in the state commission for approval of construction and renovation projects;

5.14. serves as administrator and keeper of the Republican Environmental Protection Republican Fund;

5.15. coordinates and establishes the main directions of ecological education; establishes requirements for improving the qualifications of economic specialists and local government employees;

5.16. systematically and openly informs the Republic's inhabitants about the state of the environment;

5.17. cooperates with foreign institutions, international organisations and private persons in formulating environmental policy;

5.18. encourages the formation of societal environmental protection organisations and cooperates with them.

Article 6. Rights of the RL EPC

The RL EPC and its local subsidiaries, within their competence, are rightfully entitled:

6.1. on their own initiative or at the request of local government organs, in cases when environmental laws are violated, to forbid any economic activity or the use of natural resources;

6.2. to request compensation from companies, institutions, organisations, other juridical persons and citizens as well as from foreign juridical and physical persons, for damage done to nature as a result of pollution and irrational use of resources; to assign the collected sums (including foreign hard currency) to the Environmental Protection Fund;

6.3. to review materials regarding civil violations of environmental laws, to hold the guilty parties accountable according to legally established procedures;

6.4. to encourage banks to halt financing of projects which violate environmental laws;

6.5. to monitor without hindrance compliance with environmental protection laws in any facility throughout RL territory, as well as in facilities of the USSR's Ministry of Defence, State Security Committee (KGB) and Ministry of Interior;

6.6. to board, inspect and detain any ships and other navigable vessels in RL interior and territorial waters and the Baltic Sea RL economic zone, regardless of the department or nation to which these vessels belong, if they are violating RL environmental protection laws or international standards;

6.7. to detain vehicles in order to monitor compliance with environmental protection laws;

6.8. to approve methods of monitoring environmental pollution;

6.9. to approve the conclusions of environmental impact assessments;

6.10. to receive reports from ministries, department heads and other professional staff, on questions of environmental protection and natural resource use;

6.11. to request and receive free of charge all necessary information and explanations from any juridical and physical persons within RL territory;

6.12. to form scientific-technical, expert and other consultative councils (groups, commissions) for the preparation of reports, including in them the necessary specialists.

If necessary the Committee can transfer specific above-mentioned rights to its subordinate environmental protection organs.

Article 7. Relationship of the RL EPC to the RL Council of Ministers and its subordinate administrative agencies

The RL EPC implements a unified environmental policy in the Republic both directly and through the mediation of the administrative agencies of the Council of Ministers.

The RL EPC:

7.1. informs the RL Council of Ministers of its activities and the results thereof, performed in compliance with Article 2, Section 3 and Article 6, Section 1 of this law;

7.2. participates in the preparation of the RL state plan for economic and social development and RL state budget proposals, as well as in the development of tax policy;

7.3. is entitled to represent, within its competence, the RL government in transaction with the USSR and foreign states;

7.4. submits proposals to the RL Council of Ministers on halting the activities of USSR state institutions, if these activities are in conflict with RL laws or the Republic's interests in the area of environmental protection and natural resource use;

7.5. at the request of the RL Council of Ministers, performs environmental impact assessments, provides evaluations and suggestions regarding questions of environmental protection and natural resource use;

7.6. coordinates compliance with normative rulings issued by the RL Council of Ministers and other institutions on questions of environmental protection and natural resource use.

Article 8. Relationship of the RL EPC with local government organs

The RL EPC and its territorial (local) organs, within their competence and in compliance with RL laws regarding local self-government, cooperates with township, city and county governments, businesses and organisations, reviews and evaluates their proposed environmental protection programmes.

The RL EPC is entitled to halt, pending review, implementation of any local government rulings which conflict with environmental protection laws.

Article 9. System and management of subordinate organs of the RL EPC

The RL EPC system comprises the central committee apparatus, territorial (local) and other subordinate environmental protection organs.

The RL EPC forms, reorganises and liquidates its subordinate facilities, organisations and other entities, and approves their statutes. The Committee is entitled to veto rulings issued by subordinate institutions, if these violate the law or the requirements of environmental protection and natural resource use.

Article 10. Chairman and vice-chairmen of the RL EPC

The RL EPC Chairman organises and directs the Committee's work and is personally responsible for its results.

The RL EPC Chairman:

10.1. submits proposals to the RL Supreme Council on the number and make-up of the RL EPC staff;

10.2. ensures collegiality (consensus decision-making) and openness in the working of the RL EPC; on extraordinary occasions issues rulings independently;

10.3. approves RL EPC central apparatus staff assignments, salaries and bonus system; approves the statutes of subordinate organs; determines the system for hiring and evaluating performance;

10.4. determines the rights and duties of the Vice-Chairmen and of the directors of subordinate organs.

In accordance with the division of responsibilities established by the RL EPC Chairman, the Vice-Chairmen direct the work of the Committee apparatus and subordinate organs.

In the absence of the Chairman, his/her responsibilities are carried out by the First Vice-Chairman, or in the absence of the First Vice-Chairman, by one of the Vice-Chairmen.

Article 11. Membership of the RL EPC

Members of the RL EPC staff are responsible for the spheres of activity assigned to them, and participate in Committee meetings. Committee meetings are convened and led by the Committee Chairman or First Vice-Chairman.

In its meetings the Committee resolves questions regarding improvement of environmental conditions and natural resource use in the Republic, and confirms the hiring of directors of Committee departments and subordinate organs.

If disagreements arise between the RL EPC Chairman and Committee members, the Chairman's decision takes precedence, but members have the right to express their opinion to the Supreme Council.

Article 12. Rulings and orders of the RL EPC

The RL EPC, within its competence, issues rulings and orders. RL EPC directives on questions of environmental protection and natural resource use are binding throughout the entire RL territory.

RL EPC rulings are published in the RL Supreme Council and government press, as well as in its own publications, but if broad and immediate dissemination is necessary, then they are reported through all interested mass media organs.

RL EPC rulings are signed by the RL EPC Chairman.

RL EPC directives are signed by the Committee Chairman or First Vice-Chairman, or by the Committee's Vice-Chairmen, according to established protocol.

Article 13. RL EPC State Inspectors' rights and duties

RL EPC Inspectors' rights and duties are determined by the Law on RL Environmental State Inspection, which is approved by the RL Supreme Council.

Article 14. RL EPC environmental assessments

The performance of RL EPC environmental assessments is determined by the RL Law on Environmental Assessments, which is approved by the RL Supreme Council.

The findings of RL EPC environmental assessments are final but the RL Supreme Council can order a second assessment.

Article 15. Funding of the RL EPC and its organs

The RL EPC system is funded by the RL state budget. Committee expenditures are approved by the RL Supreme Council.

Article 16. Legal status of the RL EPC

The RL EPC has the rights of a juridical person and has an official seal.

A. Gorbunovs, Chairman of the Supreme Council of the Republic of Latvia

I. Daudišs, Secretary of the Supreme Council of the Republic of Latvia

Rīga, 20 June 1990

Lithuania*

EIA regulations	Environmental Protection Department[1] Decree on Selecting Construction Sites (and Pipeline Routes), and on the Approval Procedure of Pre-feasibility and Feasibility Studies or Environmental Impact Assessment, within the EPD[1] System, No.87, December 1990 (Document A) Ministry of Construction and Urban Development and Environmental Protection Department[1] Rules for the Elaboration of the 'Environmental Protection Section' of a Study, 1993 (Document B)
EIA authority	Ministry of Environmental Protection, Board of EIA
Responsibilities for EIA	The developer covers the cost of preparing the Environmental Impact Statement. There are no licensed EIA experts.
Regulatory context for EIA	The EIA is carried out as part of the process of obtaining a siting permit, then a building permit. EIA approval is required before a building permit can be issued.
Activities subject to EIA	There is a list of projects requiring EIA.
Scoping	None.
Environmental Impact Statement	The Environmental Impact Statement is the 'Environmental Protection Section' of the project feasibility study, defined in detail in the Rules for Environment Section of a Feasibility Study, 1993.
Public participation	The law requires public access to EIA information and consultation between the EPD and the public, after review of the Environmental Impact Statement.
Review and approval	Review by the Ministry of Environmental Protection takes place within 90 days. An expert commission may be set up to assist the Ministry. Approval is given in the form of an integrated Natural Resource Use Permit.

* Reference material provided by Pēteris Zilgalvis Esq, World Bank Office for the Baltic Countries (Rīga, Latvia)

1 The Environmental Protection Department is now the Ministry of Environmental Protection.

Development consent	A Natural Resource Use Permit is required for a building permit to be issued.
Transboundary EIA	No provisions in law. Lithuania has not signed the Espoo Convention on EIA in a Transboundary Context.

1. Introduction

Population: 3.7 million
Area: 65,200 sq km
Currency: Litas

Principal environmental problems

Most environmental problems in Lithuania are concentrated in cities and at industrial facilities. Water pollution is also a serious problem affecting the Nemunas River and the Couronian Lagoon in particular. Municipal waste-water treatment facilities need to be constructed or upgraded in the major cities of Kaunas, Vilnius and Klaipėda. Vehicular air pollution, particularly in cities, needs to be addressed.

Environmental policy

The former Environmental Protection Department became the Ministry of Environmental Protection in June 1994. The environmental policy of the Lithuanian Government is subsequently being revised.

2. Legislative and institutional framework for EIA

2.1 Administrative structure and responsibilities for EIA

Lithuania is divided into 44 districts and 11 municipalities.

Central government

The central environmental authority is the Ministry of Environmental Protection. This replaced the parliamentary Environmental Protection Department in June 1994.

The role of the Ministry in relation to EIA is temporarily defined by the *Law on the Environmental Protection Department, 1990* (Document D), which will remain in force until updated. The Ministry:

- sets the limits for the use of natural resources, to determine standards and to give permits for the discharge of pollution into the environment;
- gives permits for natural resource exploration, natural resource use and waste disposal;
- submits assessments and proposals to the bodies approving industrial construction, relocation and expansion projects;
- establishes the procedure for, organises and implements EIAs;
- puts conditions on the approval of projects, so that they conform to environmental requirements;
- conducts environmental monitoring;
- halts the construction, reconstruction, and extension of facilities if environmental protection is undermined.

The Ministry has a network of eight Regional Environmental Departments, each of which covers six or seven districts. District environmental inspectors exist (see below, *Local government*). Most activity relating to EIA takes place at the Ministry in Vilnius, although the system is likely to become less centralised in the future.

The Ministry has an independent Environmental Impact Assessment Board (formerly the 'Department of Ecological Expertise'), which is responsible for EIA.

Local government

The *Interim Principal Law*, 1990 defines the competence of municipalities to coordinate and control enterprises, institutions and organisations in their own territory, including in relation to environmental protection. The *Enterprise Law*, 1990 and the *Law on the Fundamentals of Local Government, 1990* state that local governments may prohibit economic activities if they will inflict harm on the health of the population or the environment.

Only 24 of the 44 districts have employees specialising in environmental protection. Kaunas, Lithuania's pre-World War II capital, has 11 specialists and Vilnius, the present capital, has seven. In the other regions there is only one specialist or one part-time specialist.

2.2 Sources of legislation relating to EIA

2.2.1 Legislation on EIA

- Environmental Protection Department *Decree on Selecting Construction Sites (and Pipeline Routes), and on the Approval Procedure of Pre-feasibility and Feasibility Studies or Environmental Impact Assessment, within the EPD System, No.87, December 1990* (Document A)

(Referred to below as '*Decree No.87 on Site Selection and EIA, 1990*'.)

This decree defines the internal working arrangements of district environmental inspectorates and the former Environmental Protection Department (central and regional offices), in relation to approval of feasibility studies and review of EIAs, during the process of site selection. The decree now defines the work of the Ministry of Environmental Protection, until updated. Appendix 2 defines which projects are subject to EIA. Tables on the scope and contents of the Environmental Impact Statement have been updated by the following set of rules.

This is soon to be replaced by a new EIA law.

- Ministry of Construction and Urban Development and Environmental Protection Department *Rules for the Elaboration of the 'Environmental Protection Section' of a Study, 1993* (Document B)

(Referred to below as '*Rules for Environment Section of a Feasibility Study, 1993*'.)

The rules outline in detail the contents of the 'Environmental Protection Section' of a project feasibility study, which is used to obtain a construction permit.

- *Law on Environmental Protection, January 1992* (Document C)

This is a framework law which outlines the principles and jurisdictions in environmental protection. The law defines the EIA process in general terms, and requires the drafting of more detailed rules. A new EIA law is in preparation.

- *Law on the Environmental Protection Department, July 1990* (Document D)

The Law defines the role of the Environmental Protection Department (EPD), and its functions relating to EIA (see section 2.1). The Law temporarily defines the role of the Ministry of Environmental Protection, until updated.

- The Republic of Lithuania Environmental Protection Department *Order on the Rules of Determination of Environmental Pollution Standards and the Issue of Permits for the Exploitation of Natural Resources, December 1990*

The Order defines the process of applying for and granting various environmental permits. There is an integrated 'Natural Resource Use Permit', covering water consumption and discharge, air emissions from stationary sources, and storage, dumping and use of wastes. Where appropriate, permits may also be included for other activities, such as exploiting soil and mineral resources.

Limits on emissions to water and air are calculated on the basis of maximum permissible ambient concentrations. This means that emission limits are stricter in areas where there is already polluting industrial activity.

- *Interim Principal Law, March 1990*

The Law:

- establishes Lithuania's ownership of its natural resources and exclusive right to the continental shelf and economic zone in the Baltic Sea (Article 45);
- states the obligation of Lithuanian citizens to protect nature and its wealth, and to create a sound natural environment (Article 42);
- determines the competence of municipalities to coordinate and control the environmental activities of enterprises, institutions and organisations within their jurisdiction (Article 104).

The Lithuanian Constitution does not supersede this Law.

- *Government Law, March 1990*

The Law determines the competence of the Lithuanian Government in the sphere of environmental protection. The Law gives the government the right to dispose of Lithuania's natural resources according to standards and limits set by the (former) Environmental Protection Department. This responsibility has been taken over by the Ministry of Environmental Protection.

- *Law on the Fundamentals of Local Government, February 1990*

The Law determines the competencies of municipalities in environmental protection. The municipalities grant building permits and register enterprises. They also have the right to restrain or halt the activities of enterprises or organisations if environmental protection requirements are violated.

- *Enterprise Law, May 1990* and amended in July 1990

This economic legislation defines the regulation, rights, and responsibilities of enterprises in Lithuania.

An amendment in July 1990 states that enterprises must have an environmental permit from the Environmental Protection Department (now the Ministry of Environmental Protection) in order to engage in economic activity.

- *Law on the Register of Enterprises, July 1990*

In order to register as an enterprise, an environmental permit is necessary if prescribed elsewhere in Lithuanian law.

- *Law on State Natural Resources, July 1991*

The Law establishes penalties for concealing information on natural resource use – a tenfold increase of the tax rate.

- *Law on Taxes on Environmental Pollution, April 1991*

The Law establishes the penalty for concealing information on pollution discharges – a tenfold increase of the tax rate.

3. Environmental impact assessment process

3.1 Activities subject to EIA

According to the *Enterprise Law, 1990*, any activity that has an impact on the environment has to have an environmental permit from a Regional Environmental Department of the Ministry of Environmental Protection. The Regional Environmental Department decides whether an economic activity will have such an impact. If so, an EIA is required. The public can also request an EIA (Article 8.5, *Law on the Environmental Protection Department, 1990*).

According to Appendix 2 of the *Decree No.87 on Site Selection and EIA, 1990* (Document A), for certain projects, pre-feasibility and feasibility studies are to be considered as an Environmental Impact Statement which must undergo a full EIA review, undertaken by the Environmental Protection Department (now replaced by the Ministry of Environmental Protection), or a Regional Environmental Department if the projects are very simple. A list is given of such projects:

- economic plans;
- territorial, natural resource use, and environmental protection plans;
- plans for towns of national significance and for health resorts; environmental infrastructure projects;
- Ignalina Nuclear Power Plant, Mažeikiai Oil Refinery, P/A *Azotas*, *Akmencementas*, Kaišiadorys Hydro-accumulation Station, chemical plants in Kėdainiai, Lithuanian Thermal Power Plant, Klaipėda Cardboard Factory, Klaipėda State Element and Batteries Plant *Sirijus*, Panevėžys *Lietkabelis* Factory, Kaunas Synthetic Fibre Plant, expansion of toxic waste treatment plants;
- linear constructions, such as roads, gas and oil pipelines;
- joint ventures with foreign companies;
- projects involving ponds, clean-up of lakes and regulation of rivers;
- on-shore and off-shore projects in the Kuršiu Lagoon and Baltic Sea coastal areas;

- projects using natural resources (oil, iron ore, granite, etc.) and projects using common mineral resources (gravel, sand, clay, etc.) the deposits of which are larger than 500,000 m^3 in volume;
- projects in protected areas;
- investigations of groundwater resources.

Existing facilities which have no permit are required to apply for one. When permits expire, they must be renewed. In these cases, permit applications are made to the Regional Environmental Department but no EIA is needed. Instead the Regional Environmental Department carries out an 'Environmental Examination' of the site, in effect a simple EIA.

3.2 Regulatory context for EIA

EIA takes places as part of the process of obtaining siting and building permits. The first stage is obtaining a preliminary siting permit ('Act of Construction Site Permit' in *Decree No.87 on Site Selection and EIA, 1990*), in which the local, regional or national environmental authority takes part. On the basis of this, a full feasibility study is drawn up, containing an 'Environmental Protection Section', defined in detail in *Rules for Environment Section of a Feasibility Study, 1993*. For projects requiring an EIA, a review takes place at this stage.

The final siting permit ('Act of Construction Site Selection') can only be given when an integrated Natural Resource Use Permit is given. This consists of four parts:

- water use;
- discharge of pollutants in waste water;
- emissions to air from stationary sources;
- waste storage, landfills, and waste treatment.

Additional sections can be added as needed, such as mineral resource use or soil use.

3.3 Responsibilities for EIA

Consultants and experts undertaking EIAs do not need to be licensed by the authorities. The developer pays for the preparation of the feasibility study.

3.4 Scope of EIA and environmental impact statement

The purpose of the EIA is to ensure that projects comply with pollution discharge standards. When assessing the environmental impact of a project, however, the EIA also considers the 'possible impact of economic activities on the environment' (*Law on Environmental Protection, 1992*, Article 15.2). This could include the effect of a project on the landscape or cultural heritage, or indirect environmental impacts, such as traffic generation.

The process of applying for a siting permit requires the following documentation (Appendix 3, Annex 1 of *Decree No.87 on Site Selection and EIA, 1990*):

- general layout of the site with a description of the surrounding health protection zone[2];
- plan of the project, showing constructions and pollution sources;
- communications with surrounding facilities;
- basic technical/economic information;

[2] When a facility is given permission to pollute beyond maximum permissible ambient air pollution levels, a health protection zone can be set up.

- description of surrounding environment: protected areas, natural, historical and cultural assets, physical characteristics, existing environmental pollution;
- potential emissions from the project, and measures to prevent them;
- demand for natural resources and energy and intended source of supply;
- measures for treatment of water and air emissions;
- forecast changes to surrounding air and water;
- potential emissions in case of accidents;
- opinion of Hygiene Service on potential health risks of the site.

Once a preliminary siting permit is agreed, the project feasibility study is drawn up, containing an 'Environmental Protection Section'. This is defined in detail in Appendix 1, *Rules for Environment Section of a Feasibility Study, 1993* (which updates the former definition given in Annex 2 of *Decree No.87 on Site Selection and EIA, 1990*).

Project and site description:

- name of project, location, purpose, construction schedule;
- geographical description of the area, with reference to historical, recreational and cultural features, protected areas and environmental protection zones around nearby factories;
- geological/physical features of the site;
- outline of technologies to be used, and their emissions;
- natural resource consumption (a form is provided to be filled in);
- electricity and thermal heat consumption;
- potential accidents; accident prevention and mitigation measures;
- data on emissions (a form is provided to be filled in);
- environmental elements which will *not* be affected by the project (air, water, soil, flora and fauna).

Accompanying documents and data:

- site selection permit ('Act on Construction Site Selection');
- data on valuable flora on the site;
- data on insects, parasites, soil microbiology, chemical and radiological pollution (if required by the Hygiene Service) at the site;
- existing sewage and drainage systems at the site;
- existing water pollution;
- existing air pollution and emissions on the site;
- inventory of existing air emissions (for expansion or modification projects);
- opinion of the Hygiene Service of the project.

Environmental elements:

- details on water use, discharges into water, water discharge treatment; maximum allowable concentrations of water pollutants at the site[3] (forms are provided to be filled in);

[3] Ambient air and water standards are in force in Lithuania, and enterprise emissions must not lead to violation of these standards. On this basis, maximum permissible pollution levels (MPPs) for air and water are calculated for the Natural Resource Use Permit, usually valid for one year only. These are stricter in areas where ambient pollutant levels are already high. In some cases, particularly polluted areas, the permit will contain temporary permissible pollution levels (TPPs), accompanied by measures and deadlines for improvements.

- details of air emissions, measures to reduce emissions; maximum allowable concentrations of air pollutants at the site[3] (forms are provided to be filled in);
- details of agricultural land at the site, soil to be removed, methods for prevention of soil pollution;
- details of flora and fauna at the site, trees to be felled, measures to protect flora and fauna at the site;
- biotechnology measures to reduce and measure pollution;
- environmental remediation measures.

The full 'Environmental Protection Section' is not always required (Paragraph 4). A list of projects for which a reduced account of impacts on environmental elements is required is given in Appendix 2. It includes construction of houses and public buildings, agricultural facilities, communications and environmental infrastructure. For each type of project, the environmental elements that need to be covered are indicated. The Section does not need to repeat material if it is already present elsewhere in the feasibility study (Paragraph 10).

Individual state institutions can require further information (Paragraph 7).

For expansion or modification of facilities, the data should cover the whole facility (Paragraph 8).

The 'Environmental Protection Section' is to be prepared at the earliest stage of the project, and should be updated as the project is developed, and submitted for re-approval (Paragraph 3).

3.5 Review and approval

In the process of obtaining siting permission, the preliminary project documentation must be submitted to the district environmental inspectorate or Regional Environmental Department at least two weeks in advance of the meeting at which the siting permit is discussed. The environmental authority refers the matter upwards if unable to make an assessment. The Ministry of Environmental Protection is always involved if the project affects protected areas, or involves changes to water resources (Appendix 1, *Decree No.87 on Site Selection and EIA, 1990*).

The decision about the siting of the project is made by a district/municipal site selection committee. The siting permit is signed by representatives of:

- the architect;
- land management;
- State Geological Survey;
- property owner;
- local land commission;
- state hygiene centre;
- fire department;
- Ministry of Environmental Protection or its Regional Environmental Department;
- cultural heritage institution;
- design institution that drew up the project.

During application for a building permit, the 'Environmental Protection Section' of the feasibility study is presented to the district environmental inspectorate or Regional

Environmental Department (Appendix 1, *Decree No.87 on Site Selection and EIA, 1990*). If it involves a project for which an EIA is required, a full EIA review is carried out by the Ministry of Environmental Protection. This must be undertaken within 90 days. If no EIA review is required, the approval must take place within 15 days.

If the 'Environmental Protection Section' of the feasibility study is updated, approval of the updated version must be obtained (Paragraph 5, *Rules for Environment Section of a Feasibility Study, 1993*).

The feasibility study as a whole is assessed by the municipality.

Most EIAs are currently reviewed by the EIA Board at the office in Vilnius, but there are plans to give more responsibility to Regional Environmental Departments. For major projects and projects in highly polluted areas, an expert commission may be appointed to review the EIA documentation, which is then approved by the Ministry of Environmental Protection.

The project is evaluated on the basis of its compliance with pollution discharge standards. If the evaluation is favourable, a Natural Resource Use Permit (see section 3.2) is issued. The permit to handle wastes is usually valid for a year. Natural Resource Use Permits are usually valid for five years.

The Ministry's decision on the EIA is final. There is no system of appeal against its decision.

When a developer obtains a Natural Resource Use Permit, the enterprise can be registered with the local government.

3.6 Public participation

At present, the EIA process does not have any formal mechanism for public participation other than a right of public access to information before the EIA conclusion. (It is not specified how this information is to be made available.) The *Law on Environmental Protection, 1992* outlines the following measures for public participation:

- information on environmental impacts must be provided by the Ministry of Environmental Protection to the public;
- public participation will be possible after the Ministry states its opinion on the EIA;
- consultation will take place with the developer regarding the Ministry's opinion and views of the public;
- the Ministry of Economy or the municipality will consider the results of the consultation and issue a decision on the project.

The public can request an EIA (Article 8.5, *Law on the Environmental Protection Department, July 1990*).

Under the *Law on Environmental Protection, 1992* citizens have the right to obtain accurate and up to date information on environmental quality. Government has a duty to publicise plans for economic activities which may have a negative impact on the environment. The public has a right to take part in discussions on projects and demand that activities which are hazardous to the environment be terminated.

4. Monitoring

There are no specific monitoring procedures associated with projects that have required an EIA.

5. EIA in practice

EIAs are done for all economic activities which will involve the discharge of pollutants into the surrounding environment, the generation of waste or the use of natural resources. The concept of EIA in Lithuania is not yet widely understood, although as the legislation is defined more clearly, implementation will become more thorough.

Case Study: Baltic Sea oil terminal in north-west of Lithuania

The proposed project is an oil terminal to be built in north-west Lithuania on the Baltic Sea coast. This is a controversial new development, currently going through the EIA process. The first application for siting permission was refused, owing to public pressure.

The project was proposed after Lithuani declared independence, and the former USSR imposed sanctions and stopped supplying oil to Lithuania. The Ministry of Energy prepared a project for an oil terminal on the Baltic Sea coast, allowing Lithuania to import oil from other sources. From the terminal the oil would be transported further to the Mažeikiai oil refinery near the Latvian border. In the first proposal, the construction of this terminal was to occur directly north of Klaipėda, Lithuania's major port.

This proposal was supported by the relevant Lithuanian ministries, despite evident environmental drawbacks. An EIA was prepared and submitted for review in January 1991. It was a complex assessment, dealing with pollution discharges and impact on nature. As this is a major project, the review was organised at the national level by the former Environmental Protection Department (EPD).

The board of experts which reviewed the project was made up of 17 scientists and experts in various relevant fields. Two members of the board were members of the EPD. The EIA conclusion, delivered on 6 May 1991, was negative, because the project would involve reducing of the size of the beach and building an off-shore terminal facility.

After the proposal was rejected, a second proposal was drawn up to build the terminal closer to the city of Klaipėda. But an EIA was never undertaken for this proposal, because of strong opposition from the residents of Klaipėda.

Consequently a new project was formulated with two alternative sites for the proposed terminal complex – Melnrage and Butinge, near the Latvian border. The EIA for this project was submitted for review in January 1992. Once again the review was organised by the EPD at the national level. This time the board of experts had 14 members.

The board of experts presented its conclusions on 3 March 1992. It accepted the Melnrage site, but rejected the Butinge site on the following grounds:

- the investigation of potential environmental impact was not sufficient;
- the seashore in this area is not suitable for a project of this size;
- the sea-life in this area is diverse and particularly vulnerable to accidents.

The final decision about the site has still not been made though the Lithuanian Government is seeking finance for the project and a pre-feasibility study is being carried out (July 1993). The Butinge proposal could be resubmitted for review, although this would require a more extensive EIA. This alternative would also have to be discussed with the Latvian authorities, given its proximity to the Latvian border.

6. Possible changes in near future

As part of the instructions on the implementation of the *Law on Environmental Protection, 1992*, the Environmental Protection Department (now the Ministry of Environmental Protection) must prepare detailed instructions for the EIA process. A new EIA law is in preparation.

An independent EIA agency has been proposed which would:

- act as the central depository for all EIA studies and reports;
- evaluate EIA reports;
- check EIA studies for accuracy;
- approve EIAs.

There are plans to give a greater role to the Regional Environmental Department in the EIA process.

New air water standards are planned. Water quality standards of the former USSR, which are still in place, are too strict and are not implemented, while the waste standards of the former USSR are not strict enough. There is discussion about introducing new national standards for emissions to air and water, while basing environmental quality standards on EC or Nordic Council country standards.

7. Sources of further information

EIA Board
Ministry of Environmental Protection
Juozapavičius 9
232600 Vilnius
Republic of Lithuania
tel: (370-2) 35 83 12
fax: (370-2) 35 80 20
telex: 261191 gamta su

8. EIA legislation

Terms used in law	*Terms used in book*
Construction object	Project
Customer, designing company	Developer
EIA	Review
(Pre-)feasibility study	Environmental Impact Statement

LITHUANIA A

Environmental Protection Department of the Republic of Lithuania

Decree on Selecting Construction Sites (and Pipeline Routes), and on the Approval Procedure of Pre-feasibility and Feasibility Studies or Environmental Impact Assessment, within the EPD System

Decree, No.87, December 1990, Vilnius

Based on the Law of the Environmental Protection Department of the Republic of Lithuania (its Article 8.5), and aiming to find better solutions for natural environment protection problems; to the participants in construction sites (pipeline routes) selection, as well as in the approval of feasibility projects or environmental impact assessment, strictly following scientifically motivated nature resources utilisation and environmental protection standards.

I hereby order:

Article 1. that internal rules for construction sites (pipeline routes) selection, for the approval of pre-feasibility and feasibility studies or environmental impact assessment arrangements within the EPD system, as foreseen in Annex 1, be introduced;

Article 2. that a list of pre-feasibility and feasibility studies, the approval or environmental impact assessment of which shall be done or arranged by the EPD, as foreseen in Annex 2, be compiled;

Article 3. that a list of basic temporary regulatory documents to be used for the evaluation of feasibility studies' quality from the natural environment protection point of view, as foreseen in Annex 3, be compiled;

Article 4. that Decree No.5, passed by the Lithuanian SSR State Nature Protection Committee 31 January 1989, be considered invalid;

Article 5. the Expertise Board:

5.1. to arrange qualified and timely approval of feasibility studies or environmental impact assessment within the EPD system;

5.2. to provide, jointly with the EPD specialised boards (Landscape, Water, Atmosphere Boards), methodological guidance for Regional Agencies on the issues of approval of pre-feasibility and feasibility studies for construction sites (pipeline routes) selection;

5.3. to provide education and training for the staff involved in the investigation and approval of feasibility studies;

Article 6. the EPD specialised boards (Landscape, Water, Atmosphere Boards) as well as Regional Agencies, to guarantee timely and qualified investigation of feasibility studies and provision of conclusions, as foreseen in the approved 'Internal Rules', Annex 1;

Article 7. that Mr K. Zala, First Deputy Director General, be authorised to control enforcement of the Decree.

Director General, E. Vebra (signature)

Appendix 1 to the Environmental Protection Department Decree No.87, 27 December 1990

Construction sites (pipeline routes) selection, approval of pre-feasibility and feasibility studies or environmental impact assessment, arrangements within the EPD system

Internal rules

1. Construction sites (pipeline routes) selection

The customer, or a designing company authorised by the customer, shall provide primary information material on the object to be built, as well as its local natural conditions, to the Regional Agency or the District Environmental Protection Inspectorate not later than two weeks before convocation of the Commission for the selection of the construction site (pipeline route), as foreseen in Annex 1.

Having received an invitation to the Commission of the construction site selection, the District Environmental Protection Inspectorate familiarises itself with the documentation on the object to be built and its environment, and provides information to the Regional Agency together with its own judgement on how to solve the question of site selection. Having evaluated the situation, the Regional Agency takes a decision whether it is the District Environmental Protection Inspectorate that is authorised to sign the act of site selection, or a representative from the Regional Agency is to be included in the Commission, too. In the case of a complex ecological situation, or a potential overall negative impact upon the environment by the object to be built, the Regional Agency may ask the EPD for consultancy or request the participation of an EPD representative. The EPD representative is appointed by and accordingly authorised by the EPD authorities.

In case an object is planned to be built in territories under special protection (nature reserves, national and nature (regional) parks, strict nature reserves and in territories allocated for them), the Regional Agency, having received an invitation to the site selection Commission together with relevant substantiating documentation, shall immediately inform the EPD Landscape Board, which, if need be, appoints its representative to the Commission. In all instances, a representative of the Regional Agency (District Inspectorate) participates in the work of the Commission.

When a site is selected for a pond or an object related with water-level change in ponds or lakes or with their clean-up or deepening, the Regional Agency shall in all cases invite to the Commission representatives of the Hydrographic Network Board and the EPD.

To select a site it is obligatory to follow existing master plans of cities and settlements, territory layout schemes, network schemes of holiday camps and other objects, governmental decisions delimiting industrial development in certain cities and territories (in cities with no waste-water treatment plants or with ineffective ones), etc., as well as to take into consideration the public opinion of local population.

The EPD experts who participate in the Commission for site selection, having studied the documentation provided as well as all comments and suggestions for the environmental protection measures to be implemented in the construction or expansion of the object, shall jointly with the Commission, after site inspection (it is reprehensible for Commission signatures to be collected individually), provide conclusions and list them in the Act of Construction Site Selection.

The Act of Construction Site Selection can be signed only when it includes indispensable environmental protection conditions, possible ways and means for drinking and surface water supply, for sewerage water drainage ensuring its purification standards, for atmospheric air protection from pollution as well as changes in water recipient and atmosphere contamination. The above-mentioned documents together with the first version of the Act of Construction Site Selection remain with the Regional Agency. The environmental protection measures foreseen and adopted in the Act of Construction Site Selection shall serve as basis for designing. The EPD institutions do not investigate or approve of tasks for TES or designing.

In cases of planned new construction, reconstruction, expansion or new technological installations which do not require any extra territory, the customer shall jointly with the designing company seek approval, in the form of a protocol, of the interested institutions for the object designing conditions. The protocol shall be put in order in the same way as the Act of Construction Site Selection.

Considering that the selection of construction sites (pipeline routes) for new objects decides the future ecological situation of an environment, representatives of the EPD institutions shall perform this task with due responsibility. Having violated the set rules for the construction sites (pipeline routes) selection, or having taken wrong decisions (which shall be annulled), the experts shall incur disciplinary punishment.

2. *Investigations and approval of feasibility studies*

All relevant feasibility documentation concerning the objects or territory within the Regional boundaries is presented for approval to the Regional Agency, which jointly with the District Inspectorate investigates and provides approval within the limits of its competence. The scope of a feasibility study and investigation order is presented in Annex 2. In case of controversies, prompt consultation with the Regional Agencies shall be provided by the EPD Expertise Board as well as other specialised boards.

To evaluate feasibility studies of complicated objects, Regional Agencies can employ the services of paid non-staff experts and scientists.

The Regional Agency can entrust the approval of some design solutions or changes in the design to the District Inspectorate. Such approvals shall be entered in special registers in the Regional Agency, as foreseen in Annex 3.

The Regional Agency, having familiarised itself with a project for which even consultants cannot provide proper evaluations of design solutions, and having secured the agreement of the Expertise Board, forwards to it the feasibility study, together with its own comments indicating the reasons why the documentation must be investigated or given expert appraisal by the EPD.

All pre-feasibility and feasibility documentation which reaches the EPD for approval or environmental impact assessment shall be, as foreseen in Annex 4, entered in a register in the Expertise Board, which has to provide its own timely investigation and approval or environmental impact assessment. The approval period is 15 calendar days, and that of environmental impact assessment is not more than 90 calendar days.

The Expertise Board, having received (whether directly from designing institutions, clients or Regional Agencies) pre-feasibility and feasibility studies, where necessary, forwards them to the relevant specialised boards for investigation and conclusions, indicating the final deadline by which conclusions must be provided.

In cases when the negative impact is likely to affect a single sphere of the natural environment (landscape, water or atmospheric air) the feasibility study is forwarded to the relevant board, which after investigation provides complete (final) conclusions to the EPD.

The Expertise Board arranges the investigation and approval of such feasibility studies as involve matters of natural resources utilisation and environmental protection, equally concerning several specialised boards. In such cases, specialised boards forward their comments and suggestions to the Expertise Board, which conflates them and provides final conclusions.

Archives of project coordination materials are stored in Regional Agencies. District Inspectorates receive only a copy of conclusions (approvals).

Controversies between a Regional Agency (District Inspectorate), designing institution or a customer in the evaluation of design solutions are investigated by the Expertise Board.

In cases of major violations in the order approving feasibility studies, or when a project which has been given approval does not meet basic environmental protection requirements (as disclosed by random inspection or based on information received), the EPD further investigates the documentation with the customer, the designing institution and the Regional Agency, and adopts an appropriate decision (the EPD has the right to cancel the approval granted).

Every week Regional Agencies forward data (together with other relevant information) on the selected sites for major objects construction, as well as on approved pre-feasibility and feasibility studies of more complicated objects.

The Expertise Board and specialised boards shall promptly inform Regional Agencies or District Inspectorates of decisions taken in the EPD, concerning existing or would-be objects in their regions or districts, and send them relevant documentation.

3. *Pre-feasibility and feasibility studies environmental impact assessment*

In cases when, during the investigation stage of a pre-feasibility or feasibility study from a Regional Agency, in the EPD Expertise and specialised boards it turns out that an environmental impact assessment is needed for proper evaluation of decisions taken in the study, or for the estimation of potential impact upon the natural environment, the Expertise Board, or any other specialised board, addresses the EPD authorities with a suggestion that an environmental impact assessment of such a feasibility study be performed jointly with non-staff experts (scientists and specialists). With the approval of the EPD authorities, such environmental impact assessment is organised by the Expertise Board. It appoints one of its specialists responsible for the execution of environmental impact assessment to select experts and provide suggestions to the EPD authorities for the candidacies to the expert group. When the expert group is approved, agreements are made with the invited paid experts and, based on these agreements, environmental impact assessment is performed within a set time limit.

Having received comments from all EPD system staff members who participated in the investigation of the study, and conclusions from invited experts, the Expertise Board considers them with the participation of the feasibility study authors, experts and heads of respective EPD units, and provides suggestions to the EPD authorities for the final approval of the conclusions.

Copies of individual experts' conclusions and the EPD final conclusions are presented to the relevant Regional Agency and District Inspectorate.

Head of Expertise Board: R. Kunskas (signature)

Appendix 2 to the Environmental Protection Department Decree No.87, 27 December 1990

A list of pre-feasibility and feasibility studies for which the EPD provides or arranges environmental impact assessment and gives final conclusions

1. Trends, concepts, schemes in the development of national economy sectors and in the layout of production forces.

2. Territorial, complex long-term natural resources utilisation and environmental protection schemes.

3. Towns' and health-resorts' master plans, heat, water supply, sewerage (including rainwater) and other schemes, projects for water stations and waste-water treatment plants, when these are of Republican significance.

4. Ignalina Nuclear Power Plant, Mažeikiai Oil Refinery, P/A *Azotas*, P/A *Akmencementas*, Kaišiadorys Hydro-accumulation Station, chemical plants in Kėdainiai, Lithuanian Thermal Power Plant, Klaipėda Cardboard Factory, Klaipėda State Element and Batteries Plant *Sirijus*, Panevėžys *Lietkabelis* Factory, Kaunas Synthetic Fibre Plant, Toxic Waste Utilisation Plant, expansion, reconstruction and upgrading projects.

5. Special purpose and linear inter-regional objects (highways, gas, oil pipelines) projects.

6. Establishment documentation and designs of industrial objects which are joint ventures with foreign companies.

7. Projects of ponds, clean-up of lakes, regulation of rivers.

8. Projects of river-bed, Kuršių Lagoon, Baltic Sea coastal areas deepening works, as well as those of the off-shore constructions in the Kuršių Lagoon and the Baltic Sea.

9. Utilisation projects of earth deposits (oil, iron ore, granite, etc.) as well as those of common minerals (gravel, sand, clay, etc.), the deposits of which are over 500,000 m^3 in volume.

10. Feasibility studies of objects designed in territories under particular protection (nature reserves, national and nature (regional) parks, strict nature reserves and in territories reserved for them).

11. Reports on groundwater resources investigations.

Note: The EPD may authorise Regional Agencies to perform the approval of feasibility studies of certain non-complicated objects within the limits of the above list.

Appendix 3 to the Environmental Protection Department Decree No.87, 27 December 1990

Annex I to the 'Internal Rules' adopted by the Environmental Protection Department, Decree No.87, 27 December 1990

A list of documents (data) to be presented to a Regional Agency or District Environmental Protection Inspectorate prior to site selection

1. General situation layout of the selected site with sanitary protection zone description.
2. Master plan scheme with major buildings, constructions and natural environment contamination sources.
3. A scheme of external engineering network and communications with their facilities.
4. General layouts of buildings with basic construction characteristics.
5. Passports of standard and repeatedly applied projects.
6. A table of basic technical/economic indices.
7. Comments on the existing ecological situation: whether the object is in territories protected by law or planned to be protected (strict nature reserves, reserves, national parks, etc.), its location with respect to natural and cultural monuments, background contamination of the environment, evaluation of the locality from the landscape, historic and cultural, physical/geographical and meteorological points of view.
8. Comments on the potential negative impact upon the natural environment by the object and measures foreseen to avoid this, calculations of atmospheric air contamination level.
9. Demand for natural and energy resources, their sources and the capacity of these sources to supply the object with raw materials and energy.
10. Waste-water and air treatment methods and facilities, their effectiveness, quantitative and qualitative characteristics of discharged water and emitted air after treatment, utilisation of production waste.
11. Forecast of qualitative changes of discharged water recipient (open water body) and atmospheric air during the operation of the object.
12. Comments on potential pollutants discharges in case of accidents.
13. An expert assessment of the territory as a potential natural source of infectious diseases.

Note: When needed, the customer shall provide other documents as well, in agreement with the requirements of 'Basic Temporary Standards'.

Annex 2 to the 'Internal Rules' adopted by the Environmental Protection Department, Decree No.87, 27 December 1990

The scope and investigation principles of feasibility studies provided to a Regional Agency for approval

For investigation and approval, a Regional Agency shall be presented with feasibility study volumes, which deal with or have to deal with matters related to the use of natural resources or natural environment protection, as well as calculations of concentrations of hazardous substances emitted into atmospheric air. During the process of feasibility study investigation, the EPD system institutions and sub-divisions may request additional information from the customer or designing institution needed to provide considered conclusions on the potential impact of the object upon natural environment.

Together with a feasibility study the customer shall also provide the material which remains with the Regional Agency (after the feasibility study has, or has not, been given approval): the 'Nature Protection' chapter of the study, or a description of planned environmental protection measures with relevant graphic material (master plan with engineering network and facilities, zone delimitation schemes, engineering/geological data, etc.).

When the feasibility study is received for investigation and approval, attention shall be primarily paid to finding out if there is basic motivation for the object to be designed:

a. if the Site Selection Act is available, if it is approved, if it is of a set standard and volume;
b. in case the Act is not compiled according to the established order, and merely indicates the geographic situation of the site as well as its limits, the motivation for the object to be built, reconstructed, expanded, shall be checked, and whether there are any legal or governmental prohibitions for such kind of objects to be built in this locality;
c. if there are sufficient stocks of drinking and surface water to supply the object with water;
d. if the city, settlement has waste-water treatment facilities, whether their capacity is sufficient to receive an extra load from a new object;
e. if the current background atmospheric air contamination does not exceed allowable concentrations (if it does, no extra emissions can be allowed);
f. if there are conclusions on the particular feasibility study provided by other state control bodies, and if all of them are positive; if such conclusions are not available, the feasibility study is not investigated.

When it is considered that the object is being designed lawfully, the feasibility study scope and quality are examined from the environmental protection point of view.

A feasibility study shall include the following items of natural environment protection:

Atmospheric air protection

a. evaluation of the current ecological situation before the construction, reconstruction, expansion (including data of stationary observations, background concentrations), its forecast for the time the object is in operation, sanitary protection zone description, suggestions for its establishment;
b. evaluation of the basic operation technology level of the object (including that of heat and energy consumption), application of no-waste and low-waste technologies, installation of effective treatment facilities, ecological assessment based a comparison between domestic technologies and treatment facilities and those applied abroad;
c. consideration of quantitative and qualitative characteristics of hazardous substances emissions, emissions standards per unit within other branches of industry, their comparison with analogous values proposed in the project;
d. volumes of recommended raw materials, production volumes and production waste (solid, liquid, gas) utilisation, treatment, indicating concrete proposals, a comparison between domestic and foreign operating objects;
e. risk degree of the planned object upon other objects, natural environment, probability of accidents, derangements in the technological process, contamination of the natural

environment during raw materials and finished products transportation as well as foreseen remedial measures;

f. progressiveness of selected technologies with the aim of minimising the production of hazardous substances emitted into the atmosphere;
g. the effectiveness of atmospheric air protection technologies as demonstrated in functioning objects, their scientific, technical and economic effectiveness;
h. plan to reduce emissions into the atmosphere after a warning of unfavourable meteorological conditions (in cities for which such forecasts are made);
i. determination of maximum allowable concentrations for hazardous substances emissions;
k. reliability of atmospheric air pollution level calculations;
l. in the case of object reconstruction or expansion, the feasibility study shall contain a comparison of the present situation with that after the reconstruction or expansion. Whenever necessary, nature protection measures shall be foreseen for the operation period;
m. compliance of the design of the object to be reconstructed or expanded with maximum allowable emissions levels;
n. when deficit fuel, raw materials, semi-finished products are used, the planning institution's permit shall be annexed to the project;
o. quantitative and compositional characteristics of the pollutants;
p. description of quantitative and compositional control measures of pollutants.

Land use and protection

a. specific territory layout, aiming to reduce area coverage and preserve the landscape;
b. preservation of the humus layer of the soil;
c. rational layout of engineering communications, roads, electricity supply lines, etc.;
d. amounts and composition of both solid and liquid wastes, their utilisation, storage (dumping sites), measures to protect environment (including toxic and chemical substances);
e. evaluation of the area covered from the economic point of view.

Water use and protection

a. possibilities for and means of water supply;
b. rational use of drinking water, replacing it with technical water wherever possible;
c. balance of utilised and waste-water quantities in the current situation and after the expansion or reconstruction;
d. maximum application of circular and repeated water utilisation systems;
e. introduction of new technologies and no-waste processes;
f. registration of utilised and waste-water quantities by means of meters;
g. primary treatment of process-contaminated waste-water and specific streams, possibilities to re-use it in process;
h. rainwater treatment in district (group) waste-water treatment plants or in territories of enterprises, application of treated water in the process, for car washing, etc.;
i. contaminated waste-water treatment facilities, treatment technology, and the degree of treatment achieved;
k. processing of sludge in waste-water treatment plants and utilisation;

l. calculations of mixture of treated waste water with that of the recipient water body;
m. collection and storage of used oils;
n. the state of protection belts and zones near water bodies, measures to maintain them;
o. delineation and maintenance of sanitary protection zones for water intake areas;
p. quality of drained water from land reclamation areas and measures to improve it;
q. measures to eliminate the negative impact of agricultural production objects (production centres, mechanical workshops, storage, depositories, temporary storage sites, etc.) upon water bodies;
r. measures and ways to observe the impact of the object upon surface and groundwater;
s. engineering, geological and hydro-geological conditions;
t. hydro-chemical, bacteriological characteristics of surface, drainage and groundwater;
u. evaluation of pollutants migration peculiarities in the ground hydrosphere;
v. chemical composition of pollutants, bacteriological contamination, evaluation of their accumulation conditions.

Vegetation protection

a. amount and value of existing trees and bushes (on the site for construction or route), tracing those included in the Red Data Book;
b. measures to maximise preservation and promotion of growth of existing trees and bushes;
c. measures against the potential negative impact of the object upon trees and bushes to be left within the territory as well as upon valuable plants outside the territory.

Wildlife protection

a. potential negative impact of the object upon neighbouring intensive breeding sites of birds and animals (especially those included in the Red Data Book), measures to eliminate this impact;
b. potential negative impact of the discharged waste water into recipient water body upon valuable aquatic life and fishes;
c. protection of aquatic wildlife from extinction at water intake points (pumping stations);
d. negative impact of the object upon migration of fishes.

Signing of feasibility study investigation conclusions

Conclusions on the feasibility study (in case of approval or no approval) are given out to the customer or designing institution in writing, signed by: at the EPD, the First Deputy Director General or Deputy Director General, and at the Regional Agency, the Director or Deputy Director, or the Head of Project Approval Unit.

Individual non-complicated objects or project decisions can be approved by a special stamp (they will be made and distributed in a centralised way), the right for signature being granted to the Head or Deputy Head of the EPD Expertise Board, the Director or Deputy Director of a regional Agency or the Head of a Project Approval Unit.

Annex 3 to the 'Internal Rules', approved by the Environment Protection Department, Decree No.87, 27 December 1990

A register of feasibility studies or project decisions, approved by a Regional Agency, District Environmental Protection Inspection

2. Title of feasibility study
3. Reception date
4. Names of participants in investigation and approval
5. Approval date and content or date and number of the official paper
6. Notes on repeated approval
7. Notes

Annex 4 to the 'Internal Rules' approved by the Environmental Protection Department, Decree No.87, 27 December 1990

A Register

2. Title of documentation
3. Institution which handed in the documentation
4. Date of reception at the Expertise Board
5. Expertise Board specialist responsible for timely investigation of documentation and provision of conclusions
6. Names of the EPD specialists and invited experts investigating the documentation
7. Date of mailing the conclusions

LITHUANIA B

Ministry of Construction and Urban Development of the Republic of Lithuania

Environmental Protection Department of the Republic of Lithuania

Rules for the Elaboration of the 'Environmental Protection Section' of a Study

RSN 153-93

Republican construction standards
Official publication, Vilnius 1993

The Rules have been worked out by the Ministry of Construction and Urban Development (Mr A. B. Bružas), with the participation of the Environmental Protection Department (Mr J. Križčiūnas), the Republican Hygiene Centre (Mr D. Ščiupakas) as well as the design companies 'Žemprojektas' (Mr V. Cikotas) and 'Lietuvos Statybos Projektas' (Mr F. Kozlovakim).

Ministry of Construction and Urban Development of the Republic of Lithuania: Republican construction standards RSN 153-93

Environmental Protection Department of the Republic of Lithuania: Rules for the elaboration of the study section 'Environmental Protection'

Paragraph 1. The present rules are obligatory in preparing a study for a construction object where a negative impact upon the environment will occur during its construction, expansion, renovation and/or operation. Such a study shall contain a section 'Environmental Protection'.

Paragraph 2. The study section 'Environmental Protection' is an evaluation of the present ecological state, a summary of design decisions taken in all other sections of the study which have an impact upon the environment, as well as a forecast of the would-be object's impact upon the ecological state.

Paragraph 3. If the object is to be designed in several stages (e.g. 'technological project – working documentation' or 'technical/economic motivation – working study'), the study section 'Environmental Protection' is prepared in the earliest stages of the study, having obtained from the state design control institutions the designing conditions required by established order. At this stage, amounts of pollutants can be determined in an integrated form (e.g. for groups of equipment, a sector, a workshop) based on the data of analogous objects. The project stage has to be approved by a relevant environmental protection service.

During the following project stage, based on the availability of more precise data, amounts of pollutants are recalculated. If the amount of a certain pollutant or its effect is higher than that indicated at the previous stage, the study section 'Environmental Protection' at this project stage is to be revised and approved under the same order.

If at the earliest project stage there are data available that the object will not render any significant impact upon the environment, the study section 'Environmental Protection' can be prepared at a later stage upon agreement of the state design control institutions.

For confirmation provided by the Construction Science and Standards Department of the Construction and Urban Development Ministry, and the Expertise Board of the Environmental Protection Department

Confirmed by a joint Decree No.154/60 dated 6 September 1993, of the Construction and Urban Development Ministry of the Republic of Lithuania, and the Environmental Protection Department of the Republic of Lithuania

Approved by the Republican Hygiene Centre Official Letter No.05-904, dated 31 August 1993

Valid since 1 January 1994

Official publication

Paragraph 4. Recommended items for the study section 'Environmental Protection' are provided in Appendix 1. The suggested scope of the study section 'Environmental Protection' should be covered if the object may have a negative impact upon any environmental components (soil, air, water) by chemical, physical and biological pollutants emissions when the ecological state is an unfavourable one. For a definite object its feasibility study volume may be smaller as some of the factors mentioned may be absent.

Paragraph 5. Items of the study section 'Environmental Protection' of an object posing ecological threat can be specified by state design control institutions by indicating their additional requirements in the obligatory object designing conditions.

Paragraph 6. In case the object is connected to the existing engineering communications network or facilities with sufficient capacity to meet its demands, and it emits into the environment only pure ventilation air, and contains no noise-producing equipment, it is considered that the operation of the object has no negative impact upon the environment. The study section 'Environmental Protection' for such an object is not provided.

Paragraph 7. If during the operation of an object there will be no harmful impact upon any environmental components, or it will be insignificant, the scope of the study section 'Environmental Protection' may be smaller. The list of such objects is presented in Appendix 2.

Paragraph 8. The object expansion or reconstruction study section 'Environmental Protection' shall cover not only the new sector to be built or that under reconstruction, but also the existing part which has similar impacts upon the environment.

Paragraph 9. If the object expansion or reconstruction project does not include change of production, the study shall contain parameters of the current situation as well as those based upon the design.

Paragraph 10. Calculations made in other study sections are not repeated in the study section 'Environmental Protection'. Only the data used for calculations are provided, as well as the results of these calculations, and references to the study sections which include these calculations.

Paragraph 11. The study section 'Environmental Protection', together with Hygiene Service conclusions concerning the project, are forwarded for approval to the Environment Protection Department or its Regional Agency by established order. At the request of the institution which provides approval other study sections or calculations are to be presented. When approval is granted to the study section 'Environmental Protection', one copy remains irrevocably with the institution which has given approval.

Appendix 1

Recommended items of the study section 'Environmental Protection'

(Issues presented in the explanatory official paper, calculations, drawings.)

1. General data related to the object

1.1. Object description

1.1.1. Name of the object, location of construction, purpose, production, building time schedule and order of priorities.

1.1.2. Geographical situation of the construction area. Evaluation of the territory from the historical/cultural, recreational points of view, its location with respect to protected territories (state reserves, national and regional parks, strict nature reserves, protective zones and belts, territories of local significance and those of specific purpose) as well as sanitary protection zones of neighbouring enterprises.

1.1.3. Construction site description from the engineering geological point of view. Filtration and barrier properties of the soil and subsoil; horizontal and vertical fluid filtration possibilities. Geochemical, geophysical state of soil and subsoil and contamination.

1.1.4. Brief description of the technological process. Technological processes with a negative impact upon the environment. New technologies and no-waste production processes.

1.1.5. Demand for natural resources (oil, gas, etc.) and raw materials, production waste.

Table 1-1 Raw materials, waste, waste management

1	Workshop, production, equipment	
2–4	Raw materials:	
	2	Name
	3,4	Amount
	3	t/day
	4	t/year
5–10	Waste	
	5	Name
	6,7	Amount
	6	t/day
	7	t/year
	8	Aggregate state (solid, fluid, paste)
	9	Danger class*
	10	Basic components*
11–12	Waste storage in the object	
	11	Storage conditions
	12	Biggest amount
13	Management type planned (rendering harmless, recycling, dumping, etc.)	

* Danger class and basic components based on the instruction to fill in the State Statistical Report Form No.3, 'Waste'.

1.1.6. Demand for and sources of electricity and thermal energy.

1.1.7. Potential threat of the object to other objects and natural environment. Potential accidents and derangements in technological processes. Potential pollutants emissions into the environment in case of accidents. Accident prevention and potential accident after-effects combating measures.

1.1.8. Data on physical and biological pollutants emitted from the object and affecting the environment.

Table 1-2 physical and biological pollutants which have an impact upon the environment of the object

1	Name of pollutant
	Noise
	Electromagnetic radiation
	Biological pollution (micro-organisms, viruses, other pollutants of plant and animal origin)
	Other factors of physical and biological pollution
2	Name of pollution source at the object
3	Number of pollution sources
4	Background contamination of the environment
5–8	Calculated impact upon the environment by the object and measures to reduce pollution: 5 In the territory of the object (near limits) 6 In the sanitary zone of the object
	7–8 In a dwelling area, recreation territory with the estimation of background contamination 7 Without measures 8 With measures implemented
9	Measures to reduce pollution

1.1.9. Which environmental components (water, atmosphere, soil, vegetation, animal life) will not receive any impact from the object, or the impact will be so insignificant, that the study section 'Environment Protection' will not include a relevant chapter (e.g. chapter 'Water Protection', etc.).

1.2. Design documents attached
(Copies of these documents are to be included within the binder of the 'Environmental Protection' section.)

1.2.1. Act of construction site selection.

1.2.2. Data on valuable trees and other valuable plants growing on the site.

1.2.3. Data on the territory's entomological, parasitological, soil microbiological as well as chemical pollution and radiological contamination (when so indicated in the obligatory designing conditions of the Hygiene Service).

1.2.4. Conditions for connection to existing sewerage, rainwater drainage systems.

1.2.5. Data on background contamination of the surface water body recipient of the effluent.

1.2.6. Data on atmospheric air background contamination or on neighbouring enterprises' atmospheric emissions.

1.2.7. Inventory data on air pollutants emissions from an operating object (for expansion, reconstruction projects).

1.2.8. For an operating object, Chapter 1 of the latest annual statistical report Form No.2 'Atmosphere': data on pollutants emissions into the atmosphere, their treatment and utilisation (for expansion, reconstruction projects).

1.2.9. Reference from the client of waste utilisation method approval.

1.2.10. Hygiene service conclusions on the object.

2. Water protection

2.1. Water demand

2.1.1. Water demand for the object.

Table 2-1 Balance of water consumed m^3/day, m^3/year

1	Name or number of workshop, sector
2	Consumed in total (columns 3,9,10)
3–8	Fresh water consumed 3 In total 4 For household purposes 5–6 For production purposes 5 Drinking water 6 Technical quality water 7–8 To supplement circulation systems 7 Drinking water 8 Technical quality water
9–10	Repeatedly used 9 Enterprise water 10 Water from other objects
11	Remarks

2.1.2. Reasons for drinking water use for production purposes.

2.1.3. Circulation and repeated use of water systems.

2.2. Water sources

2.2.1. Water supply sources for the object (groundwater, surface water body, municipal water supply or that from another object, surface effluent, etc.), debits of intake water. In case of several options for water supply, the choice motivation shall be presented.

2.2.2. Groundwater resource as approved by the Territory Resources Commission (when the use of this water is foreseen in the project).

2.2.3. Basic data on the water-bearing horizon; its location, depth, capacity, etc. (when the use of this water in the project is foreseen).

2.2.4. Data on the quality of the intake water: microbiological, chemical and other investigations data; indicators of surface water body background contamination.

Table 2-2 Indicators of surface water body contamination

1	Name of water body, Cross section
2	Year
3	Remotest month's mean debit m^3/s of 95% probability
4–5	Background contamination
	4 Name of pollutant
	5 Concentration mg/l
6	Maximum allowable concentration (MAC) mg/l
7	Background contamination degree*
8	Sources of pollution†

* Contamination degree is the ratio of pollutant concentration with MAC.
† When data is available.

2.2.5. Registration of received and utilised water.

2.2.6. Drinking water quality control.

Table 2-3 Drinking water quality control

1	Name of indicator under control
2	Type of control
3	Periodicity
4	Basic control means, laboratory rooms, staff

2.2.7. Measures to let the surface water source sanitary debits through.

2.3. Effluent, their treatment and discharge

2.3.1. A brief description of effluent, their treatment and discharge: types of effluent (municipal, industrial contaminated, surface, etc.), amounts of effluent; contamination level of effluent, local treatment facilities (existing, to be reconstructed, to be constructed, designed individually; their capacity), discharge points of treated effluent. In the case of effluent treatment and discharge options, the choice motivation shall be presented.

Table 2-4 Balance of effluent m^3/day, m^3/year

1	Name or number of workshop, sector
2	Effluent in total (columns 3, 4, 6, 7, 8)
3–5	Discharged 3 Household water 4-5 Production water 4 In total 5 Of which untreated
6–7	Directed for recycling 6 In the current object 7 In other objects
8	Water consumption without recycling
9	Remarks

2.3.2. Primary treatment of effluent contaminated in production processes and re-use of specific treated effluent in production processes.

2.3.3. Amounts of different types of effluent from workshops and sectors, amounts of pollutants in effluent, treatment methods, composition of treatment facilities, amounts of pollutants in effluent after treatment, effluent dischargers.

Table 2-5 Volumes of contaminated effluent and their pollutants content, data on effluent treatment and discharge

1	Name of workshop, sector, effluent discharger
2	Type of effluent
3	Volumes of effluent 3 m^3/h 4 m^3/day 5 m^3/year
6–9	In effluent coming to treatment facilities or discharged without treatment 6 Name of pollutant 7 Concentration of pollutant mg/l 8–9 Amount of pollutant 8 t/day 9 t/year
10	Effluent treatment method, capacity of treatment plant, m^3/day
11–13	In effluent after discharge 11 Concentration of pollutant mg/l 12–13 Amount of pollutant 12 t/day 13 t/yea
14	Pollutant removal effect %
15	Utilisation of treated effluent, point of discharge

2.3.4. Capacity of effluent treatment facilities and treatment effectiveness. References to corresponding calculations made in another study section or to the industrial facility technical specifications source containing the data.

2.3.5. Effluent discharge. Name of effluent recipient (open water body), its background contamination; effluent dischargers, amounts of discharged effluent and their pollutants content, indicators of effluent mixture with recipient's water.

Table 2-6 Indications of discharged effluent mixture with the water of the recipient

Name of the recipient (surface water body)	
Location of calculated section	
1	Name or Number of effluent discharger
2	Distance from discharger to calculated section in water body, km
3–5	Amount of effluent 3 m^3/h 4 m^3/day 5 $m^3/year$
6–7	Pollutants in discharged effluent 6 Name of pollutant 7 Concentration of pollutant
8	Background concentration of pollutant in the calculated section of the water body, mg/l
9	Dilution degree
10	Concentration of pollutant in the calculated section of the water body after mixing, mg/l

2.3.6. Maximum allowable concentration and volume of pollutants discharged, suggested for approval as a standard.

Table Continued

11	Maximum allowable concentration of pollutant, mg/l
12–13	Maximum allowable amount of pollutant discharged, suggested for standard approval (MAP) 12 t/day 13 t/year

2.3.7. Registration of effluent and quality control. Sampling points, control methods and measures.

Table 2-7 Effluent pollutants control

1	Name of pollutant under control
2	Type of control
3	Periodicity
4	Basic control means, laboratory rooms, staff

2.4. Water contamination prevention

2.4.1. Protection belts and zones for surface water bodies, protection zones for stations and single deep wells.

2.4.2. Volumes and humidity of sludge, slime and other sediments from production, water quality improvement stations and effluent treatment facilities; their collecting, de-watering, storage, equipment, buildings, sites used for these purposes.

2.4.3. Amounts of de-watered sludge, slime and other sediments, their utilisation; amounts of hazardous substances and waste, storage, fitting out of storage sites; amount of spent oils, their collection, storage, utilisation; accumulation and utilisation of manure, slurry and silage effluent (to be included in Table 1-1).

2.4.4. Materials and types of installed pipes, fittings and reinforcement in contact with chemical substances.

2.4.5. Means to collect excess industrial water and effluent and direct them back into the process or to the treatment facilities.

2.4.6. Volumes of potential accident spills. Means to collect them without reaching aquifers or permeating the soil (dikes, anti-filtration screens, etc.).

2.4.7. Collecting and treatment of surface effluent (rainwater and melting snow) from the territory of the object.

2.4.8. Means to protect groundwater layers from contamination (filling-in of non-functioning drilling, etc.)

2.4.9. Engineering means for hydrogeological observations and measurements in the zones of groundwater layers' potential contamination.

2.4.10. Means to protect water bodies from contaminated surface effluent during the object construction period.

2.5. Drawings of the section 'Water Protection'

2.5.1. Situation plan with indicated water supply sources, intake points, effluent treatment facilities, effluent discharge points, water bodies protective belts and zones, water stations protective zones, laboratory control sampling points.

2.5.2. Construction (master) plan scheme with the indication of existing, designed buildings and those to be demolished, engineering network, equipment, storage sites of hazardous substances and waste.

2.5.3. A drawing of the territory vertical planning.

3. *Atmosphere protection*

3.1. Air pollutants coming from the object

3.1.1. Brief description of the object's stationary and mobile, organised and unorganised atmosphere pollution sources, pollutants emitted. Volley emissions of pollutants.

3.1.2. Calculations of emitted pollutants amounts (usually in the form of tables) with the indication of fuel and raw materials consumption, their sorts and marks, types of technological and energy equipment, operation regimes, calculation formulas for the amounts of pollutants or references to literature sources and methodology, coefficients, other characteristics needed for calculations and results of calculations.

3.1.3. Atmospheric pollution stationary sources and amounts of pollutants emitted from them are calculated according to Item 3.1.2. and presented in Table 3-1.

3.1.4. Amounts of pollutants emitted from mobile sources functioning in the object's territory are calculated according to Item 3.1.2. and presented in Table 3-2.

3.2. Maximum allowable concentrations of pollutants

3.2.1. Maximum allowable concentrations of pollutants emitted by the object into the atmosphere.

Table 3-1

1	Name of pollutant
2	Approximate non-hazardous level (ANL)
3–4	Maximum allowable concentration (MAC) 3 Single-time 4 Average daily

Table 3-2 Pollutants emissions from mobile sources functioning in the object's territory

1	Name, mark of pollutant source
2	Number of sources
3	Name of pollutant emitted
4	Amount emitted, t/year

3.2.2. A list of groups of pollutants which comprise emissions from the object and background contamination or that from neighbouring enterprises, and which are characterised by an add-up effect; their maximum allowable concentrations in the atmosphere.

3.2.3. Names of documents on the basis of which the Lists of Items 3.2.1. and 3.2.2. are compiled.

3.3. Measures to reduce atmospheric pollution
Amounts of emitted pollutants

3.3.1. Technical decisions taken in the design of the object to reduce atmospheric contamination (emissions reduction, treatment improvement, improvement of emissions parameters, etc.). Non-standard equipment planned to be installed, its application in functioning objects, its effectiveness. In case of options in technical decisions, the choice motivation shall be provided.

3.3.2. Gas treatment and dust trapping equipment as foreseen in the design, degree of treatment, amounts of pollutants emitted into the atmosphere.

Table 3-3 Stationary atmosphere pollution sources, pollutants produced, treatment means, pollutants emitted

1	Name, number of workshop, sector
2–4	Source of pollutants production
	2 Name, type
	3 Amount, units
	4 Work time per year, hours
5–9	Source of pollutants emission into the atmosphere
	5 Name
	6 Amount, units
	7 Number
	8 Height, m
	9 Exhaust mouth diameter
10–12	Parameters of polluted air emitted into the atmosphere
	10 Speed, m/s
	11 Amount, m^3/s
	12 Temperature, C
13–21	Coordinates X,Y (of the local system) and size of pollutants emission sources
	13–14 Point source or start of linear source, m
	15–16 End of linear source, m
17–21	Flat source
	17–18 Symmetry contour, m
	19 Length, m
	20 Width, m
	21 Angle between source length and x axis
22–26	Treatment of polluted air emitted into the atmosphere
	22 Name and type of facilities
	23 Name of trapped pollutant
	24 Availability of treatment facilities %
	25–26 Degree of treatment
	25 Designed %
	26 Existing %

Table 3-3 ***Continued***

27	Other means
28	Names of pollutants
29–32	Amount of pollutants 29–30 Produced 29 g/s 30 t/year 31–32 Emitted 31 g/s 32 t/year

Note: If the amounts of pollutants are determined for a complex (for a group of equipment, sector, workshop), based on analogous object data, then the size and coordinates of the pollutants emission centre of the relevant group of equipment, sector or workshop are to be indicated in columns 8, 9 and 13–21.

3.4. Atmospheric contamination forecast

3.4.1. Determination of pollutants for which near-the-ground concentrations have to be calculated. Determination according to Items 3.4.1.1. or 3.4.1.2.

3.4.1.1. Near-to-the-ground concentrations are calculated for those pollutants emitted from the object (or for groups of pollutants characterised by an add-up effect), which have a calculated value of parameter R (of at least one emission source of the functioning or designed production) of over 5. Parameter R is calculated by the formula

$$Rji = \frac{Dj}{Hj + Dj} \times \frac{oji}{MACi} \times 1000$$

Dj (m) is the diameter of emission source.
Hj (m) is the height of emission source above ground level.
oji is the concentration of pollutant at the mouth of the source.
MACi is the maximum allowable concentration of pollutant.

$$\text{When } Dj > 0.5\,Hj, \ \frac{Dj}{Hj + Dj} \text{ is equal to 1.}$$

3.4.1.2. Near-to-the-ground concentrations are calculated for those pollutants emitted from the object which

$$\frac{Mi}{MACi} > Fi$$

$Fi = 0.01\,H$ when $Hi > 10$ m
$Fi = 0.1\,H$ when $Hi < 10$ m

Mi (g/s) is the amount of pollutant emitted from all air pollution sources of the object.
MACi (mg/m^3) maximum allowable concentration of the pollutant.
Hi (m) average height of the pollutant emission sources.

3.4.2. Data for calculations of the highest near-to-the-ground concentrations of the object emissions:

- calculation methods, programme;
- values of stratification coefficient, of the coefficient representing the locality relief and other coefficient values;
- temperature of the environment and wind direction;
- coordinates of the rectangle delimiting the territory for which the spread of pollutants in the atmosphere is calculated.

3.4.3. Calculations of highest near-to-the-ground concentrations of the object emissions and groups of pollutants, including those from the object, which have an add-up effect;

- based on emissions from the object;
- based on emissions from the object with the estimation of background concentration or emissions from neighbouring enterprises.

Computer-based calculations attached.

3.4.4. Analysis of near-to-the-ground concentrations of pollutants calculation results and conclusions.

3.5. Sanitary protection zone

3.5.1. Sanitary protection zone (SPZ) size in metres according to standards (to be indicated which ones).

3.5.2. SPZ size specified by prevailing winds. (SPZ has to be specified when the maximum allowable concentration of a pollutant exceeds the MAC.)

3.5.3. Data on dwelling houses in the sanitary protection zone. Number of inhabitants moved from the SPZ.

3.6. Allowable pollutants emissions into the atmosphere and their control

3.6.1. Based on calculations of emissions spread from the object and the evaluation of existing air pollution, a proposal is made to approve, as a standard, maximum allowable amounts of emissions into the atmosphere from each atmospheric pollution source separately, and for the object as a whole.

Table 3-4 Suggested for approval pollutants emissions standards

Type of standards:

MAA – maximum allowable amount of pollutant emitted;
TAA – temporary allowable amount of pollutant emitted*.

1	Name of pollutant
2	Number sources of pollutants emission into the atmosphere
3	Type of standard
4–5	Allowable amount of pollutants to be emitted 4 g/s 5 t/year

Table 3-4 ***Continued***

In total (for each pollutant individually)
Pollutants in the object in total

* TAA standards are not suggested for sources under reconstruction, those undergoing technical upgrading as well as newly designed ones.

3.6.2. Methods and means for the control of pollutants emissions into the atmosphere.

Table 3-5 Atmospheric pollutants control

1	Name of pollutant under control
2	Control method
3	Periodicity
4	Main means of control, laboratory rooms, staff

3.7. Atmosphere protection measures under particularly unfavourable meteorological conditions

3.7.1. For objects in localities with particularly unfavourable meteorological conditions forecast, a plan of atmosphere protection measures under such conditions is made.

Table 3-6 Atmosphere protection measures under particularly unfavourable meteorological conditions

1	Name of workshop, sector
2	Number of the sources of pollutants emission into the atmosphere
3	Name of pollutant
4	Measures to reduce emission of the pollutant
5–6	Forecast of pollutant emission reduction
	5 g/s
	6 %

3.8. Drawings of the section 'Atmosphere Protection'

3.8.1. Situation plan covering a territory not less than 2 km in radius from the object designed. If the emission source height (H) is over 40 m, the situation plan shall cover a territory not less than 50 H in radius. The living zone, resort zone, industrial objects, the sanitary protection zone of the object designed are to be shown in the situation plan.

3.8.2. Construction (master) plan scheme with indicated sources of pollutants emissions into the atmosphere.

3.8.3. Map/scheme of highest possible concentration of air pollutants in the near-to-the-ground atmosphere layer with the object designed indicated, isolines of its SPZ and concentrations of individual pollutants as well as summary concentrations of groups of pollutants with an add-up effect exceeding MAC. (This can be shown on the situation plan.)

4. *Ground protection*

4.1. Farming land protection

4.1.1. Analysis of farming land within the object site

Type of farming land	Area (ha) Before construction	After onstruction	Area recultivated
Arable land			
Gardens			
Fallow land			
Meadows			
Pastures			
Forests			
Bushes, trees			
Wetlands			
Water			
Roads			
Yards			
Land under buildings			
Other land			
In total			

4.1.2. Area from which the fertile soil layer will be removed, thickness of the layer, volume of the soil removed. Temporary storage site of the soil removed, its application for recultivation.

4.1.3. Methods and means for soil pollutants control.

Table 4-1 Control of soil pollutants

1	Name of pollutant under control
2	Control methods
3	Periodicity
4	Main means of control, laboratory rooms, staff

4.2. Vegetation protection

4.2.1. General description of trees, bushes and other plantations on the site (species, diameter or height, state).

4.2.2. Valuable trees and bushes to be preserved, measures to protect them.

4.2.3. Number of trees to be felled, number of trees to be replanted.

4.3. Animal life protection
4.3.1. Technical measures to protect aquatic wildlife at the water intake points in open water bodies.

4.3.2. To indicate the existence or not of bird and animal intensive breeding sites, as well as bird and fish migration routes, within the object impact area. In case of existence, measures to reduce the impact are to be indicated.

4.4. Bio-technical measures
4.4.1. Greeneries to purify atmospheric air.

4.4.2. Bio-filters to purify rainwater run-off.

4.4.3. Biological indication means of water, air and soil state.

4.5. Measures to compensate the negative impact upon the environment rendered by production activity
4.5.1. Planting of trees and bushes in the enterprise's territory, construction of ponds and fountains.

4.5.2. Laying of health tracks in peripheral areas of the enterprise, adjustment of squares and parks there or their improvement.

4.5.3. Adaptation of communications routes for population needs and recreation.

4.5.4. Subsidies or financing for public and municipal facilities (parks, ponds, on-shore greeneries, etc., designed and implemented by municipality departments).

4.6. Drawings of the section 'Ground Protection'
4.6.1. A drawing of the territory management (coatings, greeneries).

Appendix 2

A list of construction objects, for which the section 'Environmental Protection' prepared is of reduced volume

Object designed	Environmental protection to be looked into		
	Water protection (see Note)	Atmosphere protection	Ground protection
1 Dwelling building (separate)	+	–	–
2 Public building (without laboratory, experimental centre)	+	–	–
3 Agricultural production building or facility:			
fodder preparation workshop, concentrated fodder storage, silos trench, milk block animal-shed, dung yard	+	–	+
barn, root-crop storage, litter shed	–	–	+
greenhouse (except those heated by gas heat generators)	+	–	+
grain storage with cleaning units	+	–	+
potato, vegetable, fruit storage	–	–	+
garage without technical service station	+	–	+
oil products storage	+	–	+
4 Engineering communications and facilities:			
water intake site, drilled well	+	–	+
water supply, sewerage, heat supply or gas pipeline collector or network	+	–	+
sewerage pumping station	+	–	+
sanitary field, animal burial place	+	–	+
electricity line, transformer room,	–	–	+
electrochemical protection gas pipeline	–	–	+
electrode boiler room	+	–	+

Note. The study section 'Environmental Protection' for these objects need not be provided if the building or facility is connected to existing water management communications and facilities of sufficient capacity.

Appendix 3

Literature recommended by the Environment Protection Department

1. Issues of a general nature
2. Atmosphere protection
3. Water protection
4. Ground protection
5. Waste management

LITHUANIA C

Law on Environmental Protection of the Republic of Lithuania

January 1992

Excerpts

Chapter 1

Article 6. The state administration of environmental protection
6.3. The Government of the Republic of Lithuania, implementing the national policy of environmental protection, shall:

6.3.1. prepare, and in conjunction with the Department of Environmental Protection, submit for approval to the Supreme Council of the Republic of Lithuania, programmes and proposals of national significance related to the utilisation of natural resources and environmental protection;

6.3.2. establish, finance and supply programmes, plans and projects for environmental protection of natural significance, and finance purposive research works;

6.3.3. keep the registration of state national resources and, within the established limits, distribute national resources to users;

6.3.4. organise ecological education and instruction;

6.3.5. prepare draft projects or norms and standards of environmental quality, and promote the introduction of ecologically safe technology and production by users of natural resources;

6.3.6. in conjunction with the Department of Environmental Protection of the Republic of Lithuania, conclude international treaties of the Republic of Lithuania related to the utilisation of natural resources and environmental protection, and implement them in accordance with their competence;

6.3.7. coordinate the activities of the bodies of state power and local governments concerning the utilisation of natural resources and environmental protection; and

6.3.8. carry out other activities prescribed by law.

6.4. Local governments, implementing the policy of environmental protection on their territories:

6.4.1. shall organise the implementation of laws on environmental protection and decisions of the Department of Environmental Protection and the Government of the Republic of Lithuania in the field of environmental protection, and within the limits of their jurisdiction, adopt decisions concerning the utilisation of natural resources and environmental protection, ascribed to them by the Government of the Republic of Lithuania, and supervise their implementation;

6.4.2. shall prepare, approve and implement the programmes, plans, and projects of environmental protection and utilisation of natural resources in the territory under their jurisdiction;

6.4.3. shall form and have at their disposal local government environmental protection funds, shall establish the amount of subsidies allocated for environmental protection, and shall document the necessity of subsidisation from the state budget;

6.4.4. shall, within the established limits, distribute national resources which are at their disposal;

6.4.5. may, in agreement with the Government of the Republic of Lithuania and the Department of Environment Protection, establish norms on their own territory which are stricter than state standards, and may create local nature preserves and monuments; and

6.4.6. shall carry out other activities prescribed to them by law.

Chapter 2. The rights and duties of citizens and public organisations of the Republic of Lithuania

Article 7. Rights and duties of citizens and public organisations
Citizens and public organisations shall have the right:

7.1. to receive accurate and up-to-date ecological information;

7.2. to take part in the discussion and implementation of programmes and projects of economic activities;

7.3. to demand that economic activities which are hazardous to the environment be terminated;

7.4. to request state ecological examinations;

7.5. to carry out public ecological examinations;

7.6. to organise public inspections or environmental protection;

7.7. to demand that the state authorities and institutions organise ecological education and instruction, and to freely advocate concepts of environmental protection, and

7.8. to insist upon the punishment of persons guilty of endangering the environment, and of officers, who have improperly carried out the duties of environmental protection ascribed to them;

Article 8. Duties of state authorities, administrators, and inspectors in guaranteeing the rights of citizens and public organisations
State authorities, administrators, and inspectors, pursuant to their jurisdiction, must:

8.1. establish ecologically based standards of environmental protection which can be achieved by technological means, supervise their changes, and inform the public thereof;

8.2. either comply with or justifiably decline the proposals of citizens or public organisations concerning environmental issues;

8.3. publicly announce plans of economic activities which may have a hazardous impact on the environment;

8.4. prevent the violation of laws, norms and standards of environmental protection by subjects engaged in economic activities;

8.5. either carry out or justifiably decline to carry out a state ecological examination if the public so requests;

8.6. evaluate the findings of state ecological examinations, and either take them up as matters of importance or justifiably turn them down;

8.7. guarantee that the damage caused to the environment by unlawful activities be redeemed, and persons guilty of these damages be punished;

8.8. organise ecological education and instruction; and

8.9. encourage the participation of citizens and public organisations in environmental protection.

Article 9. Duties of citizens and public organisations
Citizens and public organisations or the Republic of Lithuania must protect the environment, use natural resources in an economical way, and avoid violation of the rights and interests of other users of natural resources.

Article 10. Rights and duties of foreign citizens and stateless persons
Foreign citizens and stateless persons must abide by the rights and duties of the citizens of the Republic of Lithuania as established by this Law, if other laws of the Republic of Lithuania do not provide otherwise.

Chapter 3. Utilisation and registration of natural resources

Article 11. The object of the utilisation of natural resources
The object of the utilisation of natural resources shall be the existing natural resources which are in the jurisdiction of the Republic of Lithuania.

Article 12. Objects of special utilisation
12.1. The objects of special utilisation shall be:

12.1.1. protected territories: reserves of the state, national parks, regional parks, nature reserves, protective zones, and areas of local significance and special purpose;

12.1.2. the natural framework, identified and formed as the system of territories of ecological compensation, consisting of protected and other ecologically significant and sufficiently natural territories which maintain the stability of the landscape; and

12.1.3. natural monuments, species and communities of flora and fauna protected by the State.

12.2. Protection of the objects used for special purpose shall be regulated by separate laws.

Article 13. State registration of natural resources
The procedure of state registration of natural resources, as well as the custody of the cadastre shall be determined by the Government of the Republic of Lithuania and the Department of the Environmental Protection.

Article 14. Users of natural resources
14.1. Natural resources may be used by legal and natural persons.

14.2. The basis of the utilisation of natural resources shall be either the right of ownership or the right of utilisation.

The users of natural resources must:

14.2.1. evaluate the possible impact of economic activities on the environment;

14.2.2. utilise natural resources in a rational and economical way;

14.2.3. implement means of either eliminating or reducing hazardous impact on the environment;

14.2.4. take measures to avoid endangering the environment, and in the event that hazardous effects do occur, must immediately eliminate the cause of such effects and inform the appropriate officers and institutions of the occurrence;

14.2.5. avoid violation of the rights and legitimate interests of other users of natural resources;

14.2.6. redeem the damages caused by unlawful activities which have hazardously affected the environment; and

14.2.7. fulfil the legitimate requirements of environmental protection institutions and their officers.

Chapter 4. Regulations of economic activities

Article 15. Forecast of the impact on the environment
15.1. Legal and natural persons, applying for permits to engage in economic activities, shall, at their own expense, prepare and submit to the Department of the Environmental Protection of the Republic of Lithuania documents concerning possible impact of such activities on the environment.

15.2. The Department of Environmental Protection of the Republic of Lithuania shall evaluate the documents concerning the possible impact of economic activities on the environment and present a motivated conclusion, which is requisite in order for a state institution to issue a permit to engage in economic activities.

15.3. The procedure of the preparation of documents concerning the possible impact of economic activities on the environment shall be established by the Department of Environmental Protection of the Republic of Lithuania in conjunction with the Government of the Republic of Lithuania.

Article 16. Planning of economic activities
16.1. Legal and natural persons wishing to construct, reconstruct, or expand units of economic activities must prepare project documentation. Such documentation must include means to utilise natural resources rationally, to avoid industrial accidents and eliminate their causes and consequences, and to guarantee the observation of the norms of

environmental quality. Such project documentation shall be coordinated with the Department of Environmental Protection of the Republic of Lithuania.

Article 17. Construction, reconstruction or expansion of units of economic activities
17.1. Legal and natural persons may construct, reconstruct, or expand units of economic activities only if they have project documentation which is in compliance with the requirements provided for in Article 16 of this Law.

17.2. Parties involved in the construction, reconstruction, or expansion of units of economic activity who do not have project documentation as detailed in Article 16 of this law, or who are not complying with the requirements of environmental protection, or who, in the process of construction, reconstruction or expansion of these units, violate restrictions of environmental protection, shall be liable in the manner established by law.

17.3. The imposition of liability shall not prevent institutions of administration and control of environmental protection established in Article 6 of this law, as well as their officials, from discontinuing, in the established manner, activities of construction, reconstruction or expansion.

Article 18. Pre-operation review of newly built, reconstructed, or expanded units of economic activities
18.1. The operation of newly built, reconstructed, or expanded units of economic activities shall be permitted only if they comply with the requirements of environmental protection set forth in the documentation of their construction project.

18.2. Officials of the Department of Environmental Protection shall be present in the review of newly built, reconstructed, or expanded units of economic activities.

Article 19. Operation of units of economic activities
19.1. Prior to operating units of economic activities, legal and natural persons must obtain a permit (ecological passport) for the utilisation of natural resources and the discharge of pollutants into the environment in the manner established by the Department of Environmental Protection.

19.2. Legal and natural persons shall operate units of economic activities under the conditions established in the permit for the utilisation of natural resources and the discharge of pollutants into the environment and shall not exceed the norms and standards of environmental quality.

19.3. Legal and natural persons, while operating units of economic activities which are potentially hazardous to the environment, must, at their own expense, monitor the degree of environmental pollution and its impact on the environment, guarantee that information concerning the pollution be available to the public, and provide conditions for pollution control.

19.4. Legal and natural persons, while operating units of economic activities, must keep records of the utilisation of natural resources and the discharge of pollutants in the manner established by the Department of the Environmental Protection of the Republic of Lithuania.

19.5. Legal and natural persons operating units of economic activities which do not require permits for the utilisation of natural resources and the discharge of pollutants into the environment, must comply with the norms and standards of environmental quality established for such units.

Bronius Kuzmickas, Vice-President, Supreme Council, Republic of Lithuania

Vilnius, 21 January 1992, No.1-2223

LITHUANIA D

Law on the Department of Environmental Protection

July 1990

Chapter 1. General provisions

Article 1. The Department of Environmental Protection of the Republic of Lithuania shall be a state body accountable to the Supreme Council of the Republic of Lithuania and responsible for the regulation of the use of natural resources and control of environmental protection.

Article 2. The Department of Environmental Protection shall function in accordance with the Provisional Basic Law of the Republic of Lithuania, this Law, as well as other laws and legislative acts of the Republic of Lithuania.

Article 3. Decisions of the Department of Environmental Protection adopted within its jurisdiction shall be binding upon all ministries, local governments, military units, and other legal and natural persons.

Article 4. The Department of Environmental Protection of the Republic of Lithuania shall coordinate legislative acts on the issues related to the use of natural resources and environmental protection adopted by ministries, departments and local governments.

Article 5. The Department of Environmental Protection of the Republic of Lithuania shall submit an annual report to the Supreme Council of the Republic of Lithuania on the use of natural resources and the state of environmental protection.

Article 6. The Department of Environmental Protection shall prepare an estimate of expenditures which, upon its presentation by the General Director of the Department, shall be approved by the Supreme Council of the Republic of Lithuania.

Chapter 2. Objectives and functions

Article 7. The Department of Environmental Protection shall:

7.1. ensure state regulation of the use of natural resources and state monitoring of the environmental protection in the Republic, including its territorial waters, continental shelf and economic zone; and

7.2. protect the characteristic landscape of the Republic, as well as its separate areas, ecological systems, and natural objects of scientific, cognitive and historical–cultural value.

Article 8. The Department of Environmental Protection of the Republic of Lithuania shall implement state policy in the spheres of utilisation of natural resources and environmental protection, and perform the following functions:

8.1. monitor the use of natural resources and environmental protection;

8.2. at the behest of the Supreme Council of the Republic of Lithuania and on its own initiative draft laws, within the limits of its powers, adopt legislative acts, approve norms and standards for the utilisation of natural resources and environmental protection;

8.3. regulate and monitor the survey and utilisation of natural resources, establish optimum permissible utilisation of natural resources;

8.4. regulate and control human activity in protected areas and preservation zones, manage state natural reserves, compile and update the Red Book;

8.5. establish the procedure for coordinating ecological investigation and development plans, organise and implement these tasks;

8.6. prepare national special-purpose programmes of the utilisation of natural resources and environmental protection and monitor their implementation;

8.7. organise, coordinate and perform overall ecological monitoring;

8.8. organise, coordinate and carry out scientific investigation of the utilisation of natural resources and environmental protection;

8.9. create the State Environmental Protection Fund and use the moneys contained in the said Fund as prescribed by the regulations of the State Environmental Protection Fund;

8.10. cooperate with foreign countries and represent the Republic of Lithuania in international organisations and at conferences on issues related to the utilisation of natural resources and environmental protection;

8.11. monitor the implementation of international agreements on environmental protection;

8.12. inform the public on the state of the environment and coordinate public ecological education programmes; and

8.13. as needed, organise the implementation of other measures of environmental protection.

Chapter 3. Powers

Article 9. Within its powers the Department of Environmental Protection shall:

9.1. submit to the institutions responsible for the approval of projects binding recommendations on the issues of environmental protection in relation to the location, construction, reconstruction and planned expansion of economic and other facilities;

9.2. suspend the construction or reconstruction of economic and other facilities if environmental protection regulations are violated;

9.3. suspend or restrict the activities of enterprises, institutions, and organisations if they violate laws on environmental protection, fail to implement measures of environmental protection, or if their activities contradict the norms and standards of environmental protection;

9.4. submit to the Supreme Council of the Republic of Lithuania plans for the establishment of state reservations, nature reserves, national and natural parks, and other protected areas;

9.5. designate natural monuments for special protection;

9.6. file claims for damages resulting from pollution of the environment and unscientific use of natural resources; prepare and approve the procedure and tariffs for assessing damages;

9.7. investigate cases of administrative liability for the violation of laws on environmental protection and impose penalties therefor; propose the removal from office of officials responsible for gross violations of environmental protection legislation;

9.8. issue licences for prospecting and utilising natural resources, for storing and burying domestic and industrial wastes, and for discharging pollutants, as well as promulgate pollutant discharge limits and regulations;

9.9. within its powers issue permits for blasting operations and hydro-technical works, promulgate environmental protection limits for the use of motor and power boats;

9.10. stop and inspect Lithuanian and foreign ships, and other vessels in the internal and territorial waters, and in the economic zone, and exercise state environmental control;

9.11. obtain from the Government of Lithuania drafts of planned decisions and information on issues concerning utilisation of natural resources and environmental protection; apply to the Supreme Council of the Republic of Lithuania for repealing Government acts that violate regulations of environmental protection;

9.12. obtain from ministries, departments, local governments, enterprises, institutions, and organisations information and statistical and other data on issues concerning utilisation of natural resources and environmental protection; and

9.13. obtain from heads of enterprises, institutions, and organisations oral and written explanations, required certificates, and copies of documents concerning utilisation of natural resources and environmental protection.

Article 10. Officers of the Department of Environmental Protection shall have the right to enter without hindrance the territories and facilities of all enterprises, institutions, organisations, farms, and military units to perform environmental control as well as special tests and special measurements.

Article 11. The Department of Environmental Protection of the Republic of Lithuania shall consist of a central apparatus, district divisions, district inspectorates, and other organisations subordinate to it.

Article 12. The head of the Department of Environmental Protection shall be the General Director of the Department who shall be appointed or removed from office by the Supreme Council of the Republic of Lithuania.

Article 13. The General Director shall:

13.1. organise the work of the Department and be responsible for its functioning;

13.2. represent the Department of Environmental Protection of the Republic of Lithuania;

13.3. approve the structure and number of employees of the Department of Environmental Protection within the limits of funds appropriated for Department salaries, the rules and regulations of the structural subdivisions of the Department, as well as their internal rules and regulations; establish the procedure for state monitoring of environmental protection;

13.4. form commissions for the consideration of more complex issues; and

13.5. issue directives, approve instructions, regulations, and methods of functioning; adopt other decisions within the limits of his powers.

Article 14. The Department of Environmental Protection shall include the Council of the Utilisation of Natural Resources and Environmental Protection, which shall also include ex officio the General Director of the Department.
The decisions of the Council shall be implemented upon the General Director's instructions.

Article 15. The Department of Environmental Protection of the Republic of Lithuania shall have the rights of a legal person. The Department shall have its own seal with the State emblem of the Republic of Lithuania, its own emblem and other symbols.

Poland*

EIA regulations	Decree of the Environment Minister on Investments Especially Harmful to the Environment and Human Health and the Conditions for Environmental Impact Assessments for Investments and Buildings, Prepared by Experts, 23 April 1990 (Document A) Decree of the Environment Minister on Establishing the Commission for Environmental Impact Assessment, No.22, December 1989 (Document B)
EIA authorities	Ministry of Environmental Protection, Natural Resources and Forestry. District government environmental departments. Self-governing commune executive offices.
Responsibilities for EIA	The Ministry keeps a register of experts allowed to prepare an Environmental Impact Statement.
Regulatory context for EIA	EIA is part of a two-stage siting process: obtaining a *site directive* and *siting permission*. Both stages require EIA documentation. For projects 'especially harmful to the environment and human health', the EIA review takes place at the first stage. Consultations continue through the second stage, although they are not legally required. EIA can also be required for project designs.
Activities subject to EIA	List of projects 'especially harmful to the environment and human health', requiring mandatory EIA. EIAs may be required by the district authority for projects 'which may affect the environment'. EIAs may be required for existing facilities and for project designs.
Scoping	None.
Environmental Impact Statement: site directive	The developer contracts certified experts to produce an Environmental Impact Statement, the scope and format of which are defined in regulations. The Statement describes the potential environmental impacts of the project irrespective of the site.
Environmental Impact Statement: site decision	The process of drawing up the Statement is the same as above. The Statement is more detailed, describing impacts at the particular site chosen.

* Original reference material provided by Dr. Andrzej Kassenberg, Institute for Sustainable Development (Warsaw). Updated material drawn from the journal of the Commission for Environmental Impact Assessment in Poland, and provided by Dr. Stanislaw Wajda, Advisor, EC Phare Programme, Ministry of Environmental Protection, Natural Resources and Forestry (Warsaw)

Review	The first Environmental Impact Statement is reviewed by an Environmental Impact Assessment Commission of independent experts. Such Commissions exist at the national level and in three districts. If a Commission does not exist, the review takes place at a meeting of the developer, EIA expert and regional environmental authority. The Commission advises the Minister or district authority.
Public participation	The EIA Commissions involve the public in their discussions at their own discretion. There is no legal right for the public to participate.
Approval	The Minister of Environment or district environmental authority makes a decision on the EIA, taking into account the view of the Commission. Consultation continues through the siting permission stage, although not it is legally required.
Development consent	Projects for which an EIA is mandatory require EIA approval before a site can be given.
Transboundary EIA	Poland has signed the Espoo Convention on EIA in a Transboundary Context, but commitments under this convention are not yet written into legislation.

1. Introduction

Population: 38 million
Area: 323,250 sq km
Currency: Złoty

Principal environmental problems

The sources of environmental damage in Poland are confined to a limited number of sites. These sites, however, are heavily polluted and a large number of people are at risk, especially as a result of air pollution. About 50% of airborne pollution originates from 15% of the total land area, and just five enterprises in Katowice district produce over 10% of the country's particulate pollution (World Bank Report: Poland Environmental Strategy, 1992).

Water pollution is another problem area. Most pollution in the Vistula and Odra rivers originates from just three coal mines discharging saline water and brine. Water pollution aggravates a water scarcity problem – Poland has among the lowest per capita water resources in Europe.

Environmental policy

Government policy advocates market reforms, such as increased energy prices and energy conservation, as a cost-effective way of addressing environmental problems. At the same time, considerable effort is being made to preserve important natural areas, notably the north-east with its relatively untouched primeval forests.

2. Legislative and institutional framework for EIA

2.1 Administrative structure and responsibilities for EIA

Poland is divided into 49 districts (voivodships), which are further divided into 2,459 self-governing communes. The 49 districts have a total of 267 regional offices, headed by regional directors.

Central government

The *Ministry of Environmental Protection, Natural Resources and Forestry* is the highest environmental authority. It does not have district or regional departments, the environmental departments at the district level being part of district government.

The Minister has the following tasks in relation to EIA:

- reviewing and approving EIAs for projects especially harmful to the environment and human health, jointly with the Chief Sanitary Inspector;
- defining the standard form and contents of the EIA, jointly with the Chief Sanitary Inspector (the Ministry is currently revising EIA regulations);
- maintaining a list of consultants and organisations authorised to undertake EIA.

The *State Sanitary Inspectorate* reviews the impact of projects on human health.

The *Nuclear Energy Agency* must be consulted during the planning of nuclear facilities.

Districts

Districts perform general executive functions which correspond to the tasks of central government. District governors are appointed by central government.

Districts have environmental departments, which issue environmental permits and land use permits and play a role in enforcing environmental regulations. The district governor can require developers to carry out an EIA even if the project is not on the list of mandatory EIAs.

District planning authorities are also responsible for issuing land use and building permits.

Communes

Self-governing communes have executive offices with an environmental division.

The commune is responsible for issuing siting permits for all projects. The commune is also responsible for determining EIA requirements for local projects.

For local projects of all kinds, the entire siting process is the responsibility of local self-government, and EIA requirements are at the discretion of government at that level.

Environmental Impact Assessment Commission

The Environmental Impact Assessment Commission, created by the *Decree on Establishing the Commission for Environmental Impact Assessment, 1989* (Document B), reviews EIAs of projects deemed to be especially harmful to the environment and human health. The Commission is made up of 75 independent experts and representatives of environmental groups, nominated for a period of four years. For each review, between 15 and 25 members are selected. Representatives of district authorities and communes, local environmental groups and the local press are invited to each meeting of the Commission.

Future changes

Poland's administrative structure is undergoing a process of reform. It is proposed that 12 districts will replace the existing 49. Each of the districts will be divided into counties. Communes will continue to exist as self-governing authorities.

2.2 Sources of legislation relating to EIA

2.2.1 Legislation on EIA

- *Decree of the Environment Minister on Investments Especially Harmful to the Environment and Human Health and the Conditions for Environmental Impact Assessments for Investments and Buildings, Prepared by Experts, 23 April 1990* (Document A)

(Referred to below as '*EIA Decree, 1990*'.)

The Decree specifies EIA procedures. It defines categories of projects which are especially harmful to the environment and human health. It is expected that the regulation will be amended to include more projects for which an EIA is mandatory. A further amendment is expected to strengthen the independent review of EIAs.

- *Decree of the Environment Minister on Establishing the Commission for Environmental Impact Assessment, No.22, December 1989* (Document B)

The Decree defines the role, composition and responsibilities of the Commission for Environmental Impact Assessment.

- *Law on the Protection and Shaping of the Environment, January 1980*, as amended in 1983, 1987, 1989, 1990, 1991, 1993 (Document C)

The Law sets the rules governing the protection and rational management of the environment, with a view to preserving the quality of the environment for present and future generations and the right to use natural resources. The 1993 amendments made significant changes to the EIA process.

2.2.2 Legislation related to EIA

- *Law on Land Use Planning, July 1984*, amended in 1989, 1990 (Document D)

The Law deals with development planning, which involves:

- evaluating the current landscape;
- drawing up development forecasts;
- preparing development plans;
- deciding on project siting;
- monitoring the progress of project implementation.

The Law requires that the siting of projects especially harmful to the environment and human health must be discussed with the Minister of Environment and the Chief Sanitary Inspector. The Minister and the Inspector must define the EIA procedure.

- *Ordinance of the Council of Ministers on the Classification of Investments and the Scope, Principles and Procedures of their Location, June 1985* (Document E), as amended in 1990

The Ordinance establishes the procedures for siting various kinds of projects:

- national level by the Central Planning Office;
- district level by district authority;
- local level by communes.

The Ordinance obliges the developer to complete an EIA for projects especially harmful to the environment and human health. The assessment must be made at two stages: while applying for a site directive and while applying for permission to use a site.

- *Ordinance of the Council of Ministers concerning the Rules for Establishing and Managing Protection Zones, September 1980*

The Ordinance deals with establishing 'protection zones' around facilities which have an adverse environmental impact. Within a protection zone, the Ordinance prohibits the construction of houses, holiday centres, public buildings and other facilities intended for permanent human presence, and the siting of employee allotments and sports or recreation facilities. The Minister of Administration, Land Economy and Environmental Protection defines the limits and approximate standard width of protection zones. (In relation to this mandate, this minister has now been replaced by the Minister of Environmental Protection, Natural Resources and Forestry.)

If there is a possibility that the facility will exceed environmental standards, it is necessary to establish a protection zone. At present, this provision is not applied in practice, as each new, modernised or extended facility must comply with the legal environmental standards.

- *Ordinance of the Council of Ministers on Establishing Size of Protected Zones, June 1993*

The Ordinance defines protection zones for coastal waters in dune areas, cliff areas and flood zone areas.

- *Law on Forests, September 1991*

The Law establishes requirements for the conservation, protection, use and development of forest resources. Certain forests are protected more strictly than others.

- *Ordinance of the Council of Ministers concerning Detailed Rules for Protecting Forests against the Adverse Impact of Gases and Particulates, October 1980*

In the case of emissions of gas and particulates which affect forests, it is necessary to establish forest protection zones. The procedures for establishing such zones shall be defined by the Minister of Forestry and Timber Industry in consultation with the Minister of Administration, Land Economy and Environmental Protection. (In relation to this mandate, this minister has been replaced by the Minister of Environmental Protection, Natural Resources and Forestry.)

This Ordinance should be taken into account on carrying out an EIA, if it is possible that polluted air will have an adverse effect on forests.

- *Regulation of the Minister of Administration, Land Economy and Environmental Protection concerning Detailed Rules for Determining the Area, Limits and Approximate Standard Width of Protection Zones, November 1982*

On siting a facility, it is necessary to consider establishing a protection zone if it is possible that permissible environmental standards will be exceeded outside the premises of the facility. At present, this provision is not applied in practice, as each new, modernised or extended facility must comply with the legal environmental standards.

- *Ordinance of the Council of Ministers concerning Detailed Standards of Landscape Conservation, January 1987*

The Ordinance sets rules for landscape conservation. It states that district environmental departments may demand an environmental evaluation for a project which modifies the land and alters the environment.

Although the above provision is not related to EIA procedures, it is similar in character and may be applied in the case of major earth works or if the facility occupies a large area.

- *Law on Nature Conservation, October 1991*

The Law governs various aspects of the conservation, use and rehabilitation of natural resources and the environment, particularly wild plants, wild animals and ecosystems.

On carrying out an EIA, it is necessary to consider the impact of the project on natural resources and the environment, including: national parks, wildlife preserves, scenic parks, scenic preserves, protected species of plants and animals, natural monuments, data-recording stations, environmentally safe areas and natural or landscape complexes. Separate conservation standards apply to each of these natural resources.

- *Regulation of the Minister of Forestry and Timber Industry on Protecting Species of Plants, April 1983*

The Regulation lists protected species of wild plants. When conducting an EIA, it is necessary to consider the impact of the project on the various species of plants listed.

- *Regulation of the Minister of Forestry and Timber Industry on Protecting Species of Animals, April 1983*

The Regulation lists protected species of wild animals. When conducting an EIA, it is necessary to consider the impact of the project on the various animals and their habitats.

- *Water Law, October 1974*, amended in 1983, 1989, 1990, 1991

The Law governs all the aspects of water use, water conservation, flood prevention, hydro-engineering and water management.

The Law sets the standards for water conservation in protected zones near sources of water and facilities supplying drinking water. These should be considered when conducting an EIA.

- *Ordinance of the Council of Ministers on Establishing Protected Zones near Sources of Water and Water-supplying Facilities, March 1965*, amended in 1970

The Ordinance sets restrictions on the use of land and water in protected zones near sources of water and water treatment facilities. It draws a distinction between direct-protection areas and indirect-protection areas within the zones in question.

- *Regulation of the President of the Central Office of Water Management on the Classification of Rivers according to their Quality, February 1972*, amended in 1983

The Regulation lists 11 major rivers in Poland and sets their quality standards. When conducting an EIA, the project's waste-water discharge cannot alter the water quality of these 11 rivers.

- *Law on the Protection of Agricultural and Forest Land, March 1982*, amended in 1984, 1988, 1990

The Law governs various aspects of farm and forest land conservation. It includes regulations on reclaiming land for farming and forestry and changing land use.

- *Ordinance of the Council of Ministers on the Enforcement of the Law on the Protection of Agricultural and Forest Land, June 1982*

The Ordinance sets detailed rules related to: changing the purpose of farm and forest land, withdrawing land from production, preserving land from degradation, and the rules of land reclamation and land use.

The Ordinance makes it possible to calculate the costs which should be taken into account on withdrawing land from production.

- *Building Law, October 1974*, amended in 1981, 1983, 1984, 1987, 1988, 1990

The Law regulates various aspects of land use, and the design, construction, maintenance and liquidation of facilities. Facilities are defined as permanent or temporary buildings or structures such as bridges, earth works, tunnels, roads, railway lines, electricity and telecommunications networks, hydro-engineering plants, free-standing industrial and technical installations, waste treatment facilities, retaining walls, utilities, sports facilities, and structures fitted with equipment.

Facilities can be built only on land which has been set aside for this purpose, that is, in accordance with regional development plans. The Law contains a general provision related to environmental protection during the construction and utilisation of facilities, and states that a facility may not be used unless it is equipped with the necessary environmental control equipment.

- *Ordinance of the Minister of Land Economy and Environmental Protection on Urban and Construction Supervision, February 1975*, amended in 1976

The Ordinance deals with the siting and operation of projects. It outlines the responsibilities of developers and the district or commune authorities.

The Ordinance deals with environmental protection in construction, and the creation of protection zones.

- *Geological Law, November 1980*, amended in 1974, 1988, 1989, 1990, 1991

The Law sets the rules for conducting geological surveys to determine rock formations and the distribution of mineral resources and groundwater.

- *Resolution No.64 by the Council of Ministers on Determining Groundwater Supplies while Investing in the Utilisation thereof, April 1989*

The Resolution sets general rules for determining how the design of a project should be adapted to take account of the groundwater supply.

- *Law on Mining, May 1953*, amended in 1978, 1984, 1987, 1988, 1989, 1990, 1991

The Law sets the rules for issuing mining concessions and charging mining fees. It defines the jurisdiction for the design, construction, maintenance and liquidation of mines.

The Law applies to the following natural resources:

- bituminous coal, lignite, natural gas, crude oil, bituminous shales, natural mineral wax and mineral pitch;
- metals;
- rock salt, potassium or magnesium salt, sulphur, anhydride, barytes, fluorite, phosphorite and pyrite.

The Law sets general rules for mining operations to ensure that natural resources are managed and extracted in a rational way. The law aims to minimise the impact of mines on the environment and places of historical interest.

- *Ordinance of the Council of Ministers on Detailed Rules for Protecting Mining Areas, June 1978*

The Ordinance defines the rules, standards, practices and requirements for protecting mining areas.

- *Ordinance of Minister of Environmental Protection, Natural Resources and Forestry on the Procedure for Preparing and Adopting Mineral Resource Excavation Projects defined in the Law on Mining, August 1992*

This Ordinance states that an EIA is required for mining operations.

- *Ordinance of Minister of Environmental Protection, Natural Resources and Forestry on the Procedure for Preparing and Adopting Mineral Resource Excavation Projects other than those defined in the Law on Mining, August 1992*

This Ordinance states that an EIA is required for mining operations.

- *Nuclear Energy Law, April 1986*, amended in 1987

The Law deals with operations related to the use of nuclear energy for industrial and commercial purposes.

The Law contains general provisions related to maximum doses, types of nuclear facilities and siting procedures.

During the process of designing, constructing, operating and testing a facility the developer is obliged to ensure safety and protection from nuclear radiation.

In addition to the developer, other participants in the project are obliged to ensure safety and protection from nuclear radiation.

As part of the developer's application for a siting permit, the President of the Nuclear Energy Agency reviews the nuclear safety and protection measures of the project.

The siting permit is only granted when safety standards have been met.

- *Regulation of the President of the State Nuclear Energy Agency, June 1989*

The Regulation sets detailed rules and standards for nuclear safety and emergency procedures.

- *Law on Health Resorts and Health Service in Resorts, June 1966*, amended in 1987, 1989

The Law deals with the siting of health resorts and the environmental standards with which the resorts must comply.

- *Regulation of the Minister of Health and Social Welfare Listing Localities Designated as Health Resorts, July 1967*, amended in 1974

The Regulation lists localities designated as health resorts. When siting projects within or near these localities, it is necessary to comply with the stricter environmental standards which apply.

- *Ordinance of the Council of Ministers on Extending some Provisions Related to Health Resorts to Cover other Localities, December 1970*, amended in 1974, 1987

The Ordinance lists localities which could in future be classified as health resorts and where strict environmental standards apply. When siting a project within or near these areas, it is necessary to consider that the locality may become a health resort in the future.

- *Law on the State Sanitary Inspectorate, March 1985*, amended in 1989

The Law defines the roles of the State Sanitary Inspectorate.

- *Law on the State Inspectorate of Environmental Protection, July 1991*

The Law defines the functions of the State Inspectorate of Environmental Protection.

3. Environmental impact assessment process

3.1 Activities subject to EIA

There are a number of categories of projects for which EIAs are mandatory or discretionary.

- Projects 'especially harmful to the environment and human health' require mandatory EIA. These projects are mentioned in Article 39.1, *Law on Land Use Planning, 1984* (Document D) and listed in Article 2, *EIA Decree, 1990* (Document A).
- Projects 'which may harm the environment'. No definition is given of such projects. The district authority decides whether an EIA is necessary. These projects are mentioned in Articles 4.2 and 6.2, *Ordinance on the Classification of Investments and the Scope, Principles and Procedures of their Location, 1985* (Document E).
- Designs of projects 'which may harm the environment'. No definition is given of such projects. The district authority decides whether an EIA is necessary. These projects are mentioned in Article 68.5, *Law on Protecting and Shaping of the Environment, 1980* (Document C).

- District governors can require owners of existing projects to carry out an 'EIA', in effect an environmental audit (Article 7, *EIA Decree, 1990*).

Various environmental laws define requirements for environmental approvals in particular cases, for example, mining and nuclear projects. These laws are listed in section 2.2.

3.2 Regulatory framework for EIA

There is no fully coherent EIA process in Poland. Elements of EIA are defined in a variety of regulations and laws. Three kinds of EIA appear in the legislation:

- for planned projects; this EIA takes place as part of a two-stage site selection process;
- for project designs; in practice these are sometimes required by a district authority when other forms of EIA have been overlooked;
- for existing facilities, in effect an environmental audit.

EIA for planned projects: site selection

The main EIA process takes place as part of a two-stage process of selecting a site for a project (*Law on Land Use Planning, 1984*):

- obtaining a *site directive*: before a site is firmly established, a preliminary site is recommended, together with suitable alternatives, as a response to the initial application lodged by the proposer[1];
- obtaining a *site decision* – permission from the authorities to use the chosen site.

Environmental documentation must be submitted at both stages, but the law does not require a second EIA review at the second stage. In practice, consultation with the reviewing body does continue into the second stage.

(a) Applying for a site directive: According to Article 38.1, *Law on Land Use Planning, 1984*, site directives are issued by:

- the Central Planning Office for projects of national significance;
- district governor for projects of regional significance;
- the commune authority for projects of local significance.

To enable the authority to do this, the developer must first provide it with general information about the project, as outlined in Article 4.1, *Ordinance on the Classification of Investments and the Scope, Principles and Procedures of their Location, 1985*.

For projects requiring an EIA, the documentation must include information about the environmental impacts of the proposed project, irrespective of where it is located (see section 3.4). It is not possible, therefore, to be precise about the environmental impacts of the project at this stage.

Site directives cannot be issued without the necessary consultations and agreements with other 'interested institutions' or 'appropriate competent district or local authorities' (Articles 38.2, 39.1 and 2, *Law on Land Use Planning, 1984*).

The EIA review takes place at this stage of the planning process (see section 3.5).

[1] Certain types of investment do not require this procedure, provided that they do not harm the environment or human health (Article 2, Ordinance on the Classification of Investments and the Scope, Principles and Procedures of their Location, 1985).

Having obtained a site directive and after selecting a site, the investor must conclude an agreement with the district governor or the commune authority on 'mutual obligations and services' related to project implementation and future operation (Article 42, *Law on Land Use Planning, 1984*).

(b) Applying for a site decision: Having concluded the above agreement, the proposer applies for a site decision (Article 42, *Law on Land Use Planning, 1984*). The application is lodged with the district governor for projects of national significance, linear projects (roads, pipelines, etc.), projects of district significance, or projects connected with national defence. For other projects, the application is lodged with the commune authority. (Note: the authorities competent for site directives are not necessarily the same as those competent for site decisions.)

The location of projects is defined primarily by regional and local development plans.

For projects requiring an EIA, the documentation must include information about the potential impacts of the project *at that particular site*, including impacts on the 'natural beauty' of the site (see section 3.4). This is called the 'comprehensive EIA', involving more detailed information than at the first stage.

Current law does not require that the environmental authority be involved in the review of this documentation. In practice, however, consultations do continue through this stage of the planning process.

This two-stage approach is soon to be simplified to one stage (see section 6).

Environmental permits

In order to obtain a building permit, various environmental permits are required. Although applying for these permits is in practice related to the EIA procedure, in law the procedures for applications for building and location permits are separate.

All permits can contain conditions for installing and maintaining pollution control equipment and monitoring emissions.

All permits should be issued within a month, according to the *Code of Administrative Procedure*, although it often takes longer.

Air emissions
Criteria: all air emissions
Issuing authority: district
Application requirements: *Law on Protection and Shaping of the Environment, 1980*

Water use
Criteria: use of surface and groundwater above specified levels
Issuing authority: district
Application requirements: *Water Law, 1974*

Water discharge
Criteria: discharge into surface waters and the ground
Issuing authority: district
Application requirements: *Water Law, 1974*

Waste storage, treatment and disposal sites
Criteria: waste storage treatment sites have to be included in land use plans, and must have permits
Issuing authority: region
Application requirements: *Building Law, 1974*, as amended

Other sectoral permits
See legislation in section 2.2.

3.3 Responsibilities for EIA

EIA documentation must be compiled by an expert from a list drawn up by the Minister of Environment. The investor is free to choose the expert (Article 70.1, *Law on the Protection and Shaping of the Environment, 1980*, as amended in 1993). (Article 4.2 of the *Ordinance on the Classification of Investments and the Scope, Principles and Procedures of their Location, 1985* still states that the expert is chosen by the district governor, but the amended *Law on the Protection and Shaping of the Environment, 1980* is superior in law.)

EIA for existing installations allows the proposer to choose from the list of experts drawn up by the Minister of Environment (Article 70.1, *Law on the Protection and Shaping of the Environment, 1980*, as amended in 1993).

EIA for project designs can be performed by an expert chosen by the district governor. There is no reference to the list of experts (Article 68.5, *Law on the Protection and Shaping of the Environment, 1980*).

Article 70a.1 of the *Law on the Protection and Shaping of the Environment, 1980*, as amended in 1993, authorises the Minister of Environment to enact a decree defining the qualifications of experts on the list and the procedure for selecting these experts. This decree has not yet been published. Until then, a former list of EIA experts exists and will be used until replaced.

The developer must pay for the EIA (Article 70.2, *Law on the Protection and Shaping of the Environment, 1980*).

3.4 Scope of EIA and environmental impact statement

The EIA covers construction, operation and liquidation, and evaluates the following factors:

- land use plans for the area;
- general environmental regulations and standards;
- regulations particular to the site in question or particular to the type of project (for example, see laws in section 2.2);
- impacts on human health;
- impacts on 'natural beauty'.

There is no scoping process. The content of the Environmental Impact Statement is defined in the regulations. There are plans for the Environmental Impact Assessment Commission (see section 3.6) to carry out a scoping process for each EIA.

Projects especially harmful to the environment and human health

(a) Applying for a site directive: In order to enable the authority to make a choice of site, the first Environmental Impact Statement furnishes it with information about the environmental impacts of the project irrespective of where it is located (Article 4.1, EIA *Decree, 1990*).

The Environmental Impact Statement includes the following (Article 4.2, *EIA Decree, 1990*):

- description of technologies applied;
- estimate of consumption of energy and materials, and output of waste and pollutants; assessment of environmental impact;
- description of measures taken to protect the environment and minimise environmental impacts, together with an outline of their technological and economic efficiency;
- the size of the protection zone if adverse effects are not kept within prescribed limits (since other legislation forbids any such construction, this requirement is rendered void);
- forecast of possible changes in the environment resulting from the project.

(b) Applying for a site decision: Once the site has been chosen, information about the particular environmental impacts at that site is required. The Environmental Impact Statement (called the 'comprehensive EIA' is adjusted to the selected site and is more detailed (Article 5.2, *EIA Decree, 1990*):

- description of the site and the current environmental conditions there, and a list of those elements of the environment most likely to be adversely affected by the project;
- description of permissible impacts and burdens on the environment at the site – air pollution, noise and vibration levels, etc.;
- assessment of potential impacts – direct, indirect and long-term – of the project on the environment, human health and natural beauty of the area; the use of natural resources, discharge of pollution and storage of waste on the site should be assessed in this way.

Other projects

For projects categorised as possibly having an impact on the environment, a comparison with other technologies applied in the country or abroad is required (Article 6, *EIA Decree, 1990*).

Existing facilities

Environmental Impact Statements for existing facilities (environmental audits) require the following information (Article 7, *EIA Decree, 1990*):

- assessment of current and future impacts, and, where appropriate, impacts of liquidation; consideration of possible emergency situations;
- presentation of environmental data before and during operation of the facility;
- presentation of data on water consumption, waste discharge, pollutant emissions, and other adverse environmental effects of operating the facility;
- estimate of current and future impacts on environment, human health and natural beauty of the area.

3.5 Review and approval

No specific time limits exist for the review and approval of Environmental Impact Statements. The Polish *Code of Administrative Procedure* allows for one month, or two months for complicated projects. This is, however, acknowledged to be insufficient time.

Projects which are especially harmful to the environment and human health

The developer submits all the project documentation to the authority supplying the site directive (see section 3.2). This authority is required to seek agreements as follows:

- the Central Planning Office and district governors with the Minister of Environment and the Chief Sanitary Inspector;
- the commune authority with the district governor or with the authority acting on his behalf.

The authority can then submit the Environmental Impact Statement to an EIA Commission of independent experts. One such Commission exists at the national level and answers to the Minister of Environment (*Decree on Establishing the Commission for Environmental Impact Assessment, 1989* (Document B)). Three Commissions exist at the regional level.

The Minister of Environment's EIA Commission selects 15–25 people from among its 75 members for the review. Before this is done, the Environmental Impact Statement is sent to a group of consultants who express their opinion. After this, the Commission holds a public hearing (see section 3.6) and announces its findings. Typically the meeting is attended by the involved members of the Commission, the developer, the experts who carried out the EIA, representatives of local government and local environmental groups, and the media. The Commission has committed itself to review Environmental Impact Statements within three months.

The Commission can review EIAs for existing facilities, but in practice this has never taken place, because of lack of resources: the members of the Commission work free of charge.

The Commission publishes all the results of its work in a Bulletin which has a circulation of 1,500 in Poland. (A shortened English language version is also published – see section 7.)

On the basis of the decision of the EIA Commission and the opinion of other interested bodies, the Minister decides whether to approve the project. So far, the Minister has always fully endorsed the Commission's stance.

Potentially environmentally harmful projects

When the building and planning authority receives the application for a site directive and/or siting permission, it consults with its own environmental authority (rather than referring the matter upwards). The Environmental Impact Statement may then be reviewed at a meeting convened by the planning authority with the participation of the developer, the project engineer and the EIA consultant.

Appeals procedure

If a competent authority decides that an EIA should be performed, the addressee of the decision can challenge the decision before a superior authority. As a rule, the superior authority is the Minister of Environment. The decision of the Ministry can be challenged before the High Administrative Court.

An appeal against an EIA review is complicated because an EIA review is considered only as information required to take a decision on a substantive matter, the siting of a project. There is no legal basis for taking such a review to the High Administrative Court. A site directive or site decision, however, can be challenged in the normal way.

3.6 Public participation

No consultation with the public is legally required during the EIA process or the application for environmental permits, but it does take place in practice through the EIA Commission. The Commission is itself made up of 'representatives of scientific and social circles', and includes four representatives of non-governmental organisations among its 75 members. Furthermore, representatives of district and local authorities, local environmental groups and the local press are invited to the meeting at which the Commission gives its opinion. The announcement is followed by discussion, which the Commission takes into account when formulating its final opinion. This opinion is published in the Commission's Bulletin (see section 7), and is available to the general public.

The public can appeal to the Administrative Court against decisions of administrative bodies, including decisions related to project siting.

The public does not have a general right of access to environmental information about specific polluters. The 'right to know' is limited to citizens who have legal standing in the administrative proceedings.

Social organisations have the following rights:

- to file a complaint about environmentally damaging activities (Article 227, *Code of Administrative Procedures*);
- to file petitions for the improvement of the environment;
- to demand participation in administrative proceedings;
- to be part of district and commune planning committees.

4. Monitoring

Immediately before putting a facility into operation, the District Environmental Inspector checks that all environmental requirements have been satisfied.

There is no formal requirement for post-EIA monitoring. In the case of projects especially harmful to the environment and human health, monitoring requirements can be included in the siting permit, for example a post-implementation study at a specified date.

There are no specific penalties for withholding or falsifying information during the EIA process, apart from normal penalties for breaking the law.

5. EIA in practice

The EIA Commission reviewed 22 cases between its establishment in May 1990 and December 1993. In the majority of cases, initial applications have been returned for completion before being considered by the Commission. The Commission has withheld approval on five occasions, and required improvements in all 22 cases. It has been unable to do EIAs on existing facilities, on account of the lack of financial resources. Experience with assessments at the provincial level is not recorded.

The Commission publishes a bulletin in English, containing articles about EIA in Poland, and a summary of its activities (see section 7).

6. Possible changes in near future

Several amendments to laws are in preparation which relate to the siting process and the EIA process. They will bring the EIA process more into line with the EC Directive on EIA and the Espoo Convention on EIA in a Transboundary Context.

A new law on development planning will replace the current *Law on Land Use Planning, 1984*. The new law will simplify the siting process by reducing it to one stage only, granted at the local level. The final decision will be issued by the chief executive of the appropriate commune government, after all environmental requirements have been met, namely:

- approval from the Minister of Environmental Protection, Natural Resources and Forestry and the Chief Health Officer, for projects especially harmful to the environment;
- approval from the district governor and district health officer for projects which may harm the environment;
- Minister of Health and Social Welfare for projects located in or adjacent to spas.

The three-tier national/regional/local planning authority will be replaced by a one-tier process, where siting will be decided at the local level only.

The draft contains more details of the EIA process: projects for which an EIA is mandatory, and the content of the Environmental Impact Statement.

Another draft law represents a major modification of the current *Law on the Protection and Shaping of the Environment, 1980*. The draft extends the role of the EIA Commission by granting it the right to investigate each project twice: at the stage of scoping an assessment, and at the stage of reviewing it. The new law will establish regional or inter-regional Commissions.

Proposed amendments to the *EIA Decree, 1990* list a greater number of projects for which an EIA is mandatory, and strengthen the independent review of EIAs.

Poland's administrative structure is undergoing a process of reform. It is proposed that 12 districts will replace the existing 49. Each of the districts will be divided into counties. Communes will continue to exist as self-governing authorities.

7. Sources of further information

Secretary of EIA Commission
Department of Science and Education
Ministry of Environmental Protection, Natural Resources and Forestry
00-922 Warsaw
ul. Wawelska 52/54

Poland
tel: (48-22) 25 84 73
fax: (48-22) 25 39 72

Dr. Stanislaw Wajda
Advisor, EU Phare Programme
Ministry of Environmental Protection, Natural Resources and Forestry
00-922 Warsaw
ul. Wawelska 52/54
Poland
tel: (48-22) 25 88 29
fax: (48-22) 25 41 41

Andrzej Kassenberg
Director
Institute for Sustainable Development
02-078 Warsaw
ul. Krzywickiego 9
Poland
tel: (48-22) 25 25 58
fax: (48-22) 25 34 61

Bulletin of the EIA Commission
Ecobaltic Foundation
80-286 Gdańsk-Wrzeszcz
Jaskowa Dolina 76
Poland
tel/fax: (48-58) 41 00 82

Ekokonsult
80-340 Gdańsk
ul. Gospody 14 D/21
Poland
tel/fax: (48-58) 57 82 29

Proeko Sp. z o.o.
Consulting Company Ltd.
02-078 Warsaw
ul. Krzywickiego 34
Poland
tel: (48-2) 625 74 56 / 625 75 23
fax: (48-2) 625 36 48

Ekolog
04-920 Piła
ul. Wojska Polskiego 43
Poland

tel: (48-67) 12 33 99
telex: EKO 047731
(Offices in Bydgoszcz, Szczecin, Warsaw, Koszalin, Poznań)

8. EIA legislation

Terms used in law	Terms used in book
EIA	EIA Process and Environmental Impact Statement
Investor/designer/contractor	Developer
Expert examination	Expert review

POLAND A

Decree of the Environment Minister on Investments Especially Harmful to the Environment and Human Health and the Conditions for Environmental Impact Assessments for Investments and Buildings, Prepared by Experts

M.P. No.16, item 126, 23 April 1990

Unofficial translation, by Institute for Sustainable Development

By virtue of Article 39 of the Law on Development Planning of 12 July 1984 (Dz. U. of 1989, No.17, item 99, No.34, item 178 and No.35, item 192) and Article 70, section 5 of the Law on Protection and Shaping of the Environment of 31 December 1980 (Dz. U. No.3, item 6 of 1983, No.44, item 201 of 1987, No.33, item 180, and of 1989, No.26, item 139 and No.35, item 192), the following provisions shall be adopted:

Article 1. The categories of projects which pose extreme environmental and health hazards, and the plans for which have to be approved by the Minister of Environmental Protection, Natural Resources and Forestry and by the Chief Sanitary Inspector prior to giving siting recommendations, are specified herein.

Article 2

2.1. A project posing extreme environmental and health hazards is a project which may, during its construction, utilisation or liquidation:

2.1.1. emit pollutants into the air in quantities exceeding:

a. 5,000 tonnes per year of particulates and gases, jointly, in borderland areas, areas of high ecological hazard and specially protected areas, and in relation to facilities located outside the above areas, which emit pollutants affecting those areas;
b. 20,000 tonnes of particulate and gases jointly within the remaining territory of the country;

2.1.2. produce and discharge untreated waste water:

a. directly into borderland waters – irrespective of its amount;
b. into flowing waters in areas of high ecological hazard and in specially protected areas – irrespective of its amount;

c. directly into the Baltic Sea, lakes, water reservoirs and soil – in quantities exceeding 100 m^3 per day;
d. into any flowing waters in the remaining territory of the country – in quantities exceeding 5,000 m^3 per day;

2.1.3. cause the deterioration of water relations in specially protected areas and in areas of high socio-economic value;

2.1.4. produce and store hazardous waste of the first category, irrespective of its amount;

2.1.5. pollute or affect the earth's surface and soil or change the purpose of areas designated as farmland or forest land within an area of:

a. over 50 hectares in areas of high ecological hazard and specially protected areas;
b. over 100 hectares within the remaining territory of the country;

2.1.6. take water:

a. from water-supplying facilities located on borderland waters – irrespective of its amount;
b. from groundwater-supplying facilities in quantities exceeding:
 – 2,000 m^3 per day in areas of high ecological hazard and specially protected areas;
 – 5,000 m^3 per day within the remaining territory of the country;
c. from surface water supplying facilities in quantities exceeding:
 – 20,000 m^3 per day in areas of high ecological hazard and specially protected areas;
 – 40,000 m^3 per day within the remaining territory of the country;

2.1.7. generate electro-magnetic fields within the frequency range of 0.1–300,000 MHz, where the effective electric field intensity or the average energy flux density of electro-magnetic fields exceed the maximum limits for protection zones, set in separate regulations;

2.1.8. cause the noise pollution levels, set in separate regulations, to be exceeded, despite technologies applied.

2.2. Projects posing extreme environmental and health hazards are also projects such as:

2.2.1. power lines and systems whose voltage exceeds 400 kV;

2.2.2. airports;

2.2.3. motorways and main through routes;

2.2.4. railway stations and main lines;

2.2.5. nuclear power plants, heat- and power-generating plants and heat-generating plants, nuclear waste cemeteries and nuclear reactors located within city administration limits;

2.2.6. gas pipelines and oil pipelines of national and international importance;

Article 3. Environmental impact assessment shall be carried out by experts for the projects posing extreme environmental and health hazards mentioned in Article 2, and for other projects, facilities or complexes of facilities which may affect the quality of the environment.

Article 4

4.1. The environmental impact assessment referred to in Article 3 shall meet the following standards:

4.1.1. examine the following elements of the environment: air, land surface, soil, minerals, surface waters and groundwater, marine environment, plant life and animal life and their interrelations;

4.1.2. take into account the construction stage and the utilisation stage, and, where appropriate, also the liquidation stage of a project, together with supporting facilities, and take into account probable emergency situations;

4.1.3. use, where appropriate, the data and figures available, including data collected during prior environmental studies, and measurements related to the quality of the environment and other environmental hazards;

4.1.4. present the problems examined in relation to the needs resulting from the nature of the phenomena described, and ensure that their analysis and interpretation are not difficult.

4.2. The assessments referred to under 4.1 above, shall include, in particular:

4.2.1. a description of technologies applied;

4.2.2. an estimate, from the point of view of materials and energy consumed, of water consumption as well as the amounts and kinds of waste and pollutants emissions, and hazard assessment;

4.2.3. a description of methods which would minimise environmental hazards and of environmental protection facilities which would ensure the above, together with a description of their technological and economic efficiency;

4.2.4. the size of a protection zone and a description of its management techniques if the adverse effects are not eliminated or kept within the limits prescribed in spite of technologies planned or applied;

4.2.5. a forecast of the possible changes in the environment related to the operations of the projected facility and to the technologies applied or the utilisation of an existing facility or a complex of facilities.

Article 5

5.1. Apart from meeting the standards mentioned in Article 4, an environmental impact assessment, serving as a basis for siting recommendations, shall also include all project variants to be examined during the process of siting.

5.2. Apart from meeting the standards mentioned in Article 4, a comprehensive environmental impact assessment necessary for collecting opinions required on submitting an application for siting permission, shall also include:

5.2.1. a description of the area round the project site and the current quality of the environment, and, in particular, a list of those elements of the environment which the project may adversely affect in a significant way;

5.2.2. a description of permissible impact and strains on the environment;

5.2.3. an assessment of potential significant impact on various elements of the environment, on human health and on the natural beauty of the area, listing direct, indirect and long-lasting effects resulting from the utilisation of natural resources, including minerals, and resulting from pollution discharges and other adverse effects, and listing types of waste produced or stored;

5.2.4. data related to the permissible pollutant levels in the air, noise levels, vibration levels and other adverse effects on the environment, and data serving as a basis for setting out the terms and conditions on which permission to use water and discharge waste water may be granted;

5.2.5. terms and conditions for using the environment.

Article 6. An environmental impact assessment carried out for a project which could affect the quality of the environment shall comply with the standards specified in Article 4, sections 1 and 2, points 1–4, and in Article 5, section 2 and it shall also include:

6.1. a comparison of the technology applied with other technologies applied in the country or abroad in the context of minimised environmental impact or strains on the environment;

6.2. an assessment of the implementation of provisions of the siting permission which set out the conditions for using the environment or the scope and manner of eliminating the sources of environmental hazards or the conditions related to the rehabilitation of the environment.

Article 7. An environmental impact assessment carried out for an existing facility or complex of facilities shall comply with the standards specified in Article 4, section 1, point 2, and in Article 5, section 2, points 1, 2, 4 and 5, and it shall also:

7.1. take into account the current and future utilisation stages, and, where appropriate, also the liquidation stage of the facility or complex of facilities, together with supporting facilities, and take into account probable emergency situations;

7.2. use, as a basis, the data on the quality of the environment collected before the facility or complex of facilities began its operations, and that collected during their operations;

7.3. take into account the figures for water consumption, waste discharge, pollutant emissions and other adverse effects on the environment, collected during the operations of the facility or complex of facilities;

7.4. include an estimate of the current and envisaged impact on the various elements of the environment, on human health and on the natural beauty of the area.

Article 8. The Regulation by the Minister/Head of the Office for Environmental Protection and Water Economy of 27 March 1985 on projects posing extreme environmental and health hazards shall lose its binding force.

Article 9. This Regulation shall take effect 14 days after promulgation.

B. Kamiński, Minister of Environmental Protection, Natural Resources and Forestry

POLAND B

Decree of the Environment Minister on Establishing the Commission for Environmental Impact Assessment No.22, 29 December 1989

Unofficial translation, by Institute for Sustainable Development

By virtue of Article 3, section 6 of the Statutes of the Ministry of Environmental Protection, Natural Resources and Forestry, constituting a Schedule to the Resolution No.187/87 of the Council of Ministers or 14 December 1987 granting statutes to the Ministry of Environmental Protection, Natural Resources and Forestry, the following provisions shall be adopted:

Article 1

1.1. A Commission for Environmental Impact Assessment, hereafter referred to as 'the Commission', shall be established as an opinion-giving body to the Minister of Environmental Protection, Natural Resources and Forestry, hereafter referred to as 'the Minister'.

1.2. The Commission shall be composed of: the Chairman of the Commission, the Commission Secretary and 75 members appointed by the Minister for a period of four years.

1.3. The Chairman of the Commission shall be appointed by the Minister.

1.4. The Chairman of the Commission shall, within two weeks of appointment, submit to the Minister a list of candidates for appointment as members of the Commission, selected from among representatives of the world of science and voluntary organisations concerned with environmental protection and environmental impact assessment.

1.5. The Minister shall appoint the Commission from among the candidates proposed by the Chairman of the Commission, including two Deputy Chairmen and six representatives of the Minister, including the Commission Secretary.

1.6. The procedures relating to the work of the Commission shall be defined in the by-laws adopted by the Commission and approved by the Minister.

Article 2. The responsibilities of the Commission shall include, in particular:

2.1. Expressing the Commission's opinion on:

2.1.1. applications for giving siting recommendations with regard to projects which pose extreme hazards to the environment and to the rational utilisation of natural resources, or those which may affect natural resources, the quality of the environment in specially protected areas, and water economy;

2.1.2. environmental impact assessments carried out for existing facilities which considerably affect the environment and the management of natural resources, including water, sent by the Minister of Environmental Protection and Natural Resources to the Commission for consideration;

2.1.3. studies related to the environmental impact of existing facilities and to applications for siting recommendations with respect to projects which may affect the quality of the environment.

2.2. Publishing information and materials promoting the methodology of environmental impact assessment.

2.3. Encouraging environmental impact assessment training for experts.

Article 3. The Department of Environmental Science and Education shall provide clerical services for the Commission.

Article 4. Members of the Commission participating in meetings shall receive reimbursement of travelling expenses, and per diem allowances, under separate provisions, and the Chairman shall receive remuneration equal to one per diem allowance, whereas the other members shall receive remuneration equal to 3/4 of the per diem allowance.

Article 5. Expenses related to the work of the Commission shall be borne by the Ministry of Environmental Protection and Natural Resources.

Article 6. The Regulation No.11 by the Minister of Environmental Protection and Natural Resources of 27 February 1987 on establishing the Commission for Environmental Impact Assessment shall cease to apply.

Article 7. This Regulation shall enter into force upon being signed.

B. Kamiński, Minister of Environmental Protection and Natural Resources

POLAND C

Law on the Protection and Shaping of the Environment

31 January 1980 (Dz. U. of 1983, No.3, item 6; of 1987, No.44, item 201; of 1989, No.33, item 180; of 1990, No.26, item 139 , No.35, item 192, No.34, item 198 and No.39, item 222)

Excerpts

Unofficial translation, by Institute for Sustainable Development

Section 3: Implementation of environmental protection procedures

Chapter 2: Environmental protection in project construction

Article 68

68.1. The investor, the designer and the contractor, each within the scope of his responsibilities, shall be under an obligation to:

68.1.1. take into account environmental protection standards while planning and constructing a project;

68.1.2. ensure that during construction – particularly the construction of houses and public buildings – building materials and construction elements are used which will effectively protect the users of those buildings against noise and vibration and other hazards to human health.

68.2. On planning a project of an economic nature, the investor and the designer shall be under an obligation to apply technological processes which will minimise its impact on the environment, and to find rational solutions to waste management and waste-water treatment, particularly by finding ways to utilise waste and waste water.

68.3. The local body of State administration[1] responsible for siting projects, and the body deciding on the expropriation of real estate, as well as the investor and the designer, shall be under an obligation to ensure economical use of the area necessary for the project.

68.4. A newly built or modernised facility or a complex of facilities may not be put to use unless environmental protection equipment, required by law or planned for that facility, has been installed.

68.5. Designs for facilities which may pose an environmental hazard shall be examined, with regard to their environmental impact, by an expert selected by the local body of State administration at province level[2] and approved by the said body. Permission shall be given in the form of a decision.

[1] Currently 'provincial governor or a communal body' (by virtue of Article 42, sections 1 and 2 of the Law on Development Planning of 12 July 1984, Dz. Ustaw of 1989: No.17, item 99, No.34, item 178, and No.35, item 192, and of 1990 No.34, item 198; and Article 53, section 1 of the Law on Local Bodies of General State Administration of 22 March 1990, Dz. U. No.21, item 123; and Article 1, point 25, subpoint m of the Law on the Division of Powers and Responsibilities defined in Specific Laws among Communal Bodies and State Administrative Bodies and on Amendments to certain Laws of 17 May 1990, Dz. U. No.34, item 198).

[2] Currently 'the provincial governor' (by virtue of Article 53, section 1 of the above-mentioned Law of 22 March 1990).

Article 69
69.1. On siting a project, environmental protection standards shall be considered in conformity with development plans and environmental legislation.

69.2. The Council of Ministers may designate, by means of an ordinance, specially protected areas, where construction projects posing environmental hazards may not be sited unless the Minister of Administration, Land Economy and Environmental Protection[3] gives his permission.

69.3. The Council of Ministers will issue a decree to define special investment requirements relating to investment projects situated in areas subject to special environmental protection.

Article 70
70.1. The local body of State administratio[4] may decide on placing the investor and the owner or the manager of a facility or complex of facilities under an obligation to have an environmental impact assessment carried out for the facility or complex of facilities by an expert from a list of specialists drawn up by the Minister of Environmental Protection, Natural Resources and Forestry.

70.2. The cost of the assessment referred to under 70.1 above shall be borne by the investor, the owner or the manager of the facility or the complex of facilities.

70.3. If the assessment required is not submitted on time, it may be commissioned at the expense of the obligor.

Article 70(a)
70(a).1. The Minister of Environmental Protection, Natural Resources and Forestry will issue a decree to define the necessary qualifications of an expert on the list of specialists, as well as the means of verifying experts and the expenses this process will involve.

70(a).2. The aforementioned list of specialists is maintained by the Minister of Environmental Protection, Natural Resources and Forestry

Chapter 3: Restriction on the use of environment

Article 73
73.1. The following shall be prohibited:

73.1.1. constructing or extending facilities which pose an environmental hazard in specially protected areas such as: national parks, wildlife reserves, scenic parks, scenic preserves, health resort areas, tourist/holiday locations, and areas with sources of water supplied to towns, villages and settlement units;

73.1.2. constructing or extending manufacturing plants or service facilities within the city administration limits and densely built-up village areas.

73.1.3. constructing – in the vicinity of the sea, lakes, other bodies of water and water

[3] Currently 'the Minister of Environmental Protection, Natural Resources and Forestry' (by virtue of the Law establishing the Office of Minister of Environmental Protection, Natural Resources and Forestry, of 20 December 1989, Dz. U. No.73, item 433).
[4] Currently 'the provincial governor' (by virtue of Article 53, section 1 of the above-mentioned Law of 22 March 1990).

reservoirs, rivers, canals, scenic points or in areas of outstanding natural beauty – facilities which affect the natural beauty of the area, make it inaccessible or make access to water difficult or impossible for wild animals.

73.2. Suspended and subterranean cables and communication lines shall be installed in such a way as to preserve the natural beauty of the area and ensure that they do not have an adverse effect on the environment.

73.3. The restrictions specified under 1 and 2 above shall be taken into account in making development plans and in siting projects.

POLAND D

Law on Land Use Planning

12 July 1984

Based on the uniform text of the Law published as a Schedule to the announcement by the Minister of Development Planning and Construction of 28 February 1989, with later amendments (Dz. U. of 1989, No.17, item 99, No.34, item 178, and No.35, item 192, and of 1990, No.34, item 198).

Excerpts

Unofficial translation, by Institute for Sustainable Development

Chapter 6: Project siting

Article 36
36.1. The siting of a project undertaken by a unit of the socialised sector and the siting of a production facility, with the exception of farm buildings, service facilities and shops, constructed by another organised unit or a natural person, as well as places of worship and churches, constructed by churches or other religious groups and their artificial persons, shall require:

36.1.1. giving preliminary siting recommendations upon application by the investor;

36.1.2. determining conditions for the site selected;

36.1.3. granting siting permission;

36.2. The Council of Ministers shall, by means of an ordinance, define the scope, rules and procedures for siting projects.

Article 37
37.1. Siting recommendations shall contain information related to socio-economic plans and development plans drawn up for the locality or the site where the project may be constructed, and to conditions pertinent to its construction, and – in the case of projects of a linear character – to the route proposed.

37.2. Siting recommendations may be presented in the form of variants.

Article 38
38.1. Siting recommendations shall be given by:

38.1.1. The Central Planning Office – with respect to projects of national importance;

38.1.2. local bodies of State administration responsible for siting projects at province level[1] – with respect to projects of regional importance;

[1] Currently 'provincial governor' (by virtue of Article 53, section 1 of the Law on the Local Bodies of General State Administration of 22 March 1990, Dz. U. No.21, item 123).

38.1.3. local bodies of State administration responsible for siting projects at local level[2] – with respect to projects of local importance;

38.2. The bodies referred to in section 1 above shall, prior to giving siting recommendations, seek the opinions of the interested bodies and institutions, and the bodies referred to in section 1, points 1 and 2 shall also seek the opinions of the appropriate local bodies of State administration responsible for siting projects[3].

38.3. The bodies of State administration referred in section 1, point 3 shall be under an obligation to give their siting recommendations for housing projects within six months of lodging an application.

38.4. The Council of Ministers shall define the criteria for classifying projects as projects of national, regional and local importance.

Article 39

39.1. Before giving siting recommendations for projects posing extreme environmental and health hazards, the bodies referred to in Article 38, section 1, points 1 and 2, shall seek approval from the Minister of Environmental Protection and Natural Resources[4] and from the Chief Sanitary Inspector.

39.2. The bodies referred to in Article 38, section 1, point 3[5] shall seek approval for the siting recommendations mentioned in section 1 above from the appropriate bodies of a higher rank[6].

39.3. The Minister of Environmental Protection and Natural Resources[4], in consultation with the Minister of Health and Social Welfare, shall define the categories of the projects specified under 1 above, as well as standards for environmental impact assessment carried out by experts with respect to those projects.

Article 41. The investor shall carry out an analysis of the siting recommendations, and shall, within six months, lodge an application for siting permission with the appropriate body of State administration[7], notifying of that fact the body which issued the siting recommendations. In special cases, the above time limit may be extended by the body which issued the siting recommendations.

Article 42

42.1. The local body of State administration responsible for siting projects at province level[8], appropriate from the point of view of the project location, shall grant siting permission for the following projects:

[2] Currently 'communal bodies' (by virtue of Article 1, point 1 of the Law on the Division of Powers and Responsibilities defined in Specific Laws among Communal Bodies and State Administrative Bodies and on Amendments to certain Laws of 17 May 1990, Dz. U. No.34, item 198).

[3] Currently 'provincial governors and communal bodies' (by virtue of Article 53, section 1 of the above-mentioned Law of 22 March 1990, and Article 3, section 3 of the Law defining Provisions for the Implementation of the Law on Local Self-Government and the Law on Employees in Local Government, Dz. U. No.34, item 191).

[4] Currently 'the Minister of Environmental Protection, Natural Resources and Forestry' (by virtue of the Law establishing the Office of Minister of Environmental Protection, Natural Resources and Forestry of 20 December 1989, Dz. U. No.73, item 433).

[5] Currently 'communal bodies' (by virtue of Article 1, point 25, subpoint <19> of the above-mentioned Law of 17 May 1990).

[6] Currently 'provincial governors' (by virtue of Article 53, section 1 of the above-mentioned Law of 22 March 1990).

[7] Currently 'the provincial governor or the communal body' (by virtue of Article 42, sections 1 and 2 of this Law, in the light of footnotes 8 and 9 below).

[8] Currently 'the provincial governor' (by virtue of Article 53, section 1 of the above-mentioned Law of 17 May 1990).

42.1.1. projects of national importance;

42.1.2. lines and roads of regional importance;

42.1.3. projects directly related to national defence.

42.2. Siting permission for projects other than those referred to under 1 above shall be granted by the local body of State administration at local level responsible for siting projects[9].

Article 43

43.1. Siting permission shall define:

43.1.1. the lines separating the project site as well as the conditions and guidelines related to the shape of the structure erected;

43.1.2. technical conditions pertinent to construction work;

43.1.3. conditions related to the standards of environmental protection and the preservation of the cultural heritage;

43.1.4. the requirements related to the protection of the interests of third parties.

43.2. Siting permission may be granted after the opinion of other bodies of State administration[10], required under special provisions, has been obtained.

43.3. Siting permission shall become null and void if the investor fails to obtain the right to use the land or if he loses that right or fails to apply for building permission within the time limit set in the siting permission but not exceeding three years.

43.4. The local body of State administration[7] which grants siting permissions shall keep a record thereof in the manner prescribed by the Minister of Development Planning and Construction.

43.5. The local body of State administration of a higher rank[11] than the body which grants siting permissions shall, at least every five years, carry out analyses and evaluations of siting permissions in respect of their conformity with development plans.

Article 44

44.1. Siting permission for projects undertaken by enterprises and for projects undertaken by cooperatives, with the exception of communal housing projects and public utilities projects, shall be preceded by an agreement between the local body of State administration of general competence at appropriate level[7] and the investor, which shall specify project implementation conditions other than those mentioned in Article 43, section 1. In particular, this agreement shall specify mutual consideration and obligations entered into by the investor and the local body of State administration[7] with respect to the construction and future operations of the planned facility.

44.2. The local body of State administration of general competence at appropriate level[7] shall conclude the agreement referred to under 1 above also with other investors, if this is necessary from the point of view of the size and nature of the project.

[9] Currently 'the communal body' (by virtue of Article 1, point 25, subpoint m of the above-mentioned Law of 17 May 1990).

[10] Currently 'bodies' (following the reform of State administration and local self-government).

[11] Currently 'the provincial governor (with respect to projects where siting permission is granted by the communal body) and, in practice, the Central Planning Office (with respect to projects where siting permission is granted by the provincial governor)'.

Article 45. The provisions of Articles 36 to 44 shall apply accordingly to undertakings other than construction projects if those undertakings affect land management and land utilisation.

Article 46. Siting permissions or permissions altering the purpose of areas which do not comply with the local development plans shall become null and void.

POLAND E

Ordinance of the Council of Ministers on the Classification of Investments and the Scope, Principles and Procedures of their Location

27 June 1985

Based on the uniform text published as a Schedule to the announcement by the Minister of Development Planning and Construction of 16 February 1990 (Dz. U. of 1990, No.11, item 75).

Unofficial translation, by Institute for Sustainable Development

By virtue of Article 36, section 2 and Article 38, section 4 of the Law on Development Planning of 12 July 1984 (Dz. U. of 1989 No.17, item 99, No.34, item 178, and No.35, item 192), the following provisions shall be adopted:

Article 1
1.1. Construction projects of national significance are those involving:

1.1.1. construction of mines undertaking the excavation of mineral deposits which are subject to the mining law, and plants undertaking the excavation of mineral deposits which are not subject to the mining law, if the amount excavated does not exceed 500,000 tonnes per year;

1.1.2. construction of main pipelines transporting and supplying gas within the national gas network, and oil pipelines of national importance;

1.1.3. construction of nuclear power plants, power and heat generating plants and heat-generating plants;

1.1.4. construction of nuclear facilities and central radioactive-waste cemeteries;

1.1.5. manufacturing enterprise investments with an estimated/planned workforce in excess of 500 employees;

1.1.6. construction of warehouses for raw materials and food products whose storage capacity exceeds 60,000 m^3;

1.1.7. construction of main-lines of national and international importance;

1.1.8. construction of motorways and main through routes and associated construction sites and buildings;

1.1.9. construction of other national routes;

1.1.10. construction of passenger airports;

1.1.11. construction of sea ports;

1.1.12. construction of inland ports;

1.1.13. construction of power lines of 400 and more kV, within the national electricity network, including substations;

1.1.14. construction of main telecommunications lines and tele- and radio-communication facilities of national and international importance;

1.1.15. construction of stages of fall on navigable waters, navigable canals and water mains, large enough to transfer water on a regional scale;

1.1.16. construction of universities, research institutes and projects designated as State projects in the field of health care, culture and art;

1.1.17. projects related to national defence and security which involve establishing new closed areas or extending the existing ones;

1.1.18. the construction of state radio and television stations and broadcasting outlets, and radio-locating equipment at the national level;

1.2. Construction projects of regional importance are those involving:

1.2.1. Construction of facilities which pump and fractionate natural gas, facilities which extract and mix liquid gas, gas pipelines and oil pipelines which serve the needs of provinces;

1.2.3. construction of conventional heat- and power-generating plants and heat-generating plants, and other facilities supplying heat to towns;

1.2.4. construction of main-lines and main-line facilities not designated as projects of national importance;

1.2.5. construction of provincial roads and facilities related thereto;

1.2.6. construction of cargo air terminals;

1.2.7. construction of power lines of voltage lower than 400 kV but not lower than 100 kV with the exception of power lines modernised as a result of the electrification of rural areas;

1.2.8. projects related to water management and water conservation, water supply and sewerage systems of regional importance;

1.2.9. construction of irrigation facilities of regional importance or serving the needs of more than one commune (town and commune);

1.2.12. prison management investments;

1.2.13. state defence and security investments in restricted areas, and conservation areas located within them;

1.2.14. projects constructed within the areas of sea ports and inland ports;

1.2.15. establishing municipal and industrial waste dumps and sewage disposal areas serving the needs of areas larger than basic administrative units;

1.2.16. construction of industrial plants exploiting mineral deposits which are not subject to the mining law, if the amount excavated does not exceed 500,000 tonnes per year;

1.3. Construction projects of local importance are projects not mentioned in sections 1 and 2 above.

Article 2. The following shall not require siting permission provided that the construction and utilisation thereof does not affect the environment, sanitary conditions or safety of persons or property in adjacent areas:

2.1. facilities constructed in closed areas connected with national defence and security if they do not require establishing protection zones;

2.2. buildings and facilities on State forest farms, constructed in the forest areas of such farms, and other structures built on forest land;

2.3. temporary on-site facilities used by the investor or contractor – for the period of the construction work;

2.4. building extensions or additional storeys or rebuilding existing facilities;

2.5. provisional huts used during construction or geological survey examinations;

2.6. minor irrigation facilities used in farming and forestry;

2.7. land survey marks, gravimetric marks and magnetic marks and structures protecting them;

2.8. manufacturing facilities associated with agricultural production on individual farms.

Article 3
3.1. Before siting permission is granted, siting recommendations shall be obtained.

3.2. Upon applying for siting recommendations, the investor may present his own siting proposals and request that several sites be recommended to him, if the circumstances related to the siting of the project permit alternative siting.

Article 4
4.1. An application for siting recommendations shall contain a general description of the project and requirements related to its construction and future operations, in particular:

4.1.1. the size and type of the project defined in terms of the area necessary for the construction thereof, employment figures, and production figures or the scope of services provided, as well as a description of the basic buildings to be constructed;

4.1.2. requirements pertinent to transport services, electricity and water supply, and waste and waste-water disposal;

4.1.3. the proposed route for linear, network-based or road system investments;

4.1.4. other relevant information, depending on the type of project.

4.2. To the application mentioned under 4.1 above, relating to a project posing environmental and health hazards, or to a project whose construction could affect the quality of the environment, there shall be attached an environmental impact assessment carried out by the expert from the list of specialists held by the Minister of Environmental Protection, Natural Resources and Forestry;

4.3. An investor who presents his own siting proposals for a project connected with mining and processing minerals shall attach to his application the necessary information from an appropriate body on the mineral deposit he wishes to exploit.

4.4. The provision of section 4.1.1 above does not apply to projects connected with national defence and security, but the size of the area necessary for its implementation shall be specified.

4.5. An investor who presents his own siting proposals for a project connected with the construction of lines, networks or roads shall identify the sites proposed on appropriate maps.

Article 6

6.1. In order to obtain siting permission for a construction project, the investor shall submit to the appropriate body[1] an application for siting permission, attaching thereto the following documents, depending on the type of project:

6.1.1. a master plan showing the proposed development of the project site and the architectural design as well as other information required by that body before siting permission is granted;

6.1.2. a copy of a map indicating the position of the site and height levels and presenting the public utilities systems and planned investment projects;

6.1.3. a copy of the land register documents;

6.1.4. copies of documents presenting the opinion of the appropriate State administrative bodies[2], self-governing bodies or organisational units, all of which are required by specific regulations;

6.2. To the application mentioned under 1 above, relating to a project posing extreme environmental and health hazards, or to a project which could affect the quality of the environment, the investor shall attach a comprehensive environmental impact assessment.

6.4. If the proposed route of the line, network or road requires that administrative proceedings be initiated with respect to more than 50 pages the District Governor, Chief Rural Official and Mayor may notify those interested of its decisions and actions by publishing an announcement or publishing information in the local press.

6.5. The District Governor, Chief Rural Official and Mayor may demand that additional material and data be submitted which are necessary for granting siting permission.

[1] Currently 'the provincial governor or the communal body' (by virtue of Article 42, section 1 and 2 of the Law on Development Planning, Dz. U. of 1989: No.17, item 99, No.34, item 178 and No.35, item 192 and of 1990: No.34, item 198, in the light of Article 53, section 1 of the Law on Local Bodies of General State Administration, DZ. U. No.21, item 123 and Article 1, point 25, subpoint m of the Law on the Division of Powers and Responsibilities defined in Specific Laws among Communal Bodies and State Administrative Bodies of 17 May 1990, Dz. U. No.34, item 198).

[2] Currently 'bodies' (following the reform of State administration and local self-government).

Slovak Republic*

EIA regulation	None. There is no EIA process in Slovakia. An EIA regulation is in preparation. The term, 'environmental analysis' is used instead of 'EIA' in this chapter.
Environmental and building authorities	The Ministry of Environment and its 38 District Environmental Offices and 121 Sub-district Environmental Offices. Construction Offices, responsible for development planning, are part of the Sub-district Environmental Offices, and therefore part of the Ministry of Environment.
Responsibilities for environmental analysis	Only registered persons are permitted to carry out environmental analysis.
Regulatory context for environmental analysis	Environmental analysis is carried out as part of the application procedure for siting and building permits.
Activities subject to environmental analysis	Environmental analysis is required at the discretion of the building authority, in particular the Sub-district Environmental Office.
Scoping	There is no scoping process.
Environmental documentation	Application for a building permit requires information about planned environmental measures. The building authority can require further environmental information.
Public participation	Public consultation is required for applications for siting and building permits. Public opinion is taken into account during review and approval.
Review and approval	The building authority considers all project documentation and takes into account the opinions of the public before issuing the siting and building permits.
Transboundary EIA	Draft EIA legislation includes provisions for transboundary EIAs, following the Federal Act on the Environment, No.17/1992 (Articles 24–26). The Slovak Republic has signed the Espoo Convention on EIA in a Transboundary Context.

* Original reference material provided by Dr. Václav Mezřický, Institute for Environmental Policy (Prague). Updated material provided by Mary Arndtsen, Advisor at Slovak Ministry of Environment (Bratislava)

1. Introduction

Population: 5.2 million
Area: 49,000 sq km
Currency: Slovak crown

Principal environmental problems

The two main environmental problems in Slovakia are pollution by heavy industry and air pollution in cities from mobile and stationary sources. Both have significant impacts on human health. A particularly acute example of an industrial pollution problem is the aluminium smelter at Žiar nad Hronom, the environmental effects of which are both direct (soil, water, air, health) and indirect (high energy intensity).

Environmental policy

The Slovak Ministry of Environment has defined a set of policy goals.

Short-term (0–7 years): identification and removal of the main threats to the environment and human health.
Medium-term (7–15 years): development of economic and legal tools to change the behaviour of society and individuals.
Long-term (beyond 15 years): rational use of resources, re-use of resources, sustainable development, stabilisation of biodiversity, and an environmentally friendly economy.

The Ministry aims to achieve the integration of economic and environmental decision-making, through measures such as risk assessment and environmental impact assessment. Its task is to persuade other Ministries to adopt the principle of integration.

2. Legislative and institutional framework for EIA

2.1 Administrative structure and responsibilities for EIA

The Slovak Republic is divided into 38 districts, 121 sub-districts, and 2,826 self-governing municipalities.

Ministry of Environment

The central environmental authority is the Ministry of Environment which is responsible for drafting environmental legislation, formulating environmental policy and enforcing environmental laws, including EIA laws.

The Ministry of Environment enforces environmental laws through the Slovak Environmental Inspectorate. The Inspectorate is divided into departments for air, water and waste. Each department has a number of branch offices.

District and Sub-district Environmental Offices, and Construction Offices

The environmental administration consists of 38 District Environmental Offices and 121 Sub-District Environmental Offices, all of which are supervised directly by the Ministry of Environment.

Construction Offices are part of the Sub-district Environmental Offices. They make decisions on building location, use of territory, permission for construction and for using or operating a building (*Act on Land Use Planning and Construction Rules, No.50/1976*, Articles 32–42, 54–57, 78–85, 117–119).

Future changes in local administration

The structure of local administration is likely to change in the near future, when the District and Sub-district Environmental Offices and the Construction Offices are integrated into the local administration, supervised by the Ministry of Interior.

2.2 Sources of legislation relating to EIA

The Slovak National Council has adopted the laws of the former Czech and Slovak Federal Republic on water, air and waste. These define basic principles. Pre-independence Slovak laws, regulations and decrees define administrative competencies for implementing federal legislation. These are still in force in the Slovak Republic.

2.2.1 Legislation on planning

- Czechoslovak *Act on Land Use Planning and Construction Rules, No.50/1976* (Document A), amended by *Act No.262/1992*

The Act specifies basic rules for land use planning and construction. The amendment contains some details of land use planning in relation to the public interest, and in relation to expropriations and other specific circumstances.

The Act, as amended, requires the developer to supply an environmental approval issued by the competent authority with applications for a siting or land use permit.

- Czechoslovak *Decree on General Technical Requirements of Construction, No.83/1976* (Document B), as amended by *Decree No.45/1979* and *Decree No.376/1992*

The Decree outlines the criteria for selecting building sites on various kinds of land. These criteria are binding for both authorities and developers. The Decree defines general requirements for environmental protection.

- Czechoslovak *Decree on More Detailed Regulation of Land Use Planning and Construction Rules, No.85/1976* (Document C), as amended by *Decree No.378/1992*

The Decree specifies certain provisions of the *Act on Land Use Planning and Construction Rules, No.50/1976*. It sets requirements for location of buildings and for building permits.

2.2.2 Legislation on environment and on environmental permits

- Federal *Act on the Environment, No.17/1992* (Document D)

The Act has been adopted by the Slovak National Council (Parliament) and is valid as Slovak law. The law cannot be enforced, however, because of the lack of procedural legislation in the Slovak Republic. In the case of EIA, this situation will continue until the Slovak Environmental Impact Assessment law is passed by the National Council (see section 6).

The Act has an almost constitutional character, summarising the principles of environmental protection and natural resource use to be observed by the legislature of the Federation and the republics. One of these principles is pollution prevention (Article 17).

The Act states that it is necessary to evaluate human activities in terms of their impact on the environment and on natural resources. The Act specifies investment activity, as well as the introduction of new technologies, products and substances into production or into circulation.

The Act also specifies requirements for performing EIAs (Articles 20–23). It empowers Republic Parliaments to determine who carries out the EIA and which procedures they follow. In appendices it lists activities subject to EIA in the ČSFR. The appendices also outline the content of the Environmental Impact Statement. The Act incorporates the principles of the Espoo Convention on Transboundary Environmental Impact Assessment (Articles 24–26).

- Czechoslovak *Act on Human Health Care, No.20/1966*

The Act outlines basic principles for preserving sound living conditions, especially the quality of water, soil and air. It empowers bodies of the health service to uphold citizens' rights to sound living conditions by monitoring compliance with these principles.

- Czechoslovak *Regulation concerning the Safeguarding and Protection of Healthy Living Conditions, No.45/1966*, as amended by *Act No.458/1991*

Following the *Act on Public Health, No.20/1966*, the Decree specifies health criteria for the protection of the environment.

- Federal Clean Air *Act, No.309/1991*, as amended by *Act No.318/1992*

The Act defines rights and obligations relating to the protection of air, and methods for limiting the causes and mitigating the effects of pollution. The amendment specifies time limits for bringing pollution within emission limits.

- Slovak *Act on the State Administration of Air Protection, No.134/1992*

The Act specifies the responsibilities of the state administration in air pollution control.

The Act defines the responsibilities of the state administration for approving projects which will create new air pollution sources. It specifies what documentation is required when applying for siting and building permits.

- Slovak Commission for the Environment *Regulation which Specifies a List of Pollution Sources Categorisation and List of Polluting Agents and Their Limits, and which Specifies Details on Assessment of Emission Limits in Existing Pollution Sources, No.407/1992*

The Decree lists pollutants and pollution sources and establishes emission limits both for pollutants in general and for specific industries.

- Slovak Ministry of Environment *Decree on Areas Requiring Special Air Protection and Warning Systems for Smog, No.112/1993*

This Act identifies areas where stricter air pollution standards apply. These include areas where pollution limits are already exceeded and areas which need special protection, such as spas, national parks and protected areas. Appendix 2 lists the polluted areas which must develop a new regime for compliance with air pollution standards. The Act also requires

Districts to develop a warning system should pollution levels exceed permissible levels due to accidents or other incidents.

- Czechoslovak *Water Act, No.138/1973*

The Act regulates the balance between the demand for water and the capacity of water resources. It protects the quality of water, promotes its rational use, and assures protection from floods. At the same time it respects the requirements of nature conservation.

- Slovak *Act on the State Administration of Water Management, No.135/1974*

The Act defines responsibilities of water management authorities, which are empowered to issue their opinions in accordance with the *Water Act, No.138/1973.*

- Slovak Government *Order Establishing Indices of Admissible Degrees of Water Pollution, No.30/1975*

The Decree establishes ambient water quality standards. The criteria include sustainability for fish life, sight tests for algal blooms and quantitative limits for certain pollutants and heavy metals.

- Slovak *Act on the State Administration of the Environment, No.595/1990*

The Act defines responsibilities of the Ministry of Environment of the Slovak Republic, the Slovak Environmental Inspectorate, the District Environmental Offices and the Sub-district Environmental Offices.

- Federal *Waste Act, No.238/1991* and Slovak *Act on the State Administration of Waste Management, No.494/1991*

The Acts define rights and obligations for waste treatment.

- Slovak *Decree on Waste Handling, No.606/1992*

This Decree stipulates conditions for the handling, processing and disposing of waste and hazardous waste.

- Czechoslovak *Act on the Protection of the Agricultural Soil Fund, No.53/1966*, as amended

The Act protects agricultural soil as a source of food production and as a natural resource.

- Slovak *Act on the Responsibility of the Agricultural Soil Fund Protection Authorities of the Slovak Republic, No.78/1976*

The Act defines responsibilities of the agricultural land protection authorities under the Ministry of Agriculture of the Slovak Republic.

- Czechoslovak *Decree Defining Some Details of Agricultural Soil Protection, No.36/1987*, as amended and modified by later regulations

The Decree specifies measures to protect agricultural land in land use planning and in building design.

- Czechoslovak *Act on Forests, No.61/1977*

The Act protects forests and tree species as a permanent source of wood and as a fundamental natural resource.

- Slovak *Act on Forest Management, No.100/1977*, as amended and modified by later regulations, particularly *Act No.595/1990*

The Act defines forms of forest management and responsibilities of the state administration for forest management.

3. Environmental impact assessment process

There is not yet a formal EIA process in Slovakia. A new EIA law is being drafted (details in section 6). Although EIA procedures are defined in the Federal *Act on the Environment, No.17/1992* (Document D), these have not yet been implemented by Slovak legislation. The EIA terminology used in the other chapters of this book, therefore, is not used in this chapter. The phrase 'environmental analysis' is used instead of 'EIA'.

3.1 Activities subject to environmental analysis

The Sub-district Environmental Office decides when an environmental analysis is required, and can order an expert opinion on all or part of a project (Articles 34 and 35, *Act on Land Use Planning and Construction Rules, No.50/1976*). Such an analysis can be required for construction, modification, maintenance and liquidation.

Although lists of projects exist in the Federal *Act on the Environment, No.17/1992* (Document D), these provisions have not yet been implemented by Slovak legislation.

3.2 Regulatory context for environmental analysis

Environmental analysis takes place as part of the application process for siting and building permits (Czechoslovak *Act on Land Use Planning and Construction Rules, No.50/1976*, amended by *Act No.262/1992*).

A *siting permit* is required if the project involves a greenfield site or expansion of an existing facility.

A *building permit* is required for construction, modification, maintenance and removal of any building.

Siting permit

The process of siting is defined by land use plans. Applications for siting permission are reviewed by Construction Offices in relation to such plans. This planning process dates back to the socialist period. Plans may cover several settlements, individual settlements or parts of settlements. They may restrict development in the following places:

- residential areas;
- legally protected or environmentally sensitive areas;
- areas important for water management;
- 'public health protection zones' in areas where it is important to maintain clean air (spas, holiday resorts, medical facilities) and clean water (sources of public water supply).

The link between land use plans and the environment is explained in the aforementioned land use planning law:

Land use planning is a prerequisite for ensuring the lasting harmony of all natural, human and cultural aspects in a territory, in particular with respect to the environment and the protection of its main components, soil, water and air (Article 1.2).

Building permit

Applications for building permits are judged according to whether the project will abide by legal environmental and safety requirements.

Additional information about the environment may be required to apply for various environment related permits. Applications for environmental permits are part of the planning process. There is no integrated permitting procedure. (See box.)

Environmental permits

(For relevant legislation, see section 2.2.3.)

Air

Sub-district Environmental Offices grant approvals for the location, construction and modification of large and medium pollution sources. They also grant approvals for projects at large and medium-size polluting facilities which introduce new production and technology. The definitions of large and medium-size are given in the law. (*Act on the State Administration of Air Protection, No.134/1992*).

Sub-district Environmental Offices also grant approvals for the location and building of small polluting facilities which use new technologies (Article 11.1f, Federal *Clean Air Act, No.309/1991*).

Water

There are four River Basin Authorities under the Ministry of Soil Management. They issue water use permits and the District Environmental Offices issue water discharge permits, subject to approval by the River Basin Authorities (*Act on the State Administration of Water Management, No.135/1974*).

Noise and health

District Environmental Offices issue noise permits. New regulations on noise are being drafted.

Waste

Waste treatment plans need to be prepared during project planning (Federal *Waste Act, No.238/1991; Act on the State Administration of Waste Management, No.494/1991*). A later regulation states that major waste generators (annually more than 100 kg of hazardous waste or 1 tonne of special waste or 10 tonnes of other waste) must prepare a waste management plan (*Regulation on Waste Management Programmes, No.76/1992*). An emergency plan for accidents involving hazardous waste is required (*Decree on Waste Handling, No.606/1992*).

The Sub-district Environmental Office issues approval for waste storage and treatment facilities, and maintains records on waste. The District Environmental Office must approve the transport of hazardous waste. The Ministry of Environment approves transport of hazardous waste if more than one district is crossed.

Health
The District Hygiene Offices oversee compliance with the health laws, and issue a binding decision during the application for a building permit. This includes provisions for the safe handling of chemicals.

Agricultural land
The Sub-district Office must approve the removal of land from agricultural use. The approval is presented with the application for the siting and building permit (*Act on the Responsibility of the Agricultural Soil Fund Protection Authorities of the Slovak Republic, No.78/1976*).

The protection of agricultural land must be considered when planning mining projects, underground and overhead works lines, and traffic communications lines (Czechoslovak *Decree Defining Some Details of Agricultural Soil Protection, No.36/1987*, as amended and modified by the Ministry of Environment *Decree No.528/1991*).

Forests
A project which permanently or temporarily takes forest land out of use, or limits forest land use, requires the approval of the forestry authorities (Czechoslovak *Act on Forests, No.61/1977*).

The District Office:

- decides on taking forest land out use and on limiting the economic use of forests of less than two hectares;
- approves territorial decisions which will affect forests;
- issues permits for buildings which will affect forests;
- issues permits for mines affecting forests;
- approves transport systems, communications cables, and pipelines affecting forests if they do not extend beyond the border of one district.

The Ministry of Agriculture (formerly the Ministry of Forestry and Water Management) makes decisions on removing protected and special purpose forests from use, and when the area of forest is more than five hectares.

(*Act on Forest Management, No.100/1977*, as amended and modified by later regulations, particularly *Act No.595/1990*)

3.3 Responsibilities for environmental analysis

Only persons who pass a special examination by the Ministry of Environment can be registered by the Ministry as competent environmental experts. It is likely that only persons on this list will be entitled to carry out EIAs, when a formal EIA process is introduced.

The environmental analysis is prepared at the expense of the developer.

3.4 Environmental documentation

The documentation required for the siting and building permits is outlined in the *Decree on More Detailed Regulation of Land Use Planning and Construction Rules, No.85/1976.*

Part of the application for the building permit is a summary 'technological report'. This includes data on technology or production installations and on the production engineering envisaged, on environmental protection, on groundwater, sewers, water supply, heating systems and fuels. Data are also required on environmental protection measures (Articles 20–22).

The application for the building permit must also include reports on negotiations with and decisions of the authorities and all parties concerned with the project (Article 20).

The Construction Office (within the Sub-district Environmental Office) may ask the developer to supply further documents with the application (for example, maps, sketches, studies, selected parts of the preparatory documentation), in order to calculate the environmental consequences of the building or of other measures envisaged in the area.

The Construction Office can request the developer to present an environmental expert opinion on the entire project or some of its parts. However, there are no prescribed requirements concerning the expert opinion.

3.5 Public participation

Public participants are neighbours, private individuals or businesses, which may be affected by the project, and the concerned authorities (Federal *Act on the Environment, No.17/1992*, Articles 21 and 25). This may include members of non-governmental organisations. Public participation provisions were expanded in the 1992 amendment of the Czechoslovak *Act on Land Use Planning and Construction Rules, No.50/1976.*

Applications for siting and building permits must be available for public comment for a 30 day period. Although they are not required to in the legislation, in practice developers often send copies of the documentation directly to the public participants at the beginning of the 30 day consultation period.

During the 30 day period, the public and concerned authorities must make their comments. If the authorities have questions about the application, they can halt the proceedings until the questions are addressed.

The Construction Office then orders a public hearing, usually accompanied by a visit to the site. This is the last opportunity for objections to be filed.

The public has no right of veto, but it can take a dispute to court, during which the proceedings are suspended.

The Federal *Act on the Environment, No.17/1992* provides for the public's right of access to true and accurate information about the state of the environment, activities which could affect the environment, and measures taken by the authorities to prevent or remedy environmental damage. A freedom of information law relating to the environment is being discussed.

3.6 Review

Siting permit

The Construction Office (within the Sub-district Environmental Office) examines the compatibility of the project with existing land use plans, and examines whether it complies with general technical requirements and regulations concerning construction, public health, fire safety, occupational health and safety, communications, nature conservation, conservation of cultural monuments, and the protection of agricultural and forest soil. When required, the Construction Office reviews the expert environment opinion and the views of the public.

Building permit

The Construction Office examines whether the facility will have effects on the environment beyond levels permitted by law. In particular, it considers harmful emissions, noise, heat, vibrations, dust, smell, water pollution, bright light and shading.

When issuing the building permit, the Construction Office can make binding environmental conditions for the construction and use of the building.

4. Monitoring

A final approval is necessary before the developer can make a new building operational. The Construction Office examines whether the construction has followed the conditions stipulated in the building permit. It also examines further whether the building and its use will endanger the life and health of people, the environment and occupational health and safety.

If the Construction Office discovers that the requirements of the building legislation have not been complied with they can impose fines on the developer (Czechoslovak *Act on Land Use Planning and Construction Rules, No.50/1976*, Articles 105 and 106).

5. EIA in practice

Despite the absence of formal EIA legislation in the Slovak Republic, some EIAs have been carried out on a voluntary basis. In two cases – the Žilina dam and a motorway outside Bratislava – the developers conducted EIAs because of the size and sensitivity of the projects. The developers worked closely with the EIA department at the Ministry of Environment.

The Žilina dam is being constructed by a government owned company. A commission of experts was created by a consulting company to prepare the Environmental Impact Statement, which was reviewed by the Ministry of Environment. The Ministry approved the EIA without conditions. The local government, however, subsequently required some changes to the project, for example, removal of illegal landfill sites in the area and strengthening of the river banks. The EIA involved some public participation – information centres and public meetings.

In carrying out the EIA, the expert commission referred to the EC Directive on EIA and Austrian EIA legislation. International pressure to carry out an EIA was a factor. The consulting company was also keen to get experience in carrying out an EIA.

6. Possible changes in the near future

The Slovak Government has been preparing an EIA Act since 1992. The new Act is expected to be passed during 1994.

The draft EIA Act, as it stood in Summer 1993, includes provisions for mandatory and discretionary EIAs. It is not yet clear who the reviewing body will be. It is anticipated the full EIA process will take about seven months to complete.

The developer initiates the EIA by filing an initial statement, including a technical description. An independent consultant will prepare the EIA report.

Public participation is provided for in the draft EIA Act. The public must be notified and given an opportunity to comment when the project is proposed. Once the EIA has been prepared it should be distributed to the public for their comments. There is also a provision for public hearings.

An independent committee prepares an expert opinion on the applicant's report. The reviewing authority then gives its final opinion. The draft does not make the EIA recommendation binding on the construction authority; instead, it is used as one piece of evidence for the decision.

The draft EIA Act establishes procedures for evaluating transboundary effects of projects.

According to the draft EIA Act, the project must stay within the parameters of environmental damage that were specified in the EIA. If the project exceeds the limits forecast in the EIA, the developer must take remedial action.

Other forthcoming legislative changes include a regulation of the Ministry of Environment on the professional qualifications and registration of environmental experts.

7. Sources of further information

Ing. Viera Husková
Director
Department of EIA
Ministry of Environment
Hlboká 2
812 35 Bratislava
Slovak Republic
tel: (42-7) 491 843
fax: (42-7) 311 368

RNDr. Mária Kozová, CSc.
EIA Centre
Department of Landscape Ecology
Prírodovedecká Fakulta UK
Mlynská Dolina B-2
842 15 Bratislava
Slovak Republic
tel: (42-7) 720 462
fax: (42-7) 729 064

PhDr. Dagmar Petríkova & PhDr. Ivan Kusý, CSc.
EIA Centre
Faculty of Architecture

Slovak Technical University
Bratislava
Slovak Republic
tel: (42-7) 396 454

RNDr. Anton Mocik, CSc.
Pedohyg (private consulting firm which undertakes EIAs)
Prírodovedecká Fakulta UK
Mlynská Dolina B-1/304
842 15 Bratislava
Slovak Republic
tel: (42-7) 720 003 ext. 140
fax: (42-7) 720 041

8. EIA legislation

A number of Czechoslovak laws related to environmental protection continue to apply to both the Czech and Slovak Republics. As the Slovak laws relevant to EIA referred to in this chapter are currently the same as those for the Czech Republic, details of these laws can be found at the end of the chapter on the Czech Republic.

The laws are as follows:

SLOVAK A

Czechoslovak Act on Land Use Planning and Construction Rules No. 50/1976 S.B.

Excerpts of this Act can be found in Czech Republic D, page 54.

SLOVAK B

Czechoslovak Decree on General Technical Requirements of Construction No. 83/1976 S.B.

Excerpts of this Decree can be found in Czech Republic E, page 59.

SLOVAK C

Federal Ministry for Technical and Investment Development Decree on More Detailed Regulation of Land Use Planning and Construction Rules No. 85/1976 S.B. str. 364

Excerpts of this Decree can be found in Czech Republic F, page 61.

SLOVAK D

Federal Act on the Environment, Law No. 17/1992, 5 December 1991

See Czech Republic C, page 41.

Slovenia*

EIA regulation	Environmental Protection Act, 1993 (Document A). An implementing EIA regulation is in preparation.
EIA authority	Ministry of Environment and Regional Planning (MERP).
Responsibilities for EIA	An Environmental Impact Assessment can only be prepared by an authorised person or institution. The developer pays for the preparation of the Environmental Impact Statement and the public discussion.
Regulatory context for EIA	Part of application for operating licence from the local government or the MERP (the 'licensing authority').
Activities subject to EIA	A list of mandatory projects is in preparation. The MERP can require an EIA for projects not on this list, if requested by other ministries, local government, individuals or non-governmental organisations.
Scoping	The need for and scope of and extent of the EIA is determined by the licensing authority and the MERP.
Environmental Impact Statement	The developer produces a full or partial Environmental Impact Statement, as required in the previous step.
Public participation	The licensing authority makes a preliminary decision and submits this for public consultation with the project documentation. The affected public has a legal right to participate in the licensing process.
Environmental review	The preliminary decision, project documentation and results of public consultation are forwarded to the MERP for an environmental decision.
Approval	The MERP issues an 'environmental consent', and can require modifications to the project.
Development consent	For projects requiring an EIA, an 'environmental consent' is compulsory before an operating licence can be given. Modifications to the project required by the MERP must be incorporated into the licence.

* Reference material provided by Dr. Franc Lobnik, Biotechnical Faculty, Department of Agronomy (Ljubljana), and Dušan Pichler, Advisor to the Slovenian Minister of Environment

Transboundary EIA	Information about projects with transboundary impacts must be supplied to the affected countries (Environmental Protection Act, 1993, Article 63). Slovenia has not signed the Espoo Convention on EIA in a Transboundary Context.

1. Introduction

Population: 2.02 million
Area: 20,256 sq km
Currency: Tolar (SIT)

Principal environmental problems

(a) Waste: Waste is considered the first environmental priority in Slovenia. There are no facilities for processing and disposing of hazardous wastes in Slovenia. There is a shortage of landfill disposal sites (because of the prevalence of limestone as the base rock), leading to widespread illegal dumping of waste.

(b) Air: The country has one of the highest per capita emission rates in Europe. Urban air pollution resulting from domestic heating causes particular problems in cities situated in valleys, such as Ljubljana and Maribor. This is particularly the case in winter.

(c) Groundwater: All Slovenia's drinking water is taken from aquifers. Some important aquifers are becoming contaminated by agricultural pollution, for example that of Celje. There is a shortage of water during summer in the maritime regions, as a result of intensive tourism development.

(d) Surface water: All the major rivers which have their source in Slovenia or near its borders flow into the Danube Basin and are heavily polluted by the time they have passed through the country. This has a negative impact on water recreation activities, and there is evidence of long-term deterioration of groundwater quality as a result of surface water pollution.

Environmental policy

The Slovenian national report to the UNCED Conference in Rio de Janeiro (1992), outlined the following environmental policy elements:

- legislative reform;
- national environmental action plan;
- national environmental monitoring system;
- new environmental impact assessment procedures;
- legal provisions for freedom of information;
- implementation of the 'polluter pays principle', environmental taxes, creation of an environmental fund;
- waste management plan.

2. Legislative and institutional framework for EIA

2.1 Administrative structure and responsibilities for EIA

Slovenia has 62 municipalities. Restructuring of local government is being debated in Slovenia's parliament.

Environmental authority

The Ministry of Environment and Regional Planning (MERP) is the central environmental authority. It is responsible for environmental protection, water management, physical planning and housing, and nuclear safety. It has eight water management branch offices.

Licensing authority

The MERP grants operating licences for projects of national importance, and local government grants licences for all other projects. Both development planning and environmental protection at the municipal level are the responsibility of local government (*Environmental Protection Act, 1993*, Article 2.2).

EIA authority

The MERP organises the EIA process. According to the *Environmental Protection Act, 1993*, the MERP's responsibility for EIA includes:

- carrying out the EIA review and approval (Article 59.2);
- compiling a list of certified institutions that can undertake EIA studies (Article 56.4);
- participating in the inspection of facilities that require an EIA, just before the project becomes operational (Article 61.1).

The MERP can require an EIA even when not mandatory according to the law (Article 57.2).

2.2 Sources of legislation relating to EIA

2.2.1 Legislation on EIA

- *Environmental Protection Act, 1993* (Document A)

The general procedures for EIA are defined in Articles 55–63, and were drafted with reference to the EC Directive on EIA (1985).

The EIA regulations cannot be implemented until an EIA regulation is drawn up, which will define which projects must undergo an EIA, and what must be presented in the Environmental Impact Statement. Articles 101 and 102 of the Environmental Protection Act require the EIA regulation to be passed by April 1994. At the time of writing, it was still under preparation; completion is expected by the end of 1994.

2.2.2 Legislation on planning

- *Urban Planning Law, 1984*, as amended

This is a general law which defines the rules for landscape planning.

- *Law on Physical Planning and other Activities Affecting the Landscape, 1984*

This law outlines the procedure for granting an operating licence, and defines where construction can take place. A subsidiary regulation defines the level at which an operating licence is given: by the MERP for projects of national importance, and at the local level for all other projects. Projects of national significance are defined.

3. Environmental impact assessment process

3.1 Activities subject to EIA

The *Environmental Protection Act, 1993* lists projects subject to EIA (Article 55.2):

- the exploitation of soil, water, forests, minerals and other natural resources;
- construction, modification, operation, or removal of facilities and equipment;
- technological and other changes relating to the extraction, production, storage, transport and use of materials, semi-processed goods, finished products and energy;
- the introduction of new products for use or marketing;
- the trial introduction of new products and technologies.

An Environmental Impact Statement is required for mobile environmental protection facilities (Article 32.2).

The *Environmental Protection Act, 1993* requires that the Government makes a list of projects for which an EIA is mandatory, and of projects which require only a limited Environmental Impact Statement (Articles 57.1, 101.1).

Ministries, municipalities, individuals, non-governmental organisations and providers of public services all have the right to demand an EIA for projects not in these lists (Article 57.2). In such cases, the Minister of Environment decides whether an EIA should be carried out (Article 58.2).

3.2 Regulatory context for EIA

EIA is defined in the *Environmental Protection Act, 1993* (Document A). Detailed regulations for EIA will be drawn up by the Ministry of Environment and Regional Planning (MERP) (Articles 56.4, 102.1).

EIA is considered as part of the application for an operating licence (Article 55.3), and is organised by the licensing authority (see section 2.1). The licensing authority refers the project documentation, including the Environmental Impact Statement, to the MERP for an environmental decision.

Approval of an EIA is separate from other environment, health, safety and natural resource permits required by law (see, for example, *Environmental Protection Act, 1993*, Articles 21–24, 32–33).

EIAs are undertaken with reference to the physical planning components of existing long-term municipal development plans (Article 109.4). These will be replaced by 'environmental vulnerability studies', drawn up for every region and municipality in Slovenia (Articles 51–53). The studies will form the basis for all development planning in the future. They will contain an analysis of the sensitivity of various components of the environment, and define areas where development will be restricted or prohibited. On the basis of vulnerability studies, local and national authorities will draw up physical plans and sectoral plans for management of natural resources; these plans will themselves be drawn up with an EIA (Article 54).

3.3 Responsibilities for preparation of environmental impact statement

An Environmental Impact Statement may only be prepared by an authorised person or institution (Article 56.3).

The developer pays for the preparation of the Environmental Impact Statement and for the public discussion (see section 3.5) (Article 60.5).

3.4 Scope of EIA and environmental impact statement

Guidelines for the scope of the EIA, and the methodology for preparing the Environmental Impact Statement, will be defined by the MERP, in consultation with other ministries (Articles 56.4, 102.1).

The EIA covers short and long-term, direct and indirect impacts (Article 55.1).

The *Environmental Protection Act, 1993* states certain environmental requirements for all projects (Article 8.1). All projects must:

- cause the least possible change to the environment;
- present the least environmental risk;
- minimise the consumption of space, materials and energy, during construction, production, transport and utilisation;
- include consideration of the principles of replacement, recycling and regeneration;
- limit environmental impacts at their origin.

A form of scoping procedure is envisaged. When an EIA is mandatory, there is a preliminary procedure by which the licensing authority defines the conditions for granting an operating licence, and defines the scope of the Environmental Impact Statement (Article 58.1). Other ministries, municipalities, individuals, non-governmental organisations and providers of public services have the right to demand that the scope of an EIA be expanded (Article 57.2). In such cases, the Minister of Environment decides what course of action to take (Article 58.2).

In the case of projects requiring only a limited Environmental Impact Statement, the developer is able to ask the MERP about the scope of the statement (Article 58.3). This request must contain information about the type, size and nature of the project and about the environmental condition of the proposed location (Article 58.4).

The full Environmental Impact Statement consists of the following sections (Article 56.1):

- description of existing environment;
- project description, indicating conformity with technical and other regulations;
- description and assessment of anticipated environmental impacts, including a description of methods of evaluation;
- description and assessment of environmental protection methods, with reasons for the choice of technologies, accompanied by test and other certificates;
- description and assessment of overall environmental impacts of the project and predicted changes to the environment;

- description of the location and a list of all interested parties;
- limitations in the preparation of the project design and Environmental Impact Statement;
- non-technical summary.

The entire Statement must be written in a form suitable for public presentation, except when environmental components are an integral part of the project design documentation (Article 56.2).

3.5 Public participation

The public has a right to information about environmental impacts of business activity (Article 14.3). Those parties affected by a proposed project (these must be listed in the Environmental Impact Statement) have a right to participate in the licensing process, if the project encroaches on their right to a clean and healthy environment (Articles 15.4, 56.1.6).

On the basis of the Environmental Impact Statement, the licensing authority (see section 2.1) draws up a draft decision on the EIA, and presents this with the Statement to the public and organises a public discussion (Article 60.1). The form of the announcement is specified in Article 60.2. The period for public consultation must be not less than 15 days.

3.6 Review and approval

The licensing authority submits its draft decision and all the project documentation to the MERP for approval. The MERP must respond within 30 days (Article 59.1–2). If the MERP denies approval, it must give reasons and demand modification of the project (Article 59.3). The MERP may consult with other ministries before making a decision (Article 59.4).

There is no requirement for an external or independent review.

The licensing authority then announces its decision, within eight days of making it (Article 60.4), and issues an operating licence if the decision is positive.

The operating licence may include conditions, for example, a technical inspection of the project before operation, or a trial operation (Article 61.1). In such cases the MERP must establish that the project conforms to the description in the Environmental Impact Statement.

If in the period between issuing the environmental approval and issuing the operating licence there are significant changes in legislative requirements, the MERP may require the developer to amend the project and the Environmental Impact Statement (Article 62.1).

If the developer changes a project after an operating licence has been granted, the operating licence must be amended accordingly (Article 62.2). This process does not require another public consultation (Articles 60.3, 62.3).

For projects with transboundary impacts, the Ministry of Foreign Affairs informs affected countries about the project and sends the project documentation and Environmental Impact Statement (Article 63.1).

4. Monitoring

For projects which require an EIA, the MERP must establish that the project conforms to the environmental conditions set in the EIA approval (Article 61.1–2).

Failure to abide by conditions in the environmental approval will result in a fine of not less than SIT 100,000 (Article 100.1). In addition, the person responsible in the company for the offence will be fined at least SIT 10,000 (Article 100.2).

5. Experience to date

No EIAs can be undertaken under the *Environmental Protection Act, 1993* until an EIA regulation has defined which projects must undergo an EIA and what must be in the Environmental Impact Statement. EIA has, however, been in practice in Slovenia since before the *Environmental Protection Act, 1993*. An independent, non-profit organisation has prepared, on behalf of a major local state-owned bank, professional environmental evaluations of new investments financed by this bank. Since 1974, about 580 EIA reports have been conducted, about 30% of which have declared the planned activity unacceptable. However, these assessments were undertaken on a voluntary basis and did not have a specific legal significance.

6. Future developments

The *Environmental Protection Act, 1993*, enacted in June 1993 required the MERP to publish more detailed regulations on EIA by April 1994 (Article 102.1). In addition, the Government must produce a list of projects for which an EIA is mandatory, by the same date (Article 101.1).

Restructuring of local government is being debated in the Slovenian Parliament.

7. Sources of further information

EIA Department
Ministry of Environment and Regional Planning
61000 Ljubljana
Vojkova 1a
Slovenia
tel: (386-61) 327 461
fax: (386-61) 132 5263

Dr. Franc Lobnik
Biotechnical Faculty
Department of Agronomy
61000 Ljubljana
Jamnikarjeva 101
Slovenia
tel/fax: (386-61) 261 073

Fedor Gerne
Institute of Geography
61000 Ljubljana

Trg francoske revolucije 7
Slovenia
tel: (386-61) 213 458

Mitja Horvat
Faculty of Law
Institute of Public Administration
61000 Ljubljana
Kongresni trg 12
Slovenia
tel/fax: (386-61) 154 046

Dr Vida Hudnik
Chemical Institute 'Boris Kidric'
61000 Ljubljana
Hajdrihova 19
Slovenia
tel: (386-61) 263 061
fax: (386-61) 263 285

Svetozar Polic
Institute 'Jozef Stefan'
SEPO – EIA Department
61000 Ljubljana
Jamova 39
Slovenia
tel: (386-61) 266 986
fax: (386-61) 273 677

8. EIA legislation

Terms used in law	*Terms used in book*
Activity	Project
Operator	Developer
Environmental Impact Report	Environmental Impact Statement
Development consent	Licence for an activity

SLOVENIA A

Republic of Slovenia Environmental Protection Act

No.801-01/90-2/107, 2 June 1993

Excerpts

Article 2. Management of environmental protection
2.1. Environmental protection is the responsibility of the Republic of Slovenia (hereinafter 'the State'), except in matters specified by law as falling within the jurisdiction of the State but concerning the development of towns, or where matters of local character or importance are involved.

2.2. Matters of local character or importance are those pertaining to, originating, or likely to originate only in the area of a local government unit, the scope or impact of which does not reach beyond its boundaries and which can be handled, organised, managed, controlled, prevented, financed, promoted or otherwise dealt with by the local government unit itself. In particular, they include:

1. natural resources owned by a local government unit or of local importance;
2. local public services relating to environmental protection;
3. special environmental protection measures falling within its jurisdiction;
4. programming and scheduling in the domain of environmental protection;
5. subsidiary responsibility for preparing and carrying out rehabilitation;
6. the ensuring of detailed or special monitoring.

Article 4. Ensuring of environmental protection
4.1 Environmental protection shall be ensured within their respective competencies and responsibilities, by:

1. the State;
2. municipalities, urban municipalities, or wider local government units (hereinafter 'Local Authorities');
3. citizens and other members of the population, as individuals or organised in associations, professional and other organisations, and other non-governmental organisations for environmental protection;
4. enterprises and their associations engaged in environmental protection activities;
5. parties engaged in the delivery of public services, the performance of particular matters within the scope of public services, and those with public authorisations in the domain of environmental protection; and
6. parties responsible for environmental strain.

Article 8. Principle of prevention
8.1. The manner of specifying prescribed procedures, limit values, and other standards and of designing and implementing each Activity shall be such as to cause the least possible change in the environment; present the least environmental risk, minimise the consumption of space, materials, and energy during construction, production, transport, and utilisation to

the greatest extent possible; include consideration of the principles of replacement, recycling, and incineration; and forestall and limit environmental strain already at its origin.

8.2. In implementing the preceding paragraph the best concepts, technologies, equipment, and production methods which are available on the market and have been practically tested and found satisfactory shall be preferred, as well as replacement, recycling, and regeneration, even if reasonably higher costs are involved.

8.3. For reasons of precaution, any deviation from the use of the concepts, equipment, and production methods of the preceding paragraph shall only be allowed in the case of Activities which have been reliably proved on scientific grounds or otherwise to exclude the possibility of any unexpected indirect or direct environmental strain.

8.4. Where there is a danger of serious and irreparable damage to the environment, lack of scientific certainty may not be used as a reason for postponing such actions as may be necessary.

Article 14. Public access and dissemination of information

14.1. The information concerning environmental conditions and changes, the procedures and activities of bodies of the State and Local Authorities, or the parties involved in the delivery of public services, and those with public authorisations relating to the environment shall be open to the public.

14.2. The parties of the preceding paragraph shall inform the public and provide information to interested individuals and organisations in the prescribed manner not later than one month of the request for such information and at a price which may not exceed the material costs of providing the information.

14.3. Any party whose business operations should in any way or form strain the environment shall provide public access to the information concerning such environmental strain as they may cause in the manner specified in the preceding paragraph through the competent department of Local Authorities referred to in Article 92.3 hereof.

Article 15. Principle of protection of rights

15.1. In making any decision about an Activity and throughout the duration of such an Activity, everybody engaged in any such act or activity shall act in the prescribed manner and shall take all the prescribed and other reasonable measures which will ensure the exercise of the rights of others to a healthy and pure environment, without demanding for this any recompense whatsoever.

15.2. To exercise their right to a healthy and clean environment, individual citizens, their associations, unions, and organisations may file a suit with the court, demanding the termination of an Activity, if such an Activity presents or will present an immediate threat to the environment, a critical environmental strain or damage, or a direct danger to the life and health of the people, or demanding that the commencement of such an Activity may be prohibited if the likelihood of the above-mentioned effects can be demonstrated with reasonable certainty.

15.3. The court may order that the measure referred to in the preceding paragraph be taken only if it is not possible to prevent the consequences by other means.

15.4. To exercise their right to a healthy and clean environment, the parties referred to in Article 56.1.6 hereof shall have the right to take part in the procedure of deciding on granting a licence for an Activity if the decision on the matter discussed in the procedure might encroach upon this right.

15.5. Additionally, the protection of the right of citizens to a healthy environment small in accordance with law be the responsibility of the ombudsman.

Article 21. Form and payment of a concession

21.1. The State or the Local Authorities (hereinafter 'the grantor') may grant, against payment, a concession to natural resources which are their property to a legal or private person (hereinafter 'concessionaire') if the latter is capable of their management, use or exploitation.

21.2. Payment for a concession granted to natural resources which are the property of the State shall be allotted to the State and to the municipality in proportions and on the basis of criteria of the level of development of infrastructural facilities and environmental strain prescribed by the Government.

21.3. A concession may be granted to natural resources if all environmental protection conditions defined herein for Activities and for the protection of a natural treasure are fulfilled. A concession may only be granted on the basis of public tender, except in cases when public tender would not be reasonable because of the dependence of the concession on the locality.

21.4. The concession to a natural national asset may only concern the right to its management or to its specific or subsidiary use.

21.5. The concession to a natural resource shall concern the right to its economic exploitation when the exploitation is an activity of the concessionaire or when the natural resource is a dominant component of the concessionaire's activity.

21.6. The concession to a natural treasure shall concern the right to its management, use, or exploitation.

21.7. In the acquisition of a concession on the basis of public tender, priority rights may be recognised. The owner of the area comprising natural resources shall have the right of preemption in obtaining a concession, if fulfilling the conditions specified in the first paragraph of this Article. The criteria for and the method of exercising the right of preemption shall be preserved by the Government and shall give particular consideration to the needs of local population, the depopulation threat to the area, and past or existing rights of concessionary character. The Government shall also prescribe the cases and conditions under which a concession to a natural resource within the areas threatened by depopulation may be granted free of charge.

Article 22. Licences

22.1. In cases not referred to in paragraphs 4, 5, and 6 of the preceding Article a licence shall be obtained for the use and exploitation of a natural resource from the Minister responsible for that natural resource, unless provided otherwise by law.

Article 23. Deed of concession

23.1. The basis for granting a concession to natural resources shall be the deed of concession.

23.2. The deed of concession is a regulation of the Government or the Local Authorities. The deed of concession granting a concession to a foreign person may only take the form of a law.

23.3. In particular, the deed of concession shall contain the following:

1. a definition of natural resources for which the concession is given;
2. the object of the concession and a definition of the extent and possible exclusive character of the concession;
3. the definition of conditions of environmental protection, conditions of the protective regime, and the method of management, use, or exploitation of natural resources;
4. a description of the activity which may be undertaken by the concessionaire in connection with the rights which are the object of the concession;
5. conditions which must be fulfilled by the concessionaire;
6. any public authorisation of the concessionaire;
7. the commencement and duration of the concession;
8. the area to which the concession refers;
9. payment for the concession and the shares allotted to the State and to the Local Authorities;
10. authorisation for supervising the execution of the concession;
11. grounds and methods for the cessation of the concessions;
12. obligations of the concessionaire regarding rehabilitation, establishment of a new or restoration of the previous state of the environment; and
13. authorisations and conditions for concluding a concessionary contract and its effective date.

Article 24. Other questions relating to concessions

24.1. Regarding the acquisition and selection of concessionaires, public tenders, the questions relating to concessionary contract, protection of concessionaires and resolving of disputes, cessation of concessionary relationship, transfer of concession, mandatory concession, force majeure, and concessionaire's responsibility for the actions of employees, the provisions of the law governing concessions in connection with public trading services shall be applied as appropriate, unless provided otherwise by law.

Article 32. Licences for mobile facilities and tests

32.1. For the use of mobile facilities for environmental protection a licence shall be obtained from the Minister. A complaint may be lodged against the decision not to grant a licence.

32.2. An application for issuing a licence shall comprise as its integral parts an operating design and a report on the environmental impact of the operation of the facility.

32.3. For the preparation of the report referred to in the preceding paragraph, the provisions contained in Article 56 hereof shall apply. For the procedure of issuing a licence, the provisions contained in Articles 60 through 63 shall apply as and when appropriate.

32.4. If for the operation of a mobile facility appropriate Activities in the environment are required, a licence for such Activities shall be obtained in compliance with the regulations which govern the exploitation and use of space. In the case of Activities in areas having the status of natural heritage, a licence may be issued only with the consent of the competent Ministry.

32.5. The provisions of the preceding paragraphs shall also apply to the testing of operation of other facilities and of procedures for environmental protection of limited duration.

32.6. A list of facilities and procedures referred to in paragraphs 1 and 5 of this Article shall be prescribed by the Minister.

Article 33. Licences in exceptional cases
33.1. In case of emergency or occasionally, the Minister may issue to the party responsible for an environmental strain a licence temporarily or occasionally to exceed the ordinary environmental strain.

33.2. If the cases referred to in the preceding paragraph concern natural heritage areas or involve any hazard to human health, the licence may only be issued with the consent of the competent Ministry.

33.3. In matters within the jurisdiction of Local Authorities, the licence under paragraph 1 of this Article shall be issued by the competent department of Local Authorities.

33.4. The licences referred to in the preceding paragraphs may not be issued when excessive environmental strain of temporary of occasional nature is likely to lead to a critical environmental strain, hazard to the environment, or to any damage of the latter. The licence shall also specify the conditions applying to the elimination of any adverse environmental impacts.

Article 51. Environmental vulnerability study
51.1 Planning, programming, and designing of Activities and directing of regional development shall also be based on an environmental vulnerability study.

51.2. An environmental vulnerability study for each individual region of the entire territory of the State shall be prepared by the Ministry in cooperation with other Ministries.

51.3. An environmental vulnerability study shall also be prepared by a municipality for its territory if such a study is not prepared within the scope of a wider local government unit or in cooperation with other municipalities.

Article 52. Content of an environmental vulnerability study
52.1. An environmental vulnerability study shall be based on ecosystem divisions of the territory and shall incorporate qualitative and quantitative analyses of the environment and its components, its sensitivity to Activities, the regenerative and neutralising abilities of the environment, the attained levels of total and integral environmental strain and endangerment, the assessment of acceptable scope of environmental strain, and suggested levels of protection against environmental strain, including areas in which new Activities will not be allowed due to excessive environmental strain.

52.2. The principles of division on the basis of ecosystems and the methodology for the preparation of environmental vulnerability studies on national and local levels shall be prescribed by the Minister in coordination with the Ministers responsible for health, for the protection of individual natural resources, and for civil defence and rescue.

Article 53. Levels of environmental protection

53.1. On the basis of the environmental vulnerability study, the National Assembly or Local Authorities shall determine the level of environmental protection against environmental strains, which shall serve as the mandatory bases for:

1. physical planning documents of the State and the Local Authorities;
2. sector plans for the management of natural resources defined by law;
3. approvals for specific space-affecting activities and other Activities; and
4. the preparation of rehabilitation programmes.

53.2. Within the framework of environmental protection levels, areas shall be defined on which new Activities may be allowed only if collective and other measures are adopted to prevent the increase of total and integral environmental strains above or to ensure their reduction below the levels specified for the cases referred to in Article 28 hereof.

53.3. The National Assembly or the Local Authorities shall examine any decision passed in accordance with paragraph 1 of this Article at least every four years and shall modify or supplement it as necessary.

Article 54. Comprehensive assessment of environmental impact

54.1. Before adopting the documents specified in paragraphs 1.1 and 1.2 of the preceding Article, the party responsible for their preparation shall obtain the licence from the Ministry.

54.2. The Ministry shall grant the licence referred to in the previous paragraph on the basis of a comprehensive environmental impact assessment study. This study shall be prepared by the body responsible for the preparation of the physical planning document or sector plan, from the viewpoint of the environmental impact of the planned Activities and of the reciprocal influences of specific human activities.

54.3. Before issuing a licence referred to in paragraph 1 of this Article, the Ministry shall consult the Ministries responsible for health, the protection of individual natural resources, and civil defence and rescue and for other forms of protection against hazards, unless special consent be prescribed for these areas by law.

54.4. The detailed content and methodology for the preparation of a comprehensive environmental impact assessment study shall be prescribed by the Minister in cooperation with the Ministers referred to in the preceding paragraph.

Article 55. Assessment of environmental impact

55.1. To realise the principle of prevention and to assess the compatibility of an envisaged Activity with environmental characteristics of the location, an environmental impact assessment shall be carried out to determine the acceptability of the intended Activity with respect to its long and short-term, direct and indirect effects on the environment from the viewpoint of a minimum change in the natural conditions of the environment and the maximum specified environmental protection levels possible.

55.2. An assessment of environmental impact shall be carried out for those intended Activities which are subject to approval and which could significantly affect the environment. These Activities include:

1. the exploitation and use of soil, water, forests, minerals and other natural resources;
2. the construction, modification, operation, or removal of facilities and equipment;
3. technological and other changes relating to the extraction, production, storage, transport, and use of raw materials, semi-processed goods, finished products, and energy;
4. the introduction for the purpose of using or marketing of new products; and
5. the trial introduction of new products and technologies.

55.3. The assessment of environmental impact shall be based on an environmental impact report which shall be an integral part of the application for obtaining the licence for an Activity.

Article 56. Content of an environmental impact report
56.1. An environmental impact report shall include:

1. a description of the existing state of the environment which could be affected by the project, including the measurement of existing environmental strain (the zero state of the environment);
2. a description of the characteristics of the project and evidence of its conformity with technical and other regulations;
3. a description and assessment of the anticipated effects of a project on the environment, including a description of optimisation methods of evaluation;
4. a description and assessment of environmental protection measures, of the selected technologies and materials, including grounds for such selection with respect to alternative options, test and other certificates;
5. a description and assessment of environmental strains on and changes in the state of the environment which are the result of the impact of the project, including an assessment of the potential total and integral environmental strain;
6. a description of the location and a list of all parties involved in cases when special measures and stipulated restitution are prescribed for the danger to or depreciation of the environment, including an assessment of their suitability;
7. warnings regarding the comprehensiveness of the project and the report, and problems connected with their preparation; and
8. a summary of the environmental impact report containing a final judgement comprehensible to the general public.

56.2. The environmental impact report must include all the necessary technical and graphical components in a form suitable for public presentation, except in cases when these components form an integral part of the design.

56.3. The environmental impact report may only be prepared by an authorised legal or physical person.

56.4. The categories of environmental strain which must be assessed, the categories and scope of assessment, the methodology for the preparation of an environmental impact report, and conditions and procedure for obtaining the authorisation under the preceding paragraph shall be prescribed by the Minister after consultations with the Ministers referred to in Article 54.3 hereof.

Article 57. Mandatory and other environmental impact assessments

57.1. According to the size and nature of an Activity and the environmental characteristics of the location, the Government shall prescribe:

1. categories of Activities for which an environmental impact assessment is always mandatory;
2. other categories of Activities and the conditions and criteria which, if fulfilled, require a mandatory environmental impact assessment; and
3. categories of Activities for which an environmental impact assessment requires only a report containing particular analyses of specific nature or partial accounts.

57.2. At the suggestion of the Ministries or the parties specified in Articles 4.1.2, 3 and 5 hereof, the Ministry may decide in individual cases of intended Activities not covered by sub-paragraphs 2 and 3 of the preceding paragraph that an environmental impact assessment be prepared or that the scope of an environmental impact report be increased.

Article 58. Preliminary licensing procedure

58.1. When the law prescribes a preliminary procedure for setting the conditions for granting a licence for an Activity, the competent Ministry or its competent body shall also prescribe as obligatory the assessment of environmental impact and shall specify the scope of the environmental impact report for the cases referred to in the preceding Article.

58.2. In case of any doubt arising in connection with the implementation of the provisions contained in Article 57 hereof or in case of a motion proposed on the basis of paragraph 2 of the said Article, the Ministry or the body referred to in the preceding paragraph shall ask the Minister for his opinion or decision.

58.3. If the procedure referred to in paragraph 1 of this Article is not prescribed, the operator of the intended Activity may ask the Ministry to specify the environmental protection conditions and the scope of the environmental impact report in accordance with the provisions contained in Article 56 hereof.

58.4. For the purposes of the procedure referred to in paragraphs 1 and 3 of this Article, a request for specifying environmental protection conditions must include information about the type, size, and nature of the intended Activity and about the environmental characteristics of the location.

Article 59. Environmental consent

59.1. When the licensing procedure for an Activity also involves an assessment of environmental impacts in accordance with Article 57 hereof, the body competent for decisions must draw up a draft decision, ensure public announcement in accordance with Article 60.2 hereof, and submit the draft together with the design and other documentation to the Ministry for approval.

59.2. The Ministry must grant or deny the consent (hereinafter 'environmental consent') by a confirmation of the decision or by a special enactment not later than 30 days of the day when the competent body referred to in the preceding paragraph has sent to it, after carrying out a public discussion, the draft decision.

59.3. If the Ministry denies an environmental consent, it shall give reasons for considering the proposed Activity unacceptable or demand that the project be amended or modified.

59.4. If no special consent is necessary in cases of activities in the domains of the protection of health of humans, animals, and plants, safety at work, other forms of protection against danger, and the protection of natural resources prior to issuing a licence for an Activity, the competent Ministries shall, at the request of the Minister, submit to the latter their opinions within 20 days of making such a request, before an environmental consent is issued.

59.5. A licence for an Activity issued contrary to the provisions contained in paragraph 2 of this Article shall be null and void.

Article 60. Participation of the public

60.1. The body referred to in paragraph 1 of the preceding Article, which is responsible for making decisions, shall ensure public presentation of the draft decision and the report referred to in Article 56 hereof, or of the entire project, if the report does not contain all the relevant information referred to in paragraph 2 of the said Article, and shall ensure its public discussion and a public hearing of the operator of the Activity.

60.2. The public announcement including the list of concerned parties, the places and the times of the presentation, the public discussion, and the hearing referred to in the preceding paragraph shall be published in public media and announced in the usual local manner. The public announcement shall also contain a summary of the environmental impact report with final judgement and the method of contribution of opinions and comments by the public. The duration of public presentation shall not be less than 15 days.

60.3. Irrespective of the provisions of the preceding paragraphs, public presentation, discussion, and hearing are not necessary in a renewed decision-making procedure which results from an adjustment to opinions and comments given during the initial public presentation.

60.4. The body referred to in paragraph 1 of this Article shall announce its decision, including environmental consent, in public media within eight days of issuing the consent. The decision shall include a statement that the opinions and comments made during the public presentation, discussion, and hearing have been considered.

60.5. The costs of public presentation, discussion, and hearing shall be borne by the operator of the intended Activity.

Article 61. Assessment of fulfilment of environmental protection conditions

61.1. When a technical inspection, trial operation, or any other preliminary process is prescribed for issuing an operating or other licence for an Activity for which an environmental consent has been issued, the Ministry must be included in its execution in order to establish the conformity of the executed Activity with the components of the project that have been subject to environmental impact assessment.

61.2. In cases when a trial run is prescribed, the conformity referred to in the preceding paragraph shall be ascertained on the basis of operation monitoring specified in the project.

61.3. A licence referred to in paragraph 1 of this Article, which is issued contrary to the provisions contained in this Article, shall be null and void.

Article 62. Changed conditions
62.1. If upon the issuing of an environmental consent but prior to the issuing of the licence referred to in the preceding Article the environmental conditions specified by law or a regulation issued on its basis and serving as the basis for the consent will change significantly, the Ministry may require that the operator of an Activity amend the project and the report and, on this basis and with his consent, that the decision allowing the Activity be changed.

62.2. Before any change of the scope or type of operation specified in an operating licence, which would cause a change in environmental impacts, the operator shall obtain an operating licence which shall be modified in the light of the changed environmental protection conditions.

62.3. In the procedure for changing the decision referred to in paragraph 1 of this Article, the provisions of Article 60 hereof shall not be applied.

Article 63. Notification of neighbouring countries
63.1. When an intended Activity could directly influence the environment of neighbouring countries, and with the condition of reciprocity fulfilled, the Ministry shall through the Ministry of Foreign Affairs inform such countries about the intended Activity and send them the project of the intended Activity and the environmental impact report.

Article 92. General tasks of environmental protection
92.1. The general professional and related administrative tasks of environmental protection in the State shall include:

3. preparation of regulations, directives, and recommendations in the field of environmental protection;
4. preparation of environmental vulnerability studies;
5. assessment of environmental impact of planned Activities;
6. determination of environmental protection conditions for the exploitation, use, and management of natural resources, unless provided otherwise by law;
7. preparation of environmental protection measures.

92.2. The tasks specified in the preceding paragraph shall be carried out by the Institute for Environmental Protection of the Ministry.

92.3. In matters of environmental protection of local significance, the tasks specified in paragraph 1 of this Article shall be performed by a competent institution or department of one or more Local Authorities, or, in the case of urban municipalities, by a competent institution.

Article 100. Offence
100.1. A fine of not less than SIT 100,000 shall be imposed on any company or other legal person or individual committing an offence in carrying out an independent activity, for:

18. acting contrary to the elements of a project which are subject to the environmental protection consent when carrying out an Activity (Article 59);

100.2. A fine of not less than SIT 10,000 shall be imposed on the responsible person in the company or any other legal person who has committed any offence of the previous paragraph.

Article 101.1. Not later than nine months of the coming into effect of this Act, the Government shall specify or prescribe:

3. the categories of Activities for which mandatory assessment of environmental impact shall apply, and other cases of environmental impact assessment (Article 57.1).

Article 102. Regulations prepared by the Minister
102.1. Not later than nine months of the enforcement of this Act, the Minister shall harmonise the existing regulations or prescribe:

10. the principles of division on the basis of ecosystems and the methodology for the preparation of environmental vulnerability studies (Article 52.2);
11. the detailed content of and the methodology for the preparation of a comprehensive environmental impact assessment study (Article 54.4).

Article 109. Harmonisation of obligations
109.3. The provisions of this Act relating to the environmental impact assessment shall start to be applied within the time periods specified by the regulation referred to in Article 57 hereof. In the case of procedures for issuing the licence for an Activity, however, these provisions can only be applied with the consent of the operator of the Activity.

109.4. Until the environmental vulnerability study referred to in Article 51 hereof has been prepared, the maps, drawings and related documents concerning the physical planning components of long-term municipal development plans shall be deemed to be such. Until the levels of environmental strain protection have been determined, such documentation shall also serve as the mandatory bases in accordance with Article 53 hereof.

President of the National Assembly of the Republic of Slovenia, Herman Rigelnik, M.Sc.

Glossary of EIA terms

Project:	Industrial and investment activity, actual or proposed.
Developer:	Individual, company, financial institution or development organisation which prepares and submits a project for approval.
EIA:	Environmental Impact Assessment. The overall process of evaluating the environmental impacts likely to arise from a project. It can include discussion with the public.
Mandatory or discretionary EIAs:	In most countries there are lists of projects which require an EIA by law (mandatory) or which require an EIA if an environmental authority demands one (discretionary).
Scope:	The scope of an EIA is the range of issues that it must cover, for example: individual environmental elements (air, water, soil); impacts on landscape, human settlements, cultural monuments; short and long-term impacts; direct and indirect impacts. The scope also includes the number and type of alternatives to be considered. Sometimes there is a formal scoping procedure at the start of an EIA, by which the interested parties can agree the scope of the EIA before it is started.
Environmental Impact Statement:	The documentation prepared by the developer for consideration by the environmental authority.
Review and approval:	The designated environmental authority reviews the EIA documentation prior to making a decision to approve or reject the project on environmental grounds. The approval may be unconditional or be subject to conditions, such as compulsory self-monitoring, or use of specific technologies.
Development consent:	The building authority grants development consent by means of a siting, building, and operational permit, or a combination/variation of these. The building authority takes into account the decision of the environmental authority. Sometimes the environmental authority's decision is binding on the building authority.

Index